Leading in the Age of Innovations

Leading in the Age of Innovations centers on the need for a more complex process-relational-oriented approach to leadership. The complexity of leadership has grown significantly during the 21st century where the need to adapt to the escalating changes in our society and workplace forms one of the most important prerequisites to succeed. *Leading in the Age of Innovations* represents the outcomes of the lengthy scientific work that was undertaken for the past ten years and it is still an ongoing process. This book introduces a new concept of leadership based on the process and relational dimensions which resulted in the development of the Reflective Leadership concept.

The new model of leadership provides a unique concept on how to bring together various disciplines and explains the overlapping relations between them. Moreover, the proposed view on leadership reflects the current evolution around the globe highlighting the importance of change and innovation. In organizations, too much focus is on the end product and the technical details of how a product is made and distributed. Less attention is focused on how people interact, and how the human capacity is effectively supported by leaders who, on the other hand, are expected to support a culture of innovation. This behavioral interaction is governed by a set of predictable values and norms.

These relationships need to be understood for an organization to prosper and is thus far more important to the leadership process. *Leading in the Age of Innovations* seeks to establish this understanding and will be key reading to researchers, scholars and practitioners alike in the fields of leadership, organizational studies and related disciplines.

Lenka Theodoulides is an assistant professor and researcher at the Faculty of Economics, Matej Bel University, Slovakia.

Gabriela Kormancová is an assistant professor and researcher at the Faculty of Economics, Matej Bel University, Slovakia.

David Cole is an assistant professor and researcher at the Faculty of Economics, Matej Bel University, Slovakia.

Routledge Studies in Leadership Research

Women, Religion and Leadership
Female Saints as Unexpected Leaders
Edited by Barbara Denison

"Leadership Matters?"
Finding Voice, Connection and Meaning in the 21st Century
Edited by Chris Mabey and David Knights

Innovation in Environmental Leadership
Critical Perspectives
Edited by Benjamin W. Redekop, Deborah Rigling Gallagher, and Rian Satterwhite

After Leadership
Edited by Brigid Carroll, Suze Wilson, and Josh Firth

Creative Leadership
Contexts and Propsects
Edited by Charalampos Mainemelis, Olga Epitropaki, and Ronit Kark

Theoretical Perspectives of Strategic Followership
David Zoogah

Good Dividends
Responsible leadership of Business Purpose
Edited by Steve Kempster and Thomas Maak

Leading in the Age of Innovations
Change of Values and Approaches
Lenka Theodoulides, Gabriela Kormancová, and David Cole

For a full list of titles in this series, please visit www.routledge.com

Leading in the Age of Innovations

Change of Values and Approaches

Lenka Theodoulides, Gabriela Kormancová, and David Cole

Routledge
Taylor & Francis Group

LONDON AND NEW YORK

First published 2019 by Routledge

2 Park Square, Milton Park, Abingdon, Oxon, OX14 4RN

605 Third Avenue, New York, NY 10017

Routledge is an imprint of the Taylor & Francis Group, an informa business

First issued in paperback 2020

Library of Congress Cataloging-in-Publication Data
Names: Theodoulides, Lenka, author. | Kormancováa, Gabriela, author.
Title: Leading in the age of innovations : change of values and approaches / Lenka Theodoulides, Gabriela Kormancováa, and David Cole.
Description: New York : Routledge, 2019. | Series: Routledge studies in leadership research | Includes index.
Identifiers: LCCN 2018053856 | ISBN 9780815379034 (hardback) | ISBN 9781351119429 (ebook)
Subjects: LCSH: Leadership—Case studies. | Management—Technological innovations. | Organizational change.
Classification: LCC HD57.7 .T46524 2019 | DDC 658.4/092—dc23
LC record available at https://lccn.loc.gov/2018053856

ISBN: 978-0-8153-7903-4 (hbk)
ISBN: 978-0-367-78685-4 (pbk)

Typeset in Sabon
by Apex CoVantage, LLC

Contents

List of Figures   vii
List of Tables   viii
List of Abbreviations   ix
Preface   x

Introduction   1

PART I
Leadership Perspectives   15

1 Emerging Trends in Leadership   17

2 Ethical Pathologies and Cognitive Dissonance
   in Corporate Leadership   43

3 Corporate Social Responsibility From the National,
   Community, Company and Individual Levels   66

   Case Study 1 The CEE Cultures in Transition   79

PART II
Complexity View on Leadership   87

4 The Concept of the Leadership Approach Based
   on the System and Relational Theory   89

5 Designing the Concept of Reflective Leadership   111

   Case Study 2 Generational Changes in the
   Workforce Within the Socioeconomic and
   Political Context   135

PART III
Focus on Change and Innovation 147

6 Bridging the Process of Leading With Change
and Innovation 149

7 Reframing Current Leadership Approaches
to Include Diversity 174

8 How Emerging Technologies Transform Leadership 197

Case Study 3 The CEE as the Catching
Up Innovation Region 211

9 Leading in the Era of Innovations and the
Appearance of New Values: Critical Views,
Implications and Final Thoughts for Future Actions 218

Appendices 233
List of Contributors 243
Index 244

Figures

0.1	Research strategy and research design	8
1.1	Leading-Following Model	29
2.1	Ethical triad of ethics in business	62
4.1	Designing simple and clear systems	97
4.2	Understanding of the "big picture" concept	100
4.3	Complexity and reflective view	102
4.4	Sharing information and knowledge	106
5.1	The main pillars of the new leading concept	114
5.2	Learning process based on the reflection	120
5.3	Quantitative and qualitative forms of process evaluation	122
5.4	Giving and receiving feedback	124
5.5	Leading-Knowing-Following-Learning Model (LKFL Model)	130
5.6	Reflective Leadership Model	132
6.1	Typology and number of changes in 2013–2015	153
6.2	Linkage between changes and process-relational approach	158
6.3	Overlapping Kotter's model and the Reflective Leadership Model	167
6.4	Reflective Leadership Model in the process of leading change	169
9.1	Modified Reflective Leadership Model	227

Tables

1.1	Focus of transformational leadership in the age of innovation	23
1.2	Traditional concept vs. partnership concept	27
1.3	Leadership skills and roles	34
3.1	The cultural differences of four Visegrad countries prior to entry to EU before 2004	81
3.2	Perception of the corruption index	82
3.3	The GDP per capita growth in % between 2011 and 2018	82
5.1	Timeline and typology of generations	136
6.1	Typology and results of the change implementation process	154
6.2	Process of planning change	159
6.3	Process of implementing change	161
7.1	The general characteristics, habits and values of different generations	187
A1.1	Sample description—type of position	235
A1.2	Sample description—years in this position	235
A1.3	Sample description—industry	236
A1.4	Sample description—company size	236
A3.1	Evaluation matrix for Critical Reflective Analysis	241

Abbreviations

AI	artificial intelligence
CBA	cost-benefit analysis
CE	Central Europe
CEE	Central and Eastern Europe
CEO	chief executive officer
CRA	Critical Reflection Analysis
CSR	corporate social responsibility
D&I	diversity and inclusion
EU	European Union
GDP	gross domestic product
GDPR	General Data Protection Regulation
GERD	gross domestic expenditure on R&D
GII	Global Innovation Index
ICT	information and communications technology
IMF	International Monetary Fund
IPR	intellectual property rights
IT	information technology
KPI	key performance indicator
OECD	Organization for Economic Co-Operation and Development
R&D	research and development
RBV	resource-based view
SBU	strategic business units
SIT	social identity theory
SMEs	small and medium-sized enterprises
UK	United Kingdom
VAT	value-added tax

Preface

This book represents one of the outcomes of the lengthy scientific work that we have undertaken for the past ten years, and it is still an ongoing process. We have been gaining knowledge about the functions of leadership through our professional experience working in various companies as well as via educational and consulting work with all levels of managers from different sectors, both locally and internationally. This professional and international experience provides us with access and opportunity to examine the process of leadership in the work of managers.

Concepts of leadership have gained the interest of many academics and researchers over a few decades and they are still present today in many personal as well as professional discussions. There has been a lot of investment given to develop leaders in a number of organizations, which have turned out to be ineffective. One of the reasons is too much emphasis given to personal characteristics and individual behavior of potential leaders rather than seeing their actions and their impacts on other people. In contrast to traditional approaches to leadership, organizational studies suggest that leadership requires careful consideration of the social context in which leadership actions take place. We also would like to acknowledge the fact that the seeds of our interdisciplinary approach to leadership were laid while researching the leadership topic in companies in the Central and Eastern European (CEE) region (according to the Organization for Economic Co-Operation and Development [OECD], Central and Eastern European countries include Albania, Bulgaria, Croatia, the Czech Republic, Hungary, Poland, Romania, the Slovak Republic, Slovenia and the three Baltic states: Estonia, Latvia and Lithuania). This region has provided a unique observation laboratory with its almost 30-year transition from Cold War socialism to full market capitalism and later EU membership—a historic opportunity that will never be repeated. We benefited greatly from the fruitful discussions with managers and entrepreneurs whose requirements were to develop and implement the new leadership approach that will reflect on the current challenges and organizational needs. That brought our attention to study and link together social responsibility, cognitive and behavioral theories.

Our approach to leadership has been influenced by the creation of the Critical Reflective Analysis. Since 2013 this method has been implemented in many organizations in order to identify various organizational processes which arise from the challenges that leaders need to deal with.

The proposed framework of the new leadership approach is based on the process and relational dimensions which resulted in the development of the Reflective Leadership concept. Although this work replaces fundamental leadership models with an organizational view on the leading process, it does illustrate the interdependences between leadership and several organizational processes, for example, in setting up the strategic and individual goals, enhancing and implementing organizational change, identifying the role of social responsibility in any innovation and managing diverse human resources.

The proposed Reflective Leadership concept is a result of the primary research conducted in different organizations locally and internationally in the CEE region in the period 2013–2018. This work was performed in close collaboration with managers in various organizations, large corporations and SMEs. That has given us the confirmation that such a conceptual framework of leadership is needed to tackle the challenges in the digital era where change and innovation are crucial elements of the successful performance of any organization.

In this book, we propose a more complex process-relational-oriented approach to leadership. It is designed to address the current challenges through two fundamental dimensions, such as a systemic view of leadership and the role of relations, which can help to see the organization as a complex system with external and internal values and norms.

This new concept is a result of long-term consulting experience and primary research in some organizations that confirmed the need to summarize our findings and publish such a conceptual framework of leadership.

We believe this book offers a coherent concept and tools for future research in leadership theory. Theorists who are interested in the functions of leadership will gain more insight through the use of our qualitative research methods, but anyone who is interested in the leading process will also find this book valuable.

Finally, it can be beneficial to those who assess and evaluate the quality of leadership in an organization, and the proposed approaches will provide the reader with handy tools.

Introduction

At present, traditional leadership is challenged to deal with the diversity of human resources, frequently changing business conditions and the pressure to improve all organizational processes continuously. Leadership in the 21st century is not the same as leadership in the 20th century. Rapid and frequent changes, the uncertainty of the global world and fast information and communications technology (ICT) development forces the leadership process to face new challenges. Leaders are required to take actions that have more substantial consequences over future outcomes. However, these desired outcomes are often wrongly, if ever, communicated to the followers. Only partial aims are set for the followers. Moreover, the lack of the complex view, which is called the "big picture", has been acknowledged.

The complexity of leadership has grown significantly during the 21st century where the need to adapt to the escalating changes in our society and workplace forms one of the most important prerequisites to succeed. Leadership becomes a question of relations between activities that occur today and those that are expected to happen in the future.

The primary objective of this monograph is to *develop a leadership concept which explains the connections between both process-oriented and relational approaches that foster organizational innovation. This leadership approach inevitably becomes essential when the process of any change is undertaken in an organization.* This book examines leadership as a complex social process which reflects what is happening between individuals within the organization as well as its interaction in the broader organizational ecosystem.

Although there are many theories and approaches toward examining the concept of leadership, there is still a lack of good understanding of the specific interrelation between the leadership process and actions of the employees and how the leader can influence that. If we understand more accurately the mechanism of leadership and the dynamics between leaders and employees, we can discover the full potential of the process of leadership and its contribution to the overall organization performance.

A primary assumption underlying this book is that the 21st century has brought *new challenges* for organizations: a rapidly changing and turbulent environment that is knowledge-driven; an innovative global economy; and a need for a diverse workforce and new technologies. The organization is increasingly leveraging technology to modernize its business strategies. Digital era leadership capabilities are added to traditional leadership skills. According to *Global Leadership Forecast 2018*, the new skills, identified as leading with digitalization, driving execution, hyper-collaboration, identifying and developing future talent, and 360-degree thinking have the greatest impact on performance and are considered as key competencies in the digital era.

In the latest work of Hickman (2016), it is stressed that a new era in organization is needed to meet the environmental challenges through dedication of a commonly held purpose. This is achieved when all the organization's members develop the capacity to share responsibility for leading. In this book, a different perspective and view on leadership are offered. First, the current challenges identified by our research will be understood through two fundamental dimensions, such as a systemic view of leadership and the role of relations, which can help to see the organization as a complex system with values and norms. Second, the new leadership approach will be introduced based on the understanding of the world around us which will propose how to interact in the environment with the goal of unleashing creativity, change and innovations among individuals in an organization. At the same time, several concepts, tools and guidelines will be introduced which can help leaders to achieve high performance and effectively act in a digital era.

Finally, the necessity to be able to bring together various perspectives will result in the proposed concept of Reflective Leadership. This includes new perspectives on learning, coping and benefiting from diversity and elimination of traditional leadership approaches. Successful digital leaders will not only need to have a technical mindset but also the ability and vision on how to bring together the technology and human factors to enable an organization's success.

Why the CEE Region?

We chose the CEE region for our research because of its specific features compared to other European countries. The common communist past and the process of economic, social and political transition shaped these countries considerably. This consequently has influenced their capability to innovate and the leadership style as well. Even after more than 30 years of being considered as modern democratic states, the burden of their shared history is still present.

There are many approaches on how to define the CEE. For the purposes of this book, we use the definition of the Organization for Economic

Co-Operation and Development (OECD), where the Central and Eastern European countries include Albania, Bulgaria, Croatia, the Czech Republic, Hungary, Poland, Romania, the Slovak Republic, Slovenia and the three Baltic states: Estonia, Latvia and Lithuania.

The collapse of communism in Eastern Europe was precipitated by the growing gulf between the vibrant and wealthy economies of the West and the stagnant economies of the communist East. In looking for alternatives to the socialist model, the populations of these countries could not have failed to notice that representative democracies governed most of the world's strongest economies.

Central Europe's period under the auspices of communism was profoundly ideological in its approach to modernity. This approach, called high modernity, can be described as a strong confidence in scientific and technological progress; a reliance on experts (scientists, engineers, bureaucrats, etc.); an attempt to master nature to meet human needs; spatial ordering (city planning, housing and transportation); and a disregard for historical, geographical and social context in development (Scott, 1998). This ideology of modernity had a rather dark vision of the future and it materialized in the real world as a form of brutalism seen in concrete tower blocks, utilitarian design and general dull-gray tedium. Even non-socialist Western countries were enamored with high modernity as the post-war period flirted with the idea of a Malthusian future of ever-increasing shortages due to ever-increasing population (e.g. Le Corbusier and his brutalist protégés).

The shift toward a market-based economic system often entails a number of steps: deregulation, privatization and creation of a legal system to safeguard property rights (Hill, 2011).

Deregulation involves removing legal restrictions to the free play of markets, establishing private enterprises and operating private enterprises in different ways. This opens the door to privatization, which transfers the ownership of state property into the hands of private individuals, frequently by the sale of state assets through auction. The well-functioning market economy requires laws protecting private property rights and providing a mechanism for contract enforcement. Many CEE countries lacked the necessary legal structure to protect property rights. For example, the titles to urban and agricultural property were often uncertain because of incomplete and inaccurate records, multiple pledges on the same property and unsettled claims resulting from demands for restitution from owners in the pre-communist era. The government policymakers and implementers also faced (and sometimes created) uncertain situations in which they had neither the experience nor the education to operate effectively.

Since 1989 the studied region of CEE countries experienced significant political and economic turnover toward market economies with some form of democratic or semi-democratic government. There was some pessimism about these countries' capabilities to complete the needed reform; several countries developed consolidated democratic systems, functioning economies with extensive welfare policies, well-established educational systems and relatively low inequality (Ekiert, 2012).

At the beginning of the 1990s most of the companies in the CEE region started to integrate themselves into the world economy. Later, the majority of these countries had the ambition to join the European Union, which required the fulfillment of macroeconomic goals and several reforms. Despite all of the changes over the last decades, economic and political instability and uncertainty over government regulations and legislation remain serious concerns for businesses. Company leaders consider the uncertainty related to the political and economic landscape to be a major business challenge. CEE countries ranked from 16th place in the world on the Heritage Foundation's Index of Economic Freedom (Heritage Foundation, 2017) all the way down to 116th out of 186 countries included in the index (Purg et al., 2018).

Looking at economic growth, for example, Slovakia in the period 2004–2006 was considered the "CEE economic tiger" when the growth rate was on average 7%. Extremely high growth was also seen in the Baltic region in 2011 where those three countries had GDP per capita growth around 8%. After the global economic recession in 2008, the GDP per capita growth percentage gradually increased in most CEE countries (World Bank data).

In spite of favorable economic development, the CEE countries still lag behind in innovation compared to their European counterparts. The *European Innovation Scoreboard* (2017) reveals that the EU's innovation performance continues to increase, especially due to improvements in human resources, the innovation-friendly environment, own-resource investments and attractive research systems. Sweden remains the EU innovation leader, followed by Denmark, Finland, the Netherlands, the United Kingdom and Germany. Lithuania, Malta, the United Kingdom, the Netherlands and Austria are the fastest growing innovators. On the contrary, CEE countries (e.g. Slovakia, together with Poland, Hungary, the Czech Republic and the Baltic states) are still considered *moderate innovators*. In addition, Romania and Bulgaria are the least innovative CEE countries in the European Union.

The business leaders make decisions and act in accordance to what is happening in their environment. In 2017, Price Waterhouse Coopers conducted a survey on Central and Eastern European CEOs as to how they foresee the global economy and their company's performance. The results show that they are more pessimistic than their global peers (only 45% predict improvement in global growth, compared to 57% of global CEOs). As far as their confidence about the organization's prospects in the next three years, just 32% reported that they are "very confident", compared to 45% of their global peers. The reason for that can be seen in the CEE history from the past 25 years. CEOs in this region have managed to survive a complete economic and political transformation along with war (in the former Yugoslavia), hyperinflation, booms, busts and wrenching social change.

Another reason is linked to general geopolitical concern considering ongoing tension between Russia and Ukraine. CEE countries are also anxious about how Brexit may disrupt the labor markets and supply chains.

Conducted research among CEOs and study of the CEE region reveals how business leaders recognize the process of leading and how they are aware of several challenges which the digital era brings to organizations.

Concept Building Approach

We understand leadership as a series of complex events that are important for individuals and for the entire organization. It also reflects on what is happening in the external environment and what impact it makes on the organizational environment.

The *concept building approach* is based on the new theory construction that enables us to study processes in depth and identify the main challenges which leaders have to face. The conceptual approach helps us to present a leadership context as a system and as a process with a strong orientation on building the relations within the internal and external environments of the organization.

In contrast to traditional approaches to leadership, we suggest that the study of leadership requires careful consideration of the social context in which leadership takes place. Leadership is a mosaic of social processes which reflect on what is happening with individuals within the organizational ecosystem. The proposed view of leadership encapsulates the current evolution around the globe, highlighting the importance of change and innovation and what challenges leaders have to cope with. Thus, the research assumptions were formulated in order to reflect the externalities of the current business environment as well as the challenges which leaders have to face currently. These assumptions are formulated as follows:

1. The environment (external and internal) is changing dramatically and is making an impact on organizational systems and leadership actions.
2. The changing structure and quality of human resources requires new leadership approaches.
3. To address the global challenges, it is inevitable that the leading process focuses on continuous enhancement of innovation and change.

Leading organizations toward any improvements and changes requires a more profound analysis of both processes and relational content of the leadership. This kind of analysis produces findings, concepts and hypotheses that are not possible to ascertain by statistical methods. Therefore, since 2013, qualitative research has been used to a large extent. To develop a new leadership approach (which may satisfy the requirements and adjust to differences that the digital era has brought to organizations), we used the grounded theory method—an interactive and comparative qualitative approach to research. It seeks to build theoretical explanations of observed phenomena by constructing these explanations from the data itself (as opposed to theory testing).

Strauss and Corbin (1989) originally constructed this method in order to increase the abstract level and explanatory power by going back and forth between gathering specific data and analyzing them. As discussed later in Glase's work (1992), the method creates concepts from data and relates them to each other. It is a means of qualitative analysis derived from a comparative method in which researchers make constant comparisons throughout the process of analysis. Continual comparison, which is achieved through a coding process, leads to the construction of theoretical explanations of observed phenomena. Observed phenomena encompasses the entire data of the representatives of this phenomena.

Silverman (2016) provides several reasons to adopt this for our research approach: to move the analysis beyond description; to develop new concepts, rather than rely on earlier theories; and to study processes. The lengthy interviews conducted directly at the leaders' premises provided us with a considerable amount of inside information and allowed us to get into the corporate world and its climate. Gaining a closer view and interactions with research participants fostered our knowledge about the organizational processes and an understanding of what the organizational systems and leaders' actions within them are.

Reflection Approach

This is an empirical approach which has been developed in order to assess and evaluate the processes. All these processes are related to key leadership actions and those elaborated broadly in the context of change and innovation.

The reflection approach started with the development of the Critical Reflection Analysis (CRA) in 2013. The primary purpose for the use of this method is to critically assess and evaluate the processes which resulted from grounded theory analysis. It has been used to analyze the process of changes implemented in a number of companies and to reflect the various leadership actions performed by different managers across the CEE region.

To accomplish these purposes, there are key aims which guide the implementation of the CRA in our research activities:

1. Introduce the new method which combines the both quantitative and qualitative analysis of the examined processes in organizations.

2. Promote a tool for managers to assess and evaluate any performance.
3. Determine the correlation between critical thinking, reflecting and learning processes which develop complex narratives of the leadership process.
4. Construct and test guidelines for deeper and objective understandings of the organization as a system.

It has been implemented in a number of case studies as an effective tool to establish an objective judgment on the resources and conditions which make an impact on the development of the strategic direction for an organization. The framework of the CRA and its implementation within research methodology is described in Appendix II and Appendix III.

The Research Philosophy, Chosen Strategy and Its Implementation

Referring to both practitioners' and as well as researchers' comments that more qualitative data focused on senior leaders is needed to better understand the scope of organizational transformation, the associated processes and practices of leadership (Gordon and Yukl, 2004; Beck, 2014), we have designed the qualitative research framework. The research philosophy is presented through the flow of connected findings based upon the research assumptions and design of two main qualitative approaches (i.e. case studies and grounded theory).

Currently, more focus is given to the content of innovations and changes rather than to provide an in-depth understanding of the process of leading innovation. Our research philosophy for this book is to identify *what* leading approach is suitable for the digital era where the innovation plays the key role and *how* it can be implemented in the diverse organizational environment.

The research aimed to find out how people interact (work in diverse teams with the different perception of ethical behavior) and how human capacity is adequately supported by leaders who are expected to enhance a culture of innovation. The research underlines the interdisciplinary scope of the leading processes overlapping various disciplines (sociology, philosophy, economics and informatics) and explains the relations among them.

The scientific objective of this book is to provide the target audience with a new theoretical and leadership concept as well as practical tools; therefore, our research strategy based on qualitative research fits best.

Since the nature of qualitative data is rather exploratory and qualitative analysis often deals with a considerable amount of raw data, a clear plan of specific steps is essential (Wilson, 2014), as proposed in Figure 0.1. Another reason to develop a valid path toward gathering and analyzing the data was to make the qualitative analytical process a bit more explicit and easier to understand for any reader.

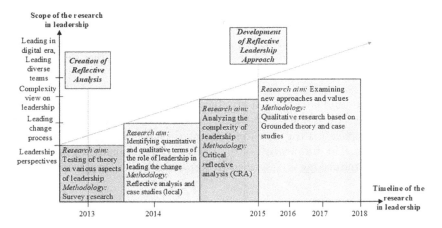

Figure 0.1 Research strategy and research design
Source: Authors.

However, to discover the present challenges and to propose the new leadership model, it is crucial to raise the following fundamental questions:

- What are the leadership challenges in the digital era?
- How do the organizations reflect the digital era and how do they deal with it?
- How does diversity contribute to creativity and innovation?
- What is the role of leadership in supporting change and innovation?
- What are the core values and approaches of the new leadership process?

This qualitative research was designed as the sequence of four parts starting in 2013 and finishing in 2018. Each research stage reflects the externalities of the CEE region of that period. The implementation of different qualitative research methods provides an assessment and evaluation of all examined processes and insights of the leadership challenges. The proposed research methods are considered to be rather innovative and not widely used in qualitative research. The Critical Reflection Analysis (CRA) was developed and published originally by the authors in 2013. It provides a guided process to assess and evaluate specific social processes and increase the potential for positive outcomes.

The first part of the longitudinal and systematic research started in 2013 when the CRA was designed and used for the first time to assess and evaluate the impact of leadership on organizational performance. Additionally, the CRA was implemented to examine the process of leading change in several companies. It aimed to identify what the change flow is and how the process of leading the change is performed. This part of the research was conducted via 123 case studies during three years from 2013 to 2015. The Critical Reflection Analysis was implemented in order to investigate what type of changes were implemented and how changes were led across all the processes within the organizational system. The findings from this analysis contributed to the reflection approach which helps us to identify the multiple and complex features of any change.

The results from this first part brought our attention to proceed toward the second stage run in 2016. We intended to examine more deeply the leadership role when leading the organization toward any transformation process. The data were collected through semi-structured interviews with 77 leaders from the CEE region (the 12 CEE countries plus Russia and Macedonia).

The structure of the questionnaire corresponds with the philosophy of the Critical Reflection Analysis to reflect on the challenges that leaders have to face and the support to the employees in order to cope with the changing environment efficiently.

The key results are highlighted in Chapter 9. The process of analysis contributed to a conceptualization approach toward the new leadership model.

The results from this research show what the crucial features of the leading process are, how it can be performed in an organization and what support leaders might provide to their followers.

In the third part of our ongoing research sequence, grounded theory has been used to discover how leadership has been changing and what new challenges are being faced by organizations and leaders in the so-called digital era. The lengthy interviews (each lasted one and a half hours on average) were conducted in confidence by young researchers. The interviewing process started in mid-September 2017 and was completed in December 2017. The data gathered from interviews were transcribed and analyzed by using the grounded theory method. The process of coding and the results contributed to Chapters 2–8.

The coding analysis of interviews with 65 leaders from both international and local companies provided a new view of the leadership process and current challenges which the new era has brought about (for a detailed research description, see Appendix I).

The workforce became more globalized, diverse and also structurally modified. New generations Y and Z entered the labor market with their own system of values and ways of tackling tasks. The structured surveys were distributed to 100 representatives of these two generations which will represent the primary human resources in the future.

Finally, we intended to merge the research findings and find out how discovered categories of the modified process of leading in the digital era are performed, what support leaders provide to their followers and how this fits with the young labor force's expectations. Therefore, verifying interviews (each lasting over two hours on average) with five selected multinational leaders were conducted in February and March 2018. These six top managers (HR, innovation managers and CEOs) of highly innovative international companies from different industries (machinery, printing, global logistics, automotive and financial sectors) were asked to reflect the research results of the key categories resulting from the coding process of the grounded theory analysis. Their insights, experiences and best practices enriched the content of Chapters 2–8 as well.

In the appendices, the detailed description of the overall research methodology is developed, which was gathered through all four stages.

Outline of the Book

The structure of the book is divided into three parts in order to reflect the three main assumptions: (1) internal and external challenges; (2) changing the structure and quality of human resources; and (3) the necessity to enhance innovation and change in every industry in the digital era.

Each part can be seen as the conceptual base of the key concepts which are linked and elaborated in individual chapters. At the end of each part, a case study is developed where the political and socioeconomic events together with cultural differences of the examined CEE region are presented and explained. We intend to show those events and features and what a significant impact they have made on the organizations and people of the studied geographical region. Part I provides an overview of key aspects of theories and concepts as the starting base for the further discussion of leading the new era organizations through the rest of the book.

In Chapter 1, we describe the fundamental theories and research on leadership, focusing mainly on the challenges of the 20th and 21st centuries. These concepts focus primarily on personal characteristics of leaders; they also provide shared knowledge to the latest responsibilities and requirements of leaders in an organizational environment. None by itself can give insight into the dynamics of the relationship between leader and followers and its processual dimension. This shortcoming encourages us to describe the role of leadership within the organizational ecosystem and to underline the main challenges that leaders have to face nowadays. Attention is given to theory development spotlighting the importance of rapid and frequent changes, global uncertainty and fast ICT development. All this means that the leadership process will revolve around new challenges. Currently traditional leadership has to deal with the increasing need for flexibility, diversity of human resources, frequently changing business conditions and pressure on the permanent improvement of all organizational processes. Chapter 1 provides an overview of the core concepts and summary of key debates. We want to question some leaders' actions since the followers' performance is a result of those actions. This can have a significant impact on future organizational performance.

Chapter 2 explores the various ethical pathologies and cognitive dissonance in corporate leadership that is a part of the field of behavioral economics. This includes subjects like psychopathic behavior, groupthink, cognitive bias and hubris. In order to process the sheer volume of information they encounter on a daily basis, individuals create simple mental efficiency rules that psychologists refer to as heuristics. Each individual must make order from the chaos around them and create a reality that minimizes emotional stress. This reality is not always logical or even rational, and the decision-making process is subjugated to one's own experiences based on historical environmental factors. As such, rationality can be distorted not only on an individual level but also on a societal one. One such problem is myopia that can occur from the lack of a diverse group of individuals, and with it a more extensive variety of opinions. This chapter describes how cognitive biases could lead an individual or organization toward unethical practices, unsustainable growth or a quick corporate downfall. With the insights mentioned above, we develop a conceptual triad of ethics based on transparency, accountability and universality. The main goal of this concept is to decrease the environmental factors that foster selfish behavior and at the same time establish social cues that reinforce concerns for others. This concept is also forward-looking with regard to the future sustainability of the organization.

Chapter 3 turns our attention to social responsibility in organizations as the result of the leadership actions. Much of the focus of corporate social responsibility (CSR) has centered on the needs of stockholders and the various stakeholders both inside and outside of the company. This historical response to CSR has been altered by the new global and digital order. Companies could perform the perfunctory duties of standard CSR and still create negative externalities for the country as a whole. At the same time the sovereign individual is often overlooked by the standard measurement of CSR. This chapter explores a version of CSR that is intended to serve the intuitive good, putting the individual citizen in the forefront.

Part I concludes with the first case study which focuses on the past and current changes in CEE countries. The purpose of this case study is to explore the historical background of the entire CEE post-communist region and how it impacts on its culture. In particular, it links the socio-economic and political development during the transition period before most CEE countries joined the European Union.

Part II explores (in two chapters) the complexity of leadership consisting of simultaneously running processes within the organizational ecosystem as well as the dynamic interactions and relations between actors. The concept of Reflective Leadership is designed here as a significant outcome of our qualitative research with 77 managers in CEE countries.

Chapter 4 sets the scene for the new concept of leadership, outlining our intention to study the complexity in leadership which is an output of previously discussed theories as well as the results of conducted research. Based on studies of everyday work and leadership, we argue that there is a complicated interplay between current activities, historical events and performance expectations, setting up the strategy and the perceived need to exercise leadership in organizations. Managing complexity is an essential leadership skill. In particular, in this chapter the concept of the "big picture" is introduced that helps to understand the complexity of the organizational system. Leaders influence and design the internal organizational systems which need to reflect the dynamism and changes coming from the external environment. Those systems have to be clear, purposeful and consistent. Leadership in the context of all events and developments is vital for individuals and the entire organization. Leadership as a system and as a process is presented with a strong orientation on building relations within and outside the organizational environment. Such a process-relational view of leadership may inspire higher individual performance, change organizational settings, form effective workplace relationships and create a sense of strategic direction.

Chapter 5 continues to synthesize the conceptual frameworks presented in previous chapters. We argue that there is a significant impact on what leaders really do and how their followers perceive it. This interplay is presented within the flow of four actions (i.e. Leading-Knowing-Following-Learning). The relations between leaders and followers are built by three essential techniques which framed the new concept of leadership for the digital era: critical thinking, reflection and the implementation of the process of feedback. Dynamic two-way discussions between leaders and followers based on critical thinking result in more effective decisions and accompanying innovations and improvements in organizational performance. Reflection in the process of leading is carefully thought out with critical consideration of all processes that make impacts on the organization's performance as well as on individuals' performance and further learning and development. We also explore the process of feedback which consists of two separate techniques: providing and receiving feedback. This chapter shows the results of conducted research where Critical Reflective Analysis was implemented in order to assess and evaluate different leaders' actions. The leadership approach emphasizes the social and metacognitive processes where the creation of interactions and networks are the key tasks for leaders. Here ethical issues, transparency of leaders' actions and interpersonal relations become crucial elements of the organizational ecosystem. It results in Reflective Leadership as the proposed concept which reflects on the challenges brought by the digital era.

Part II ends with Case Study 2, which is focused on introducing the significant differences between generations which are performing together in the current work environment. It discusses how leaders have to reflect those differences and how to cope with the generation gap.

In Part III, the content of change and innovation from the different perspectives is explored. First, in Chapter 6 the core attributes of change dynamism are examined. This chapter looks at the key leadership theories that focused on change and innovation, mainly those presented by John Kotter, the outstanding author of a vast number of publications describing the process of leading change. He states that nowadays strong leadership is needed to capitalize on unpredictable opportunities to catch up with innovation and create a change-driven organization.

As the business environment becomes more complex and is continuously changing, organizations need to be more flexible and alert. The dynamic external environment is a major driver of change and innovation. Organizations can thrive in this environment if leaders and followers identify emerging patterns and seize opportunities presented by these external changes. Technology, economic conditions, labor conditions and social and cultural diversity have significantly influenced leadership in recent times where most organizations function under the high turbulence and uncertainty of their environment. This chapter focuses on case studies where the processes of forming and implementing various types of changes are presented. Next, the concept of Reflective Leadership is applied in the process of leading change. The chapter ends with proposed guidelines on how to develop a change-driven organization.

Chapter 7 opens the discussion associated with the concept of diversity. Here we concentrate on the *diversity features* in organizations. Moreover, the influence of diversity on business will be analyzed—more precisely, the contribution of diversity to innovation and creativity. The *four layered diversity model* will be presented in order to explore diversity features in the researched organization. In this chapter we follow the broader understanding of diversity which is based not only on demographic characteristics but also includes informational differences, reflecting a person's education and experience, as well as values and goals. We want to find out how organizations perceive diversity and moreover if a positive or negative perception prevails. Nowadays, various generations are represented in the workplace, each with their own values and priorities. This provides a unique opportunity to increase productivity, creativity, problem solving and learning. Finally, the role of leadership in supporting innovation and creativity is examined.

Chapter 8 deals with leadership challenges triggered by digitalization and examines how organizations deal with them—more precisely, how organizations embrace new ideas, accommodate different styles of thinking, create a more flexible work environment, enable people to connect and collaborate and encourage different leadership approaches. There is also a high level of complexity which leads to the necessity of interactivity among all innovative actors. The constantly changing environment has triggered the so-called new teams: virtual, global and self-managing. This development has been strongly influenced by growing computer literacy and the explosion of ICT. Our process-relational leadership model explains which skills are required to tackle these challenges. New technologies such as social networking and virtual collaboration play a crucial role in the leadership process. Increasingly, more interactions are occurring in cyberspace than in the real environment. This revolution has brought potential benefits, such as a reduction of particular costs for the organization, and fostered the capabilities of a diverse workforce.

The final chapter pinpoints the main findings from previous chapters and proposes future research questions. The relevant aspects which shape future leadership development are discussed, including creativity, innovativeness and diversity. The current evolution requires a different leadership approach highlighting the importance of social identities of all workforce members and their relations within and outside of the organization. In the digital age, we want to improve our skills using IT applications, but there are still some restraints that are neglected, especially those regarding soft skills (networking, leading, giving and receiving feedback). One line that surfaced throughout this chapter is that the past and the present can direct us to the possible future. By identifying the new Reflective Leadership concept and reframing existing approaches toward diversity, change and innovation, we can provide not only new knowledge and research about leadership framework (which fits the new era) but also consider its application for leaders and organizations.

The third part closes with Case Study 3 reflecting innovation and ICT development in the studied CEE countries. We summarized "best practices" from different sectors to highlight the fact that the digital era offers a vast variety of tools to leaders for developing better interactions and relations with their employees.

Part I
Leadership Perspectives

1 Emerging Trends in Leadership

Introduction

This chapter highlights the *emerging features of the current leadership* approach. Effective leadership is the key to the future success and survival of an organization. Then the question is raised whether the leadership of the 21st century is the same as the leadership of the previous century. We draw attention to theory development spotlighting the importance of rapid and frequent changes, global uncertainty and fast ICT development. The leadership process will revolve around these new challenges. Currently, traditional leadership has to deal with the increasing need for flexibility, diversity of manpower, frequently changing business conditions and pressure on the permanent improvement of all organizational processes. In the broad interdisciplinary context, this chapter attempts to merge the theoretical and empirical knowledge generated from the distinctive social science disciplines. On the basis of the theoretical background of the system and relational theories, this chapter offers a modified view of leadership.

The essential part of this chapter is to provide an overview of the core concepts and summary of key debates. We want to question some of the leaders' actions since the followers' performance is a result of their actions. This can have a significant impact on future organizational performance.

Theories, Philosophies and Traditional Approaches in Leadership

The word leadership is one of the world's oldest concepts. In earlier times, words meaning "head of state", "military commander", "principal", "chief" or "king" were very common in most societies; these words differentiated the ruler from other members of society (Bass, 1997).

Historical management theories of leadership include inspiring, engaging and motivating employees so they would work harder and achieve organizational goals. There are various opinions among researchers as well as many definitions of leadership.

James MacGregor Burns (1978) argues that a study of the definition of the leadership world reveals 130 definitions. Some fundamental definitions originate from his work, where leadership is characterized as collective, causative and a morally purposeful action. It is a notion that a one-person leadership is "a contradiction in terms" because both leaders and followers must exist. Also, an organization may have multiple leaders all acting in correspondence with one another. Leadership is causative. True leadership affects the motives of individuals and groups of people and alters the course of organizational history. It causes positive change. It is goal oriented, with leaders and followers pointing the way to some future state of organization with plans about how those goals might be met.

The earliest approaches to leadership are descriptive and based on providing the personal characteristics and charisma of leaders. A lot of emphasis has been given to the leader's ability to influence others through his or her personal authority. Bass (1997, p. 131) explains that leadership is a combination of many definitions, such

> as a matter of personality, as a matter of including compliance, as the exercise of influence, as a particular behavior, as a form of persuasion, as a power of relation, as an instrument to achieve goals, as an effect of interaction, and as initiation of structure.

There are many other approaches presented in leadership theory. The classification has been provided by Grint (2010), where core leadership concepts are identified:

- Leadership as a *position* (leaders are defined by the position they are in, usually taking the form of authority based on formal hierarchy).
- Leadership as a *person* (people become leaders based on their character; it is their personality which makes them a leader).
- Leadership as a *result* (character is not enough; results make up a leader).
- Leadership as a *process* (considers relationships between leader and practice; how leaders get things done).

Traditional literature on leadership focuses mainly on "characteristics" of good leaders. These characteristics, however, are often too general to have practical value to someone trying to become a better leader. For instance, to say that good leaders are "gifted optimists" or are "honest" and "inspiring" provides little practical basis for specific skill development or improvement. These are typically judgments about our behavior made by others. In its broadest sense, leadership can be defined as the ability to influence others toward the accomplishment of some goal. That is, a leader leads a collaborator or a group of collaborators toward the desired end.

Much of the early leadership literature was focused on middle managers, but recently the interest has shifted toward strategic leaders. This reflects the understanding of how senior managers are able to cope with globalization, increasing international competition and accelerating innovation and radical change. But the innovation is not created in one person's head. It results from a collective effort, as a transformation, and that requires an adjustment in people's behavior.

Few leaders from the interviewed group revealed that the leader is expected to be an initiator of change. Another group of interviewed leaders stated that they just formulate the purpose of innovation, set goals and provide support to staff. People are a valuable source for improvements. We realized that expectations of leadership that have been effective in a particular business, culture or environment may be ineffective in another environment or in a different culture.

Some studies of leadership focus on the outcomes of effective leadership, pointing out that good leaders "create the vision", "mobilize commitment", "recognize needs" and so forth (Hamel and Green, 2007). However, simply knowing about these goals is not enough. The key to actually achieving them involves having the mental and behavioral skills required to put them into practice. The process of learning to be a good leader has been suggested by Collins (2001) though the Level Five Leadership Model. It is based on the idea that respect toward people, self-awareness of the leader and strong, powerful commitment to achieve results bring out the best in subordinates. The ability to use leadership skills in everyday work is not an easy task for many leaders. Senge (1990, p. 216) argues that

> leadership is about influence when there is a genuine vision; people excel and learn, not because they are told to, but because they want to. Many leaders have personal visions that never get translated into shared visions that galvanize an organization.

The literature on leadership is vast, yet it offers models and theories about leader behavior and different styles, and answers how those skills can be developed or which leadership style to use. A dramatic shift from ego- and personality-centered leadership during the 1980s and 1990s toward contingency approaches has been observed and was later called the post-heroic approach in leadership with an emphasis on the occurrence of emotional intelligence.

A new credo for leadership was presented by Bennis and Nanus (1997), who launched the idea that a primary role of leadership is to create meaning for co-workers. They state that leaders should create and communicate a shared vision and future direction of the company. They point to a new set of tools and techniques that leaders need to master in order to be successful. Leaders need to invent and implement daily the images, metaphors, stories and new business models that provide focus on new intentions.

Our approach to studying leadership with the focus on its processual character was influenced by the point of view presented by Wilson (2010), who states that the research on leadership has been too scientific for this highly interpretative subject matter. Leadership might be considered an art rather than a science, and there are no recipes to guarantee success. This opinion has a certain bias since art cannot be learned; it is something we are born with, and thus leadership skills would be difficult to practice. If no good leader is born, who would come and lead the organization? Then would there be no future vision formed?

Our primary interest in leadership theory analysis is to identify the process feature of leading action and to deconstruct the key attribute of this process with the main focus on developing the relations between all actors in the organizational environment. The process view on leadership provides a better understanding of *what* has to be done in line with *how* to conduct leadership actions in order to make an impact on organizational performance.

The process view on leadership started by Blanchard (2009) argues that leadership is defined as an influence process for many years. Evans (2008) adds to the idea of leadership as a process, explaining that this happens as an interaction between all individuals and it can be documented and adapted to any organizational environment.

These two parameters (process and relations) are essential for the leader to understand the organizational ecosystem. The leader needs to consider a different way of communication with the organization and other stakeholders. In the light of fast-changing technology, it is much harder for a leader to decide what information, sources and data are relevant to consider and what are not. The research results indicate the dyadic and somewhat controversial tasks for leaders. On the one hand, the implementation of ICT across all organizational operations is inevitable, thus it reduces costs and simplifies the work. The pacing of the latest digitalization trends and their fast implementation as a process of the change continuum represents one of the key leadership challenges in the digital era. Contrary to this, the understanding of real leadership by respondents is to help people understand and adjust to new conditions, accept changes and actively participate in new processes. They are aware that the speed of change, its implementation and adequate leadership action make a significant impact on the organization's performance and its competitiveness.

For that, leaders challenge the complexity of the external and internal environment and they should continuously search for new ways to engage with all stakeholders. That is all about joint communication, where the focus of their interactions should be about organizational vision, strategy and goals and how they are communicated with the workforce and external stakeholders. It should not be about the leader's personal agenda.

This corresponds with another leadership action which has been pointed out by respondents. They understand that the leadership role is to be in contact with employees, customers and other stakeholders and to build relations with them. The respondents perceive these personal contacts and relations to be important sources of innovation.

Studying all those views, shifting from the leaders' personal characteristics to their actions and relationships that bond leaders to different actors, along with process content of leadership, reveals our view of leadership as a social influencing process in which the leadership seeks the involvement of all stakeholders in an effort to formulate the organizational goals and strategy.

All those mentioned approaches focus on *what* leaders should do, however they are not able to address the complexity and dynamics of the leadership process. In a number of organizations which emphasize operating and controlling activities, there is a lack of a leading function. The vision and strategy are developed as a single exercise of one individual, usually by the executive manager, without sharing it through the entire organization and with no support of other people. This leadership is called a top-down approach. As such, leadership is performed by giving directions and does not foster any mutual collaboration and active contribution of other members in the organization. Very often people do not understand the purpose and meaning of the leader's actions. This prevents the acceptance of any change or innovation, and results in a lack of coordinated learning and its adaptations in complex organizational systems.

The role of leadership is to create a shared and jointly discussed vision of where the organization is aiming to go and to formulate strategies to bring about the changes needed to achieve that vision. It is a difficult process nowadays, when the traditional theories of management are not offering expected results, and the new generation of employees born in the digital era is expected to implement more innovative approaches.

Among all the selected ideas and examined theories about leadership, three aspects stand out: people, influence and vision. The contemporary view sees the role of leadership as a need of the organization to seek transformation and continuous change. This can be achieved only by building relationships with people within the entire organization.

Human resources are very much influenced by ICT, both positively and negatively. They need to be developed and guided on how to cope with the digital era. Managers are expected to select the right information and share it with their people, as this is an important condition for following trends and developing innovation.

In the emerging views of leadership, leaders are committed to creating an environment in which employees thrive and perform. This commitment demands a special set of skills and abilities in order to effectively and ecologically manifest the visions which guide those committed to change. It involves communication, interaction and managing relationships within an organization, network or social system to move toward one's highest aspirations. These aspects are covered in the most recently developed leadership theories which are based on relations. The relational-based theories are built on the social-exchange theory, which states that both leader and followers commit to working together; that is, the followers are willing to be led and the leader is willing to provide direction and support as long as members find the relationship mutually satisfying (Cleveland et al., 2000).

The earliest approach to relation-based leadership theory is the transformational leadership concept, where the role of the leader in the process of change and formulation of the strategy first appeared. In the next section, we discuss the core ideas which contributed to our research focus of leadership on innovation and change.

Transformational Leadership

This concept is tracked back to the development of transactional and transformative leadership by Burns (1978), where he provides the foundation for revolutionary thinking about the role and purpose of leadership. He explains that transactional leadership takes place when one person takes initiative in contacting others for the purpose of an exchange of valued things. The transactional leadership can exist between leaders of two or more organizations, or between leaders and members within the same organization. On the other hand, the transforming leadership occurs when one or more persons engage with others in such a way that leaders and followers encourage one another to a higher level of motivation and morality. Although Burns feels that transforming leadership cannot work in bureaucratic organizations, it is possible that it can exist where organizational leaders and members aspire to generate collective purpose and transforming processes that are ultimately linked to social change (Hickman, 2016).

Bass (1985) extends the work of Burns (1978) by explaining the psychological mechanisms that underlie transforming and transactional leadership, thus developing what is today referred to as Bass's Transformational Leadership Theory. He separates Burns's link to social change from his theory of transforming leadership and finds that qualitative change in performance and relationships occurs to the benefit of the individual and the organization. He introduced the term "transformational" in place of "transforming". Bass also adds an explanation of how transformational leadership could be measured, as well as how it impacts follower motivation and performance. The extent to which a leader is transformational is measured first in terms of the leader's influence on the followers. The followers of such a leader feel trust, admiration, loyalty and respect for the leader, and because of the qualities of the transformational leader they are willing to work harder than originally expected. These outcomes occur because the transformational leader offers to the followers something more than just working for self-gain; the leader provides followers with an inspiring mission and vision and gives them an identity.

In the age of innovation, where continuous change is considered to be the key competitive advantage, the leadership approach is mainly transformational. Even though the impact of ICT in all sectors is extremely high and leaders often use technical knowledge to determine the change process, the necessity of a transformational approach is crucial to successfully implement and cope with all those innovations and changes. The transformational leadership focuses on the followers; it develops their potential, and stimulates and inspires them to be creative and proactive.

The transformational leadership model gets the attention of many other theorists. In contrast to Burns's (1978) distinction, Bass does not consider transactional and transformational leadership to be at opposite ends but as along a continuum. A number of researches conducted by Avolio and Bass (1991, 1995) and Bass (1985, 1997) indicate that transformational and transactional behavior can be displayed by the same leader in different amounts, intensities and various situations and complement each other. In the historical background of transformational leadership, it has

Table 1.1 Focus of transformational leadership in the age of innovation

Focus	Transformational Leadership
Key actions toward followers	• Arouse emotions in their followers, which motivates them to act beyond the framework of what may be described as exchange relations. • Be proactive and form new expectations in followers. • Provide and receive feedback.
Motivation	• Distinguish the incentives which fit culture, industry or specific group of employees to inspire them, provide individualized consideration, intellectual stimulation and idealized influence to their followers.
Performance	• Set strategic goals, create learning opportunities, stimulate followers to solve problems and coach them to achieve the desired performance outcomes.
Core leadership capabilities	• Possess good visioning, rhetorical and managerial skills. • Develop strong emotional bonds with followers.
The approach in process of leading the change	• Search for adaptive solutions to engage hearts and minds in the change process.

Source: Authors.

much in common with charismatic leadership, but charisma is only a part of transformational leadership as it has been described in more modern concepts (Conger and Kanugo, 1987; Shamir and House, 1993).

Bass (1985) argues that charisma alone is insufficient for transformational leadership. In later studies, Bass and Avolio (1993) develop the four critical factors which are essential for transformational leadership, where inspiration is a subfactor of charisma and later described as a separate component design to motivate. That can also be understood like the dimension of communication where transformational leaders communicate high expectations, use symbols to focus effort and express important purposes in simple ways.

Even though the role of communication is often repeated and seemed to be "the general recipe", in our research leaders acknowledge the specific features of communication in supporting the innovativeness of their employees, for instance:

> Regular communication encourages people to express their ideas with confidence.
> More frequent and friendly personal contact with employees establishes better relations and working environment.
> Leaders need to listen, avoid criticism and to be open to any idea and proposals. They use a variety of tools and techniques in order to encourage people to talk freely, and not be afraid of failure or making mistakes.

This corresponds with the work of Bass and Riggio (2006) who state that leaders encourage followers to come up with new and unique ideas by challenging the status quo. Therefore, the entire concept of transformational leadership is composed of the four I's:

1. *Idealized influence*, which serves as a positive model for followers.
2. *Inspirational motivation*, which motivates and inspires followers by providing meaning and challenge and articulating a compelling vision of the future (charisma).
3. *Intellectual stimulation*, which stimulates followers' efforts to be innovative and creative by questioning assumptions, reframing problems and approaching old situations in new ways.
4. *Individualized consideration*, which pays special attention to individual followers' needs for achievement and growth by acting as a coach or mentor.

Transformational leadership is essential when an organization is changing and/or creating a new vision. As a result, transformational leadership has an important impact upon the high involvement of individuals, guiding them to consider not just their self-interests but also reflecting implications of their actions and goals on the organization's performance. Thus, transformational leadership can become a viable form of leading the organization toward continuous real change and innovation. Leadership as a process contributes to building the strategic architecture, partnerships and relations inside as well as outside the organization.

More research related to transformational leadership is primarily concentrated on highlighting the effects of this type of leadership on individual performance, satisfaction and effectiveness. Less attention is given to evaluating other key factors that may explain and moderate the impact of transformational leadership on the overall organization's performance. It includes the actions of the leader and the context in which the leader and his or her followers operate (e.g. the level of support for innovation, coping with changes and/or developing high-performing teams). In addition, little attention is paid to various theories and research which examine the relationships between key variables of the process of leadership, such as formulation and implementation of the strategy, development and coaching to reach a higher level of performance and satisfied individuals. This approach is further developed in the next chapters of this monograph, where emphasis is given to what the ethics and responsibility of leaders are when fostering innovation and how they impact the organization's environment.

The Role of Leadership in the Current Business Environment

Any leadership action is performed as the reflection on what is going on in the external environment and how that makes an impact on the internal environment. The organizational environment can be described at three main levels:

1. The macro-environment, which includes the overall external impacts that may affect an organization.
2. The micro-environment, which is set up by businesses and individuals with whom the organization interacts and which directly affect the organization's activity.
3. The inner environment, which consists of all processes conducted inside the organization.

Three layers of the environment are seen as the sources for the continuous change process in which leaders play a crucial role. These connections with their overlapping actions are provided by the latest organizational concept of Hickman (2016). He points out the essential role for leadership throughout all levels of an environment is to establish strategic foresight and purpose and create passion and energy among the employees.

In order to fulfill the expected result of the leadership—which means understanding of the business, being well informed of dynamic changes and assessing potential impacts on products, services, stakeholders and the environment—the joint effort of all people within the organization is required.

Such complexity is described by defining all of the stakeholders in both the external as well as the internal environment which influence leadership action. This gives a broad perspective for an era of innovation, currently defined as the digital era, which requires leadership to be substantially different from its traditional point of view.

Organizations in the digital era function as complex ecosystems where the need for new leadership values and approaches arise. They share both the social responsibility and ethics for leading the organization and they frame the role of leaders and the behavior of followers.

Instead of extending the dyadic theories of leadership to explain organizational processes, it is more useful to develop new conceptual frameworks that are more comprehensive and complex. Related ideas can be found in several emerging theories of organizational leadership which focus on how leadership impacts individual and organizational performance, followership theories and the importance of strategic leadership (e.g. Kotter, 2014; Yukl, 2010; Beerel, 2009; Goleman, 1995; Hickman, 2016). This is bringing our focus onto the system view of organizations.

For the first time, this view occurred in Senge's concept (1990) of "learning organization" where the essentials of how to understand the organizational system depended on a person's time horizon. On the one hand, if the horizon is too short, the leader will ignore essential feedback loops and come up with short-term fixes that won't work in the long run. On the other hand, if the leader's horizon is long enough, they will have a chance of seeing more of the key systems of action.

The organization functions as a system and is surrounded by the external environment as well as a number of different interactions coming from within. In the emerging views of leadership, leaders are people who are committed to creating a world to which people want to belong. This commitment requires a special set of models and abilities in order to effectively and ecologically manifest the visions which guide those committed to change. It involves communicating, interacting and managing relationships within and outside an organization, network or social system to move toward one's highest aspirations.

In Table 1.2, the difference between the traditional type of relationship and the newly discussed partnership concept of the relationship is presented.

The partnership concept calls for a set of complex leadership skills and abilities, including relationships, negotiating mutually rewarding deals, finding the "right" partners with compatible values and goals, and providing the partnered organizations with the appropriate balance of

Table 1.2 Traditional concept vs. partnership concept

Characteristics	Traditional Concept	Partnership Concept
Time frame	Short/term, renewable	Long/term, sustainable
Strategic orientation	Subcontracting	Strategic outsourcing
Inter-firm relationship	Superior-subordinate	Leader–team member
Information flow	One-way	Two-way
Decision making	Precise, unilateral	Guidelines, consensus oriented
Planning	Few executives, experts	Many managers, line and staff
Product improvement	Defined by contract	Ever-changing, fluid
Control	Traditional hierarchy	Multi-disciplinary teamwork
Primary objective	Price	Quality, price, timing
Profit orientation	Buyer controlled	Mutually controlled

Source: Authors.

freedom and control. The main actions that are expected from leaders are a result of the aforementioned latest theories and include:

- Acting as a broker, securing and negotiating relationships with other firms.
- Recognizing their independence and willingness to share information and co-operate with their partners.
- Understanding other interests, cultures and diversity, accepting another members' independence.
- Encouraging innovation of products or services and customizing them on a continual basis to maintain the mutually beneficial partnership.
- Investing in the development of inter-firm capabilities, human resources and trusting the individual, team, company and partnership at all levels.

Thus, understanding and the ability to manage inter-unit dynamics and interactions between partners become crucial for the success of such a strategic partnership outside and inside the organization. Negotiating and discussing the partnership deal is a long and difficult project. Some of the managers or owners of the companies who faced such a challenge admitted that creating a partnership was a learning and self-discovering process.

The people's view of leadership in an organization is influenced by the knowledge of their performance and by the extent of how they are organized and thus provide information on what action is required and what work needs to be done.

The previously discussed content of transformational leadership has brought attention to the leaders' commitment to create a vision and formulate and implement a strategy. Within the action of transformational leadership, the leader envisions the changes of the company and sets the strategic goals for the entire organization and for subordinates. The latest theories focus on transformational leadership with an articulation of the vision and recognizing the patterns of how things are done. Because it includes showing of direction, pacing and directing the action for followers, it is described more as a process rather than a pattern of behavior.

Eriksson-Zetterquist et al. (2011) state that leadership is one of the more important groups of activities carried out in an organization and is linked to formal aspects of organizing. The formal structure is part of the context in which leadership is realized. It is a broad concept which consists of a wide range of aspects that can shape the conditions for leadership—formal structures, people, relations, culture, legislation and technology are a few examples. There are two important contextual factors that show how intimately leadership and organizations are connected. The first factor, *organizational structures*, has leadership carried out by people set in formal positions in a formal structure, usually referred to as *managers*. The second factor, *values*, deals with societal trends that influence the way leadership is exercised and how it is accepted by people, referred to as *followership*. This describes relations between leaders and followers and also how leaders can develop an understanding of their followers and how to help them to be most effective (Daft et al., 2010).

Under this approach, the relationships between a leader and followers are interpreted as the behavioral Leading-Following framework, influenced also by external and internal environments (see Figure 1.1). The relationship is developed both ways and the interaction process includes both business transactions and social exchanges taking place in the entire organizational environment. According to this framework, the interacting parties are seen as individuals or groups that work in an organization. The groups can be viewed in terms of size, structure, strategy and the individuals in terms of experience and behavior.

There are no good leaders without good followers. The interactions between leaders and followers are presented in Figure 1.1, where the key is to understand the two interdependent processes of leading and following. The Leading-Following Model is based on several observations:

- Critical and careful thinking of a leader is required in developing an understanding of the environmental conditions in which an organization exists.
- Interactions between leadership and followership are systematic and explore all distributed process within a team or organization.
- A good leading process involves the following process which both tracks and deals with the environment.

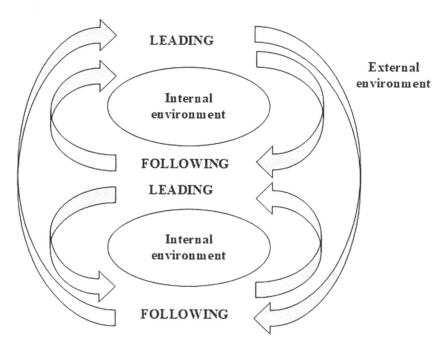

Figure 1.1 Leading-Following Model
Source: Authors.

The current trend fosters the leaders' commitment toward reflecting and envisioning the changes outside and inside the organization. It requires inspiring followers to commit to a shared vision and goals for an organization or unit, challenging them to be innovative problem solvers, and developing followers' leadership capacity via coaching, questioning, feedback and provision of both challenge and support.

Describing the quality of followership, Kelley (1992) explains it within two dimensions. The first dimension is the quality of independent, critical thinking versus dependent, uncritical thinking. Independent critical thinkers are mindful of the effects of their own and others' behavior on achieving goals. They can weigh the impact of their bosses's and their own decisions and offer constructive criticism, creativity and innovation. Conversely, a dependent, uncritical thinker does not consider possibilities beyond what he or she is told, does not contribute to the cultivation of the organization and accepts the supervisor's ideas without thinking. The second dimension of followership is active versus passive behavior. An active follower participates fully in the organization, engages in behavior that is beyond the limits of the job, demonstrates a sense of ownership and initiates problem solving and decision making. A passive follower, by contrast, is characterized by a need for constant supervision and avoids taking responsibility (Daft et al., 2010).

People are considered to be an important resource for any organization that can create a distinctive capability as a prerequisite to achieving a competitive advantage providing they are led and developed properly.

If the organization identifies its people as an important resource and provides them with high-quality leadership and further development possibilities, it will find itself at a competitive advantage. In such occasions, learning and knowledge sharing make a crucial impact on leading the people toward the achievement of their goals. The leaders are often in the roles of coaches, mentors or even teachers of their subordinates. The individuals are an essential part of the social process of which quality is predetermined by the ability and readiness of the leaders to implement and use the reflection in this process. This is a new way of leading the organizations where the complexity of all processes, interactions and relations has to overlap in order to perform successfully.

What Do We Expect From Leadership in the Organizational Environment?

The debate on transactional and transformational leadership still continues many years after it was developed by Burns. The reasons are clear: transformational style generates a higher level of engagement and brings better results. It is also a very effective way of fostering transformation, which can occur in a number of various forms such as radical change, innovation or high-quality improvements in organizations. Certain threats of the transformational approach are indicated by Pendleton and Furnham (2012), who argue that followers might suffer from unreasonable expectations or become dependent on their leaders. Such leaders expect unity of purpose—those who do not fit will leave, with the consequences of limiting effective diversity.

The question regarding what leadership approach is the most suitable for organizations in the 21st century is often raised. A simple answer is not provided. Avery (2004) develops the argument that the future of leadership development is organic, that is, organizations might not need single leaders but leadership as a cooperative action closely linked to an organization's direction and purpose. It appears in multiple forms of joint actions which refer to formulating and executing the strategy, decision-making and problem-solving processes.

Leadership in organizations is a process that involves many formal and informal leaders at all levels and in different subunits of the organization. The fates of different leaders are closely intertwined in complex ways and the overall performance of the organization is likely to suffer if decisions made by different leaders are not compatible with each other. Even though top executives have primary responsibility for strategic decisions, they are unlikely to be implemented successfully without the support and commitment of middle and lower-level leaders in the organization (Beer and Eisenstat, 1996; Huy, 2002).

Strategic leadership is required to show direction and guides the actions of followers. This is described more as a process than just a pattern of behavior or a certain leadership style. In the book *Blue Ocean Strategy*, Kim and Mauborgne (2005) advocate three elements for gaining the cooperation and commitment of people involved in the execution of strategy: (1) engagement and involvement, (2) explanation and understanding and (3) clarity of expectation, which is built on clarification of standards, responsibility and consequences.

Some authors acknowledge that the increased interest in strategic leadership reflects the importance of understanding how leaders help the organization to cope with globalization, increasing international competition and more rapid technological and social changes (Cannella and Monroe, 1997). This, of course, recognizes the role of strategic leadership to anticipate events, envision possibilities, maintain flexibility and empower others to create strategic change (Hoskinsson et al., 2013). This view is also supported by Yukl's (2010) concept which provides an answer on how leaders can influence the overall effectiveness of large organizations. Interest is more closely linked to examining how this influence is actually achieved rather than providing a general description of what the leader's influence is on organizational performance. He states that organizational effectiveness depends on three performance determinants, which are (1) efficiency and process reliability, (2) human relations and resources and (3) adaptation to the environment. There are three general leadership behaviors that are differentiated by their primary objective. Task-oriented behavior is used primarily to improve efficiency and process reliability. Change-oriented behavior is used primarily to improve adaptation to the external environment. Relations-oriented behavior is used to improve human relations and resources.

The present business environment requires their leaders to simultaneously reflect on technological trends while controlling the efficiency of all organizational processes, and at the same time involve a diverse labor force. This makes it difficult to separately implement the different leadership styles and behaviors. Some of the major leadership theories, including the trait theories (Bass, 2000), contingency theories (Fiedler, 1967), leader-member exchange theories (Graen and Uhl-Bien, 1995) and leadership styles (Bass and Avolio, 1993; Burns, 1978), have largely sought universal dimensions to characterize leader behavior and attributes. In the 21st century, leaders and members find themselves in heterogeneous contexts within organizations. Leaders need to be prepared to lead a diverse workforce, confront complex situations that are influenced by diverse communities and lead in ways that are culturally responsive and competent (Chin and Trimble, 2015).

Based on the amount of research conducted on the nature of leadership, leadership theorists began to redefine the criteria for effective leadership that reflect current challenges. The results show that as leaders reach higher levels in an organization structure, the need for interpersonal skills becomes equivalent to the need for conceptual skills. The need for technical skills becomes proportionally less important (Zaccaro and Klimovski, 2002), and more flexibility in thinking and responsiveness to a changing world is required (Chin and Trimble, 2015).

At the strategic level, the leader faces a set of challenges combining the guiding of the organization in a global and changing marketplace, meeting the demands of owners and stakeholders, and helping employees to perform and develop themselves. The leading process focuses on initiating and setting externally referenced challenges which are connected to the key attributes of strategic management (i.e. vision, mission and strategic goals). That also requires the top executives to express a clear understanding of the strategic architecture through action and constructive dialogue where appropriate activities are built.

Such features are an essential part of the work of Pendleton and Furnham (2012) which characterize outstanding leaders. These leaders think and act systematically and perceive relationships as a route to enhance performance in others. They give huge amounts of their time and focus on people and the climate of the organization.

Overall, all these concepts and most of all the strategic leadership theory do not explain much about the nature of those relationships, or about how to accomplish all the aforementioned tasks. All these issues trigger the discussion on *what* is expected from leaders nowadays and *how* they can accomplish these things without in-depth analysis of the underlying mechanisms. Many questions still remain regarding what main parameters the leading process should establish and how the leaders form the relationships and the transformation of these relationships into specific outcomes.

Several reports and studies have been conducted recently in order to identify future trends in leadership development. The studies *Future Trends in Leadership Development* (Petrie, 2014) and *The State of Leadership Development Study* (2016) conducted by Harvard Business School, describe the environment that leaders are currently working in. They use the US Army acronym *VUCA* (Global Leadership Forecast 2014/15, published by Development Dimensions International, 2014) to define the main features of the outside and inside organizational world. VUCA stands for:

- *Volatile*: change happens rapidly and on a large scale.
- *Uncertain*: the future cannot be predicted with any precision.

- *Complex*: challenges are complicated by many factors and there are few single causes or solutions.
- *Ambiguous*: there is little clarity on what events mean and what effect they may have.

Based on various reports and studies, the dynamic changing environment and the uncertainty of the external environment are affecting leadership performance to a certain extent. According to the report *Future of Jobs* provided by the World Economic Forum (2016), the main drivers of change are demographic, socioeconomic and technological trends. In addition to these general characteristics, several studies pointed out that areas related to *human resources* and *information technologies* are the biggest driving forces of many challenges that leaders need to face (Global Human Capital Trends, 2016; National Ethics Business Survey, Ethics Resource Center, 2013).

The *Global Leadership Forecasts* from 2014/2015 (Sinar et al., 2015) and 2018 (published by Development Dimensions International, 2018) define the readiness of leader in four key areas which they claim is comprised of the VUCA index, which is further used in determining the business environment in these crucial leadership roles: anticipating and reacting to the nature and speed of change; acting decisively without always having clear direction and certainty; navigating through complexity, chaos and confusion; maintaining effectiveness despite constant surprises; and a lack of predictability.

Other results provided by the report *Succeeding in the VUCA Paradigm* (2016) showed that leaders spent most of their time doing the following tasks: managing complexity and contradictions (67%), articulating a shared vision (64%), guiding and supporting change execution (54%) and addressing change resistance (52%). Researchers concluded that one of the most important activities of leaders in the VUCA environment is to manage complexity, the other two actions are addressing the process of change consisting of guiding, supporting change as well as coping with the resistance to change. Taking into consideration the general perspectives on leadership skills which are presented in Table 1.1, there are some contradictions. We compare two significant worldwide studies. In the first one, *High Resolution Leadership* (Sinar et al., 2016), 15,000 respondents covering all hierarchical organizational levels from leaders on the frontline up to strategic executives and C-suite executives identified the top ten leadership skills (ordered based on priority). In the second study, the *State of Leadership Development* (2016), 700 respondents' business-line managers and learning and development managers identified the biggest gaps in essential leadership skills (ordered from highest to lowest).

Both studies provided a totally different perspective on what leaders should do and what capabilities are needed. They only focus on change

Table 1.3 Leadership skills and roles

High-Resolution Leadership Study	State of Leadership Development
Operational decision making	Coaching in the moment
Customer focus	Emotional strength
Cultivating networks	Agility
Leading change	Social intelligence
Driving execution	Change agent
Empowerment/delegation	Innovation
Establishing a strategic direction	Visionary
Coaching and developing others	Team building
Entrepreneurship	Data analysis
Building organizational talent	Technologically savvy

Source: Authors on the basis of Sinar et al. (2016) study on *High Resolution Leadership* (2016) and the *State of Leadership Development* (2016) study of Harvard Business Report.

that is considered to have similar importance since it appears almost at the same place.

Another study conducted, called *CEO Challenge* (Mitchell et al., 2014), provides us with the results on the top five essential global traits and behaviors that future leaders must exhibit: integrity, leading change, managing complexity, entrepreneurial mindset and retaining and developing talent.

Finally, we can conclude that among the most important attributes of leadership actions are managing complexity, leading change and developing human capital.

After studying various approaches and theories, also based on the research on secondary data where the respondents were the leaders of all organizational levels and positions and from various industries, we can summarize that regardless of managerial position or industry, the new concept of the leadership process should reflect current challenges and demonstrate the following six qualities:

> *Collaborative*: the best strategies, plans, products and processes emerge from a collective effort. Leaders allocate and develop valuable resources and actively seek out others' ideas and opinion and convey enthusiasm about achieving important goals. They believe that collaboration motivates people to do their best and establishes the basis for learning, knowledge creation and sharing processes.
>
> *Inventive*: there are always new and different ways to serve people, to be more efficient and to make work easier. Leaders question traditional methods and look for unconventional solutions to unmet dilemmas and needs.
>
> *Change oriented*: understanding the change continuum as the engine for the organization's improvement and success. Leaders enhance, successfully introduce, guide and monitor the process of change.

Skilled: the presence requires balancing the demands of multiple critical tasks, with both technical and interpersonal skills being crucial in achieving results. Leaders view learning as a lifelong process for themselves as well as for all people, as it takes continued practice and experience to becoming fully competent and capable in diversified jobs.

Visionary: foreseeing and painting an inspiring and better future for the organization and people around it. Leaders believe that others should contribute to the future and participate in its realization. Leaders inspire and motivate people with both actions and words.

Mindful: respecting human needs and realizing others' feelings are important. Leaders have a strong sense of organizational values and act in alignment with them. The long-term best interests of others and the organization are at the center of their decisions and actions (Theodoulides, in Raguz et al., 2016).

The transformational concept recently gained certain doubts due to a strong emphasis on the role of a single leader. As already described, the environment of new era organizations is inclusive of the social identities and lived experiences of a diverse workforce which shape the leader-follower exchange, which in turn influences how the organization implements its strategy and adapts its structure to external changes. This diverse organizational framework goes from an individual/dyadic perspective to a group/social perspective and from a situational to systemic leadership perspective.

New Leadership Challenges: Transforming Business Models

Previously described leadership concepts have been characterized as complex and dynamic with a humanistic perspective where interactions between the leaders and their people are at the center of the organizational environment. Every organization can be seen as a system where leadership is expected to perform complex tasks in order to lead the organization the right way. In a number of theories (Senge, 2006; Ackoff, 2006; Latham, 2013) there is the experience and applied knowledge about the leadership process based on contextual factors where key elements of an organization system have been described in general. Although the context of leadership changes significantly when new generations step into the labor market, the content of leadership remains the same. In addition to that, little empirical evidence exists on the systemic view of leadership where the process and the relations jointly executed would impact the staff's performance. There are many processes conducted in every organization. The rapid technological progress forces the organization to keep up with innovation, and change becomes an everyday topic for leaders.

A new era of leadership for the first time appears in Hickman's Leading Organizations (2010). He offers a holistic approach on how to understand and analyzes the role of leadership in a post-industrial society of new era organizations. In his opinion, leaders and participants must innovate and create value beyond the organization's usual boundaries. He points out the key responsibilities and actions for the new era leadership, which are as follows:

- Ensuring that the organization is well positioned economically.
- Acquiring, developing and managing key resources including human capital and effective organizational culture.
- Developing and managing relationships with external stakeholders.
- Determining and communicating strategic direction together with establishing values and ethical practices.
- Overseeing the formulation and implementation of specific strategies.
- Establishing balanced controls (Hickman, 2016).

Our research follows up on all of the above findings and provides us with the view of what behavior and actions of leaders are needed in organizations in the digital era. Two perspectives of leadership are proposed. The first one focuses on the point of view of *processes* in order to:

- Understand the technology to modernize their business strategy and operations.
- Be aware of a complex digital landscape by accepting the purpose of innovation and its broader impact (economic, ethical, social, etc.).
- Seek opportunities across complex ecosystems.

The second perspective which was identified by our respondents is based on *relations*, where the key task of the leader is to:

- Understand what is going on in the external environment and then translate it into the organizational environment accordingly.
- Balance people and technology.
- Help people adapt to different situations and adjust their behavior to new circumstances.
- Search for innovation possibilities via cultural and intellectual curiosity.
- Be aware that leading is a skill to identify and develop talents.

Leaders never get extraordinary results by themselves. Leadership is a relationship between those who mobilize others to accomplish things and those who agree to follow. Sometimes that requires a high degree of reflection, critical thinking and a learning mindset.

Our respondents emphasize the rise of the role of technology today in enabling strong human resources development. Technology can help companies break out of the traditional leadership approach (top-down) that many still have. The fast-paced digital era helps leaders in day-to-day interactions with their followers both on the national and international levels. Companies invest into various ICT tools and platforms which support organizational interactions that accelerate the processes and make them more effective. That helps leaders engage with more people as they seek to foster learning, understand organizational strategies, and encourage their creativity and involvement in the decision-making process (a bottom-up approach).

As the pace of change increases, so does the need for the innovation of all organizational products, services and processes. The coding analysis used in our qualitative research based on grounded theory generates several responses to the current leadership challenges:

> *It is all about innovation and right information. Digitalization and continuous improvement of all processes offer the solution to: reduce costs, increase profit, deal with the lack of labor and make the work easier.*

On the other hand, the changes caused by innovation are so rapid that it pushes the management to implement a different approach. Several questions have been raised in order to highlight the importance of leadership transformation. For instance, will the changes and their implementation be successful? Are people still considered to be the key organizational source? Will the new leadership uncover opportunities, and will it attract and retain the right talent?

In our research respondents acknowledge a new role of leadership which fits better to the new era. Organizations need leaders who are quick to recognize emerging challenges and inspire organizational responses. That ability of leaders is crucial today, in areas such as digitalization, the increasing power of data as a competitive advantage and utilizing ICT to impact the workplace and enhance business performance. These technology-driven shifts create an imperative for most organizations to understand that despite the ICT pressure, people are still a very important organizational resource. The key role of leadership in the digital era is to make people more involved in organizational processes and to build relations by using all sorts of influencing forms. The role of leadership in the digital era will be elaborated further in Chapter 8, focusing on emerging technologies. Innovation drives the organizations' performance and currently several contradictory observations occur, for instance:

- Automatization and technology reduce costs and simplify the work but also requires the continuous training and development of human resources.
- Digitalization means a higher level of competence that will become an expectation of leaders as well as the workforce.

- Despite the ICT pressure, people are still considered to be the most important organizational resource.
- Continuous change flow becomes a competitive advantage which is the task of everyone and requires all people to contribute.
- Diversity enriches creativity but can cause some conflicts that make it more difficult to manage.
- The character and behavior of new generations Y and Z entering into the labor market requires a different leadership approach and it is in conflict with generation X (which most of the leaders represent).

We identify the key features of leadership values and approaches for the digital era that can be summarized as follows:

- Guide the people in line with the organizational goals and strategies on an everyday basis and encourage and lead idea creation to fit internal processes and procedures.
- Use a proactive and positive approach toward trends, envision the process of change and help people to understand and implement it successfully.
- Establish a regular two-way communication system by using various motivational tools that create an organizational environment that supports and enhances innovation and creativity.
- Trust in an organization as a system as well as mutual trustworthy relations between leaders and followers based on moral and ethical principles are the fundamental bricks for every organization.

Conclusion

The outcomes of reviewing selected theories related to various attributes of leadership together with the research findings establish a fundamental base to highlight what is expected from leaders in the digital era. The presented diversity of meanings attached to the theory of leadership reveals the complexity that is required in order to advance theoretical thinking and empirical evidence in this scientific field. It is important to merge and synthesize distant theoretical concepts that have contributed to our interpretation of new leadership approaches which might reflect the features of the new era. The digital era is seen as a strong creator of innovation and change. The main paradox of balancing technological progress and the human factor has appeared. So how to link the process of forming and implementing innovation with the development of a capable and dedicated human workforce? The work of many scholars focuses on how defying the role of transformational leadership in the process of change could provide an answer to this dilemma. However, the dynamism and uncertainty of the external environment affects organizational performance. In order to sustain competitiveness, leaders are urged to search for sources of any innovation in both the internal as well as the external environment. The presented model of interactions between leading and following actions in those two environments is essential to see the organizations as a living system which will be further elaborated on in Chapter 4.

Before that, we will elaborate more on the insights which occurred in the conducted research. It underlines the broader understanding of how cognitive processes influence leadership actions both positively and negatively. Therefore, the next chapter will discuss the role of leaders to guide their people to act in such a way that will contribute to successful organizational performance and will be in accordance with the expectations of the external world.

Bibliography

20th CEO Survey 2017, PwC. Retrieved from: www.pwc.com/gx/en/ceo-sur vey/2017/pwc-ceo-20th-survey-report-2017.pdf [Accessed 5 September 2018.]

Ackoff, R. L. (2006). Why Few Organizations Adopt System Thinking. *System Research and Behavioral Science*, 23(5), 705–708.

Avery, G. C. (2004). *Understanding Leadership: Paradigms and Cases*. Los Angeles: Sage.

Avolio, B. J., Bass, B. M. (1991). *The Full Range of Leadership Development. Basic and Advanced Manuals*. Binghamton, NY: Bass, Avolio, & Associates.

Avolio, B. J., Bass, B. M. (1995). Individual Consideration Viewed at Multiple Levels of Analysis: A Multilevel Framework for Examining the Influence of Transformational Leadership. *The Leadership Quarterly*, 6(2), p. 199–218.

Bass, B. M. (1985). *Leadership and Performance Beyond Expectations*. New York: Free Press.

Bass, B. M. (1997). Does the Transactional/Transformational Leadership Paradigm Transcend Organizational and National Boundaries? *American Psychologist*, 52(2), 130–139.

Bass, B. M., Avolio, B. J. (1993). Transformational Leadership and Organizational Culture. *PAQ*, 17(1), 112–121.

Bass, B. M. (2000). The Future of Leadership in Learning Organizations. *Journal of Leadership & Organizational Studies*, 7(3), 18–40.

Bass, B. M., Riggio, R. E. (2006). *Transformational Leadership*. London: Lawrence Erlbaum Associates.

Beck, C. D. (2014). Antecedents of Servant Leadership: A Mixed Methods Study. *Journal of Leadership and Organizational Studies*, 21(3), 299–314.

Beer, M., Eisenstat, R. A. (1996). Developing an Organization Capable of Implementing Strategy and Learning. *Human Relations*, 49(5), 597–620.

Beerel, A. (2009). *Leadership and Change Management*. London: Sage.

Bennis, W. G., Nanus, B. (1997). *Leaders: The Strategies for Taking Charge*. New York: Harper & Row.

Blanchard, K. (2009). *Leadership and Creating High Performing Organizations*. New Jersey: FT Press.

Burns, J. M. (1978). *Leadership*. New York: Harper & Row.

Cannella, A. A., Monroe, M. J. (1997). Contrasting Perspectives on Strategic Leaders: Towards a More Realistic View of Top Managers. *Journal of Management*, 23(3), 213–237.

Chin, J. L., Trimble, J. E. (2015). *Diversity and Leadership*. Thousand Oaks, CA: Sage.

Cleveland, J. N., Stockdale, M., Murphy, K. R. (2000). *Applied Psychology Series. Women and Men in Organizations: Sex and Gender Issues at Work*. Mahwah, NJ: Lawrence Erlbaum Associates Publishers.

Collins, J. (2001). *Good to Great*. New York: Harper Collins.

Conger, J. A., Kanugo, R. N. (1987). Toward a Behavioral Theory of Charismatic Leadership in Organizational Settings. *Academy of Management Review*. 12(4), 637–647.

Daft, R. L., Kendrick, M., Vershinina, N. (2010). *Management*. Andover: South-Western/Cengage Learning.

Ekiert, G. (2012). *Eastern Europe's Postcommunist Transformations*. Retrieved from: www.worldpoliticsreview.com/articles/11749/eastern-europes-postcommunist-transformations [Accessed 4 September 2018.]

Eriksson-Zetterquist, U., Mullern, T., Styhre, A. (2011). *Organization Theory. A Practice—Based Approach*. New York: Oxford University Press.

European Innovation Scoreboard 2017. Retrieved from: http://ec.europa.eu/growth/industry/innovation/facts-figures/scoreboards_en [Accessed 8 June 2018.]

Evans, J. (2008). Dual-Processing Accounts of Reasoning, Judgment, and Social Cognition. *Annual Review of Psychology*, 59, 255–278.

Fiedler, F. E. (1967). *A Theory of Leadership Effectiveness*. New York: McGraw-Hill.

Future of Jobs. (2016). *Global Challenge Insight Report, World Economic Forum*. Retrieved from: http://www3.weforum.org/docs/WEF_Future_of_Jobs.pdf [Accessed 29 October 2018.]

GDP per capita. The World Bank. Retrieved from: https://data.worldbank.org/indicator/NY.GDP.PCAP.CD [Accessed 4 September 2018.]

Global Human Capital Trends. (2016). Deloitte University Press. Retrieved from: https://www2.deloitte.com/content/dam/Deloitte/global/Documents/HumanCapital/gx-dup-global-human-capital-trends-2016.pdf [Accessed 29 October 2018.]

Global Leadership Forecast 2014/15. (2014). Development Dimensions International, Inc., Retrieved from: https://www.ddiworld.com/DDI/media/trend-research/glf2014-findings/vuca-vortex_glf2014_ddi.pdf [Accessed 14 December 2018.]

Global Leadership Forecast 2018. (2018). Development Dimensions International, Inc., The Conference Board Inc., EYGM Limited. Retrieved from: www.ddiworld.com/glf2018 [Accessed 23 October 2018.]

Glossary of Statistical Term. (2001). OECD, Retrieved from: https://stats.oecd.org/glossary/detail.asp?ID=303 [Accessed 4 September 2018.]

Goleman, D. (1995). *Emotional Intelligence*. Praha: Columbus.

Gordon, A., Yukl, G. A. (2004). The Future of Leadership Research: Challenges and Opportunities. *German Journal of Human Resource Research*, 18(3), 359–365.

Graen, G. B., Uhl-Bien, M. (1995). Relationship—Based Approach to Leadership: Applying a Multi-Level Multi-Domain Perspective. *The Leadership Quarterly*, 6(2), 219–247.

Grint, K. (2010). *Leadership. A Very Short Introduction*. New York: Oxford University Press.

Hamel, G., Green, B. (2007). *Future of Management*. Praha: Management Press.
Hickman, G. R. (2010). *Leading Organizations: Perspectives for a New Era*. 2nd edition. Thousand Oaks, CA: Sage.
Hickman, G. R. (2016). *Leading Organizations: Perspectives for a New Era*. 3rd edition. Thousand Oaks, CA: Sage.
Hill, C. W. L. (2011). *International Business: Competing in the Global Marketplace*. New York: McGraw-Hill Irwin.
Hoskinsson, R. E., Hitt, M. A., Ireland, R. D., Harrison, J. (2013). *Competing for Advantage*. South-Western, Mason, OH: Cengage Learning.
Huy, Q. (2002). Emotional Balancing of Organizational Continuity and Radical Change: The Contribution of Middle Managers. *Administrative Science Quarterly*, 47, 31–69.
Index of Economic Freedom. (2017). The Heritage Foundation. Retrieved from: www.heritage.org/index/ranking [Accessed 4 September 2018.]
Kelley, R. E. (1992). *The Power of Followership: How to Create Leaders People Want to Follow, and Followers Who Lead Themselves*. New York: Doubleday.
Kim, W. C., Mauborgne, R. (2005). Blue Ocean Strategy: From Theory to Practice. *California Management Review*, 47(3), 105–121.
Kotter, J. (2014). *Strategy Acceleration Tool*. Boston, MA: Kotter International Inc.
Latham, J. R. (2013). A Framework for Leading the Transformation to Performance Excellence Part I. *The Quality Management Journal*, 20(2), 12–18.
Mitchell, C., Ray, R. L., Van Ark, B. (2014). *CEO Challenge 2014* (Research report R-1537–14-RR). Retrieved from: www.conference-board.org/retrieve file.cfm?filename=TCB_R-1537-14-RR1.pdf&type=subsite [Accessed 29 October 2018.]
National Ethics Business Survey. (2013). Ethics Resource Center. Retrieved from: www.ibe.org.uk/userassets/surveys/nbes2013.pdf [Accessed 29 October 2017.]
Pendleton, D., Furnham, A. (2012). *Leadership. All You Need to Know*. New York: Palgrave Macmillan.
Petrie, N. (2014). *Future Trends in Leadership Development*. Center for Creative Leadership. Retrieved from: www.ccl.org/wp-content/uploads/2015/04/future Trends.pdf [Accessed 5 December 2017.]
Purg, D., Bracek-Lalic, A., Pope, J. A. (2018). *Business and Society: Making Management Education Relevant for the 21st Century*. Switzerland: Springer.
Raguz, I. V., et al. (2016). *Neostrategic Management. An International Perspective on Trends and Challenges*. Switzerland: Springer.
Scott, J. C. (1998). *Seeing Like a State*. Yale: Yale University Press.
Senge, P. M. (1990). *Fifth Discipline. The Art and Practice of the Learning Organization*. Praha: Management Press.
Senge, P. M. (2006). *Learning for Sustainability*. Cambridge, MA: The Society for Organizational Learning Inc.
Shamir, B., House, R. J., (1993). The Motivational Effects of Charismatic Leadership: A Self-Concept-Based Theory. *Organization Science*, 4(4), 577–594.
Silverman, D. (2016). *Qualitative Research*. London: Sage.
Sinar, E., Wellins, R., Paese, M., Smith, A. Watt, B. (2016). *High Resolution Leadership. Development Dimensions International*. Retrieved from: http://ddiworld.com/DDI/media/trend-research/high-resolution-leadership.pdf [Accessed 9 May 2017.]

Sinar, E., Wellins, R., Ray, R., Abel, A.L., Neal, S. (2015). *Global Leadership Forecast 2014/2015*. Development Dimensions International, Retrieved from: www.ddiworld.com/DDI/media/trend-research/global-leadership-forecast.pdf [Accessed 4 May 2017.]

The state of leadership development. (2016). Harvard Business Publishing. Retrieved from: www.hardvardbusiness.org [Accessed 21 May 2017.]

Strauss, A.L., Corbin, J. (1989). *Basics of Qualitative Research: Techniques and Procedures for Developing Grounded Theory*. Thousand Oaks, CA: Sage.

Succeeding in the VUCA paradigm. (2016). Ernst & Young LLP. Retrieved from: www.ey.com/Publication?vwLUAAssets/ey-succeeding-i-the-vuca-paradugm-making-change-happen.pdf [Accessed 14 May 2017.]

Wilson, F.M. (2010). *Organizational Behavior and Work*. New York: Oxford University Press.

Wilson, S. (2014). Using Secondary Analysis to Maintain a Critically Reflexive Approach to Qualitative Research. *Sociological Research Online,* 19(3), 1–12.

World bank data. The World Bank. Retrieved from: https://data.worldbank.org/country/ [Accessed 19 October 2018.]

Yukl, G.A. (2010). *Leadership in Organizations*. Upper Saddle River, NY: Prentice-Hall.

Zaccaro, S.J. Klimovski, R. (2002). The Interface of Leadership and Team Process. *Group and Organization Management*, 27(1), 4–13.

2 Ethical Pathologies and Cognitive Dissonance in Corporate Leadership

Introduction

It would seem that much of the old battles in ethics have been won and there are in place generally accepted rules for behavior. Outwardly discriminatory practices against women, people of color, sexual orientation and so forth are taboos that most businesses would readily reject today. Engaging in criminal behaviors such as bribes and creative bookkeeping are forbidden with rules against these practices established and well enforced. There would seem to be little need to focus on ethical practices in corporate leadership. All one would need to do is create an ethical policy and have everyone sign it and everything will be fine. If there is a problem, then a digital solution could be found. This could not be further from the truth. In fact, it is these very same "digital app solutions" that could amplify the myopic vision of the world, leading to a brutal mediocrity that we wish to avoid. The danger today is that we become completely unaware of our own biases as tribalism increases unabated. With modern technology, it has never been so easy to set up our own echo chamber with a continuous feedback loop of what we think is right. As such, it is important to explore how our cognitive processes work, especially from an ethical framework. This chapter explores these cognitive processes and how they could lead to rather tragic consequences.

It would be a cliché to state that the nature of work and company organization is changing due to globalization and innovations. This is rather self-evident. It needs to be remembered that these changes and even more significant changes have occurred throughout history. Today's car has much in common with the cars from 60 years ago with rather incremental improvements. In fact, a car journey today is more likely to take longer than in the past due to traffic congestion. As such, changes today are rather mild compared to previous times.

Instead of a new glorious future for ourselves and our children, many feel a sense of foreboding. While it is true that the new global economy has, in aggregate, brought higher living standards across the world, it has also been destructive to some local communities, especially in developed countries. A pervasive fear among individuals today is the idea that they may someday become irrelevant. Ethical issues have greater consequences than ever before. A modern leader needs to be aware of these fears and what drives them.

Pathologies in Corporate Leadership

For the most part of the late 20th century, businesses have also moved toward greater ethical consciousness with more equality, accountability and potential for greater good for mankind. Unfortunately, the start of the new century has been marred with some spectacular ethical failures that makes one wonder "how corporate leaders could do something so wrong". Consider the following examples:

- The 2008 financial crisis, caused by speculative bubbles in real estate that led to the greatest recession since the Great Depression.
- The Volkswagen diesel scandal (in 2015), where designers and engineers colluded to create a cheat-device to thwart emission standards, leading to dirtier cars and a decline of air quality in metropolitan centers.
- Social media with the promise of openness has led to the spread of "fake news", unscrupulous data collection, hate speech and child-hood addiction to computer devices.
- A drug company's promise of safe pain relief with a synthetic opioid ended with the addiction of millions and deaths of thousands of users.

Before embarking upon the details related to business practices and relationships between the various stakeholders, a basic tenet of individual motivation needs to be established. Neoclassical economic theory suggests that people have rational preferences among outcomes; individuals maximize utility and firms maximize profits; and people act independently on the basis of full and relevant information. Over the years, this thought has been discounted far too often, as humans make choices that go against their economic self-interest either now or in the future. Man is more than an economic creature; he is a social animal. Deep down, all individuals are looking for a respectable legacy for themselves.

Sociologist Anthony Giddens (1991) refers to this search as the life-narrative. He asserts:

A person's identity is not to be found in behavior, nor—important though this is—in the reactions of others, but in the capacity to keep a particular narrative going. Individuals' biographies, if they are to maintain regular interaction with others in the day-to-day world, cannot be wholly fictive. It must continually integrate events which occur in the external world, and sort them into the ongoing "story" about the self.

For all individuals, we are each writing the book of ourselves. This book will hopefully demonstrate that our lives have meaning and purpose. This narrative extends also to our children. Most individuals wish to be seen in a positive light and as such are not inherently evil and keeping this positive narrative going becomes paramount. The new generations Z and Alfa are no different from their predecessors in this regard, yet a few "experts" are trumpeting a postmodernist vision stating the young are different with less desire for the traditional markers to success (get an education, get married, buy a house, have children and grandchildren, retire, etc.). Despite the outward appearance, the young want an existence with meaning and would not be content with "swiping away" their life on the digital gadget of the moment. The story changes through the generations, but the narrative structure remains the same.

The narrative in the "book of ourselves" can be threatened in two ways: (1) the decision produces an undesirable outcome with negative consequences or (2) external factors limit our ability to continue this narrative in the way we desire. People in organizations are often faced with two powerful competing impulses. They want to be viewed as honorable people but, on the other hand, they also want to get the things they need (i.e. money and what it buys). With dishonesty there is a calculation of both cost and benefit. The theory of cost-benefit analysis (CBA) is a systematic approach to estimating the strengths and weaknesses of alternatives. It is a technique that is used to determine options which provide the best result in terms of benefits (Boardman, 2006). CBA theory suggests that the benefit of a decision is greater than the cost of the risk. On the other hand, if the cost of the risk is too high, it is unlikely that the particular decision will be made.

If a person thinks there is a good chance they will be caught cheating and if there is a big penalty for being caught, then it is less likely that people will cheat. Leadership is more than just simply creating the penalties for cheating, and the official rules do not give corporate leaders immunity for fault if the rules are broken. It does no good to create rules (the penalty) against cheating while at the same time providing incentives (a benefit) for secretly breaking the rules.

The proverb "one bad apple spoils the whole barrel" states that in a group, one bad person can make others bad. If this were true, a company should concentrate on finding the evildoer that instigates theft, cheating and general unethical behavior and have that person removed. In doing so, the whole organization could be saved from this ethical rot. Most all know the ethical rules of an organization and would categorically state an allegiance to the rules. This is revealed through the stated preference, that is, asking people what they would do in certain situations to gain an understanding of an individual's moral turpitude.

Rational choice theory states that people will make rational decisions that will provide the greatest utility with the least amount of effort from the available choices. It assumes that it would be irrational to do things that could have potential long-term damage to this utility, that is, no one would want to jeopardize their future by engaging in illegal activities. One experiment at the Massachusetts Institute of Technology found that people will behave irrationally and often will do so in predictable ways (Mazar et al., 2008). They designed a study that would give the subject a chance to cheat without the subject knowing that they were being observed. The subjects were given a financial reward for overstating their success in a math test. What the study found was most people cheated a little and very few people cheated a lot. It was clear from the subject's point of view that "the more correct answers I have, the more money I will receive—after all, no one will know". The ratio did not change even after they were offered more money for the correct answers. A clear benefit to cheating was clearly seen. The conclusion can be made that since we want to feel that we are basically honest, it is OK to cheat a little, but we feel less comfortable when we cheat a lot. Ariely (2013) concluded that people are caught between two desires: to make money and to remain honest. There is a balance between these two desires, that is, we would only cheat up to a level which still makes us feel good about ourselves. This is what Ariely named a *fudge factor*.

In a similar experiment (Gino and Ariely, 2011), subjects were interviewed to determine if they were creative. Then the subjects were given a test where they had an opportunity to cheat. The researchers found that creative people were more likely to cheat because creative people are likely to be able to tell better stories, which would allow them to cheat more on the one hand, but not feel worse about it on the other hand. The researchers concluded that charismatic people would have a higher ability to become good cheaters. Charismatic leaders would have a higher chance of affecting their followers due to their ability to tell a good story. From this research, it can be seen that charisma cannot be the main marker for honesty in leadership.

The Importance of Social and Market Norms in Leadership

All citizens of a society are brought up to respect the *social norms* of that society. These norms govern how we should behave in relation to what society expects. Social norms include friendly requests such as "Will you help me move my furniture?" With a request like this, instant payback is not required, which means if you helped your friend move his furniture, he does not have to come right over and help you move yours. Social norms are like opening doors for other people: the pleasure is on both sides and reciprocity is not necessary.

This is not the same, however, with *market norms*, which have a different set of rules. Market rules are based on the cost-benefit concept; they are a simple exchange of goods or services for a monetary price. This does not mean that market norms are bad, as they offer qualities like inventiveness and self-reliance. When people function on market norms, they "get what they are paid for".

When social and market norms are clearly distinguished and separated, no problems are expected. However, as soon as they collide, we set out for trouble. Social norms often disregard monetary terms and instead focus on societal expectation.

Facebook, a company promoting social connectivity, is also a marketing platform for business. Because of its low regard for privacy, the website became known for abusive ads, fake news, conspiracy theories and racism, among other things. This cavalier attitude toward privacy and unchecked freedom of speech has led many firms to pull back on advertising on this platform as the market norm became entwined with the social norm, and not in a good way. Very few companies would want their products marketed to or endorsed by the Ku Klux Klan, for example, and Facebook was unable to guarantee this from happening. This accumulated into the largest one-day loss in market value by any company in US stock market history, a sum of US$119 billion in 2018. Conflating social norms and market norms has a cost.

A study of a day care center by Gneezy and Rustichini (2000) very clearly illustrates how social and market norms can change. Parents were often late in picking up children from a day care center and felt guilty for being late. As such, they often took great care to be on time, which was dictated by a social norm. In order to discourage late parents, the school decided to penalize them for being late by imposing a relatively small, but not insignificant, penalty. The penalty was per child, which meant that parents with more children would pay more money if late. The results were surprising: the number of late-coming parents increased and parents came even later to pick up their children. Before the penalty, the parents felt guilty for being late and tried to be there on time. After the penalties were introduced, the social norm was replaced with the market norm, so parents no longer felt the need to be on time, assuming they were paying for the service. Later, the penalty was removed and parents were not charged for being late, however, the social norm did not come back. The market norm stayed with the parents with no penalties for being late, and even more parents were late picking up their children.

Social norms take a long time to cultivate, whereas market norms are immediate. Once market norms are established, they are hard to eliminate.

Ann Tenbrunsel (2005) states that we are sometimes unable to see the ethical big picture in what she calls *bounded ethicality*. Bounded ethicality refers to the systematic and predictable ways in which humans act unethically beyond their own awareness. According to Tenbrunsel, traditional approaches to ethics do not take into consideration the unintentional reason why people make unethical decisions. This applies when a person's decision harms others and this decision is not consistent with his/her beliefs, a *conflict of interest*. People are not able to see the conflict of interest (i.e. the bigger picture) because of their strong psychological motivations to maintain a certain view about themselves. She also claims that how a decision is framed makes a big difference in how the decision is reached. The main question to ask is "Was it a business decision or was it an ethical decision?"

According to Tenbrunsel, the business frame cognitively activates one set of goals (i.e. to be competent and successful) while the ethics frame triggers other goals (i.e. act in accordance to my personal view of myself). Once a person is in a business frame, they become much focused on meeting the business goals, and other goals can completely fade from view (Tenbrunsel, 2005).

Gains can have the effect of making people stingier, that is, people become greedier. The *endowment effect* states that people ascribe more value to things merely because they own them (Roeckelein, 2006), which makes them reluctant to sell something they own for a lower price. A person, however, would expect to buy the same good that is owned by someone else only if it is cheaper. Sellers of homes are more likely to list their house's value at a much higher rate than a buyer would be willing to pay.

Patricia Greenfield (2013) found that as people get richer, they become more individualistic and less family and community oriented. Individualism happens in subtle ways. For example, the monthly barbeque with neighbors could be a tradition that connects a person to his community. As a man becomes wealthier, there is a higher likelihood that he would not be engaging in the neighborhood barbeque. Gradually, this individual becomes less connected with the community and less likely to feel the need to give back to the community. Greenfield also proved that as individuals were becoming wealthier and more individualistic, the language used in books also changed. For example, words that show individualistic orientation, such as "get", "self" or "unique" increased in use over the years, and words like "give", "obliged" or "belong" decreased.

The Problem of Leadership Biases and Corporate Charisma

The discussion related to transformational leadership in the previous chapter brings our attention to why some people tend to follow leaders and under what circumstances they do not. This has been studied in Stanley Milgram's electric shock experiments (1963) and presented in significant research where his intention was to see how far a person would go under the orders of a strong authority. Milgram (1973, p. 76) stated that the need to follow the rules of authority is greater than the need to follow one's moral conscience. He stated:

> Ordinary people, simply doing their jobs, and without any hostility on their part, can become members in a terrible destructive process. Moreover, even when the destructive effects of their work become very clear and they are asked to carry out actions that go against their standards of morality, relatively few people have the capabilities needed to resist authority.
>
> (Milgram, 1973, p. 76)

For the business environment, the message is clear: moral and ethical standards are set by the leaders. Replication of this experiment in its original form would be impossible today because of the ethical concerns for the subject, as the experience was quite traumatic. A modified version of the experiment, however, was recently conducted in Poland (Doliński et al., 2017), where 90% would have presumably given a lethal shock to the learner, an actor and confederate of the experimenter. This experiment, however, was conducted on a smaller scale with only 80 participants. One could presume that the CEE region is more prone to authoritativeness.

Robert Jackall (2010) illustrates this point in *Moral Mazes*, where he explores how corporate bureaucracies shape moral consciousness. Probably the most important finding of Jackall's book is that is that successful managers are skillful symbol manipulators. Mid-level managers are not evil in their everyday lives, but when it comes to work, there is a separate moral code. Jackall names this phenomenon the *fundamental rules of corporate life*, which he defines as follows:

- You never go around your boss.
- You tell your boss what he wants to hear, even when your boss claims that he wants to hear the opposite.
- If your boss wants something stopped, you stop it.
- You are sensitive to your boss's wishes so that you anticipate what he wants; you do not force him (i.e. act as a boss).
- Your job is not to report something that your boss does not want reported, but rather to cover it up.
- You do your job and you keep your mouth shut.

To succeed, managers constantly adapt to the social environments of their companies. This does not allow room for abstract ethical principles, but rather for bureaucratic conformity. The power in corporations is centralized in the CEO, while the responsibility is pushed down to lower levels as far as possible. This takes the burden from the shoulders of top management and gives managers opportunity to blame subordinates when something goes wrong.

As life is full of important decisions, each individual must make order from chaos and create a reality that minimizes emotional distress. This reality is not always created in a logical fashion and individuals create their own "subjective social reality" from their perception of the information (Bless et al., 2004). Individuals create simple mental efficiency rules to process information and assign value to this data. All individuals will find some information to be more important than others. Decision making involves focusing on some aspects of complex problems while ignoring other aspects (Nevid, 2012).

Not all decisions, however, result in rational choices. Nobel laureates Tversky and Kahneman noted that the cognitive thought process can sometimes create severe errors in judgment (1974). These judgments could lead to unethical decision making. In other words, individuals have such preset notions about what is correct that it becomes difficult to truly form an unbiased opinion.

As life is full of choices, it is important to feel comfortable with the choices we make. This helps prevent *cognitive dissonance*, a condition of mental stress or discomfort caused by two beliefs that are in contradiction to each other (Festinger and Carlsmith, 1959). Cognitive dissonance refers to a situation which involves *conflicting attitudes, beliefs* or *behaviors.*

Psychologically, living with dissonance is uncomfortable, and as such, ways are found to try to reduce it. This leads to avoidance of the situations and information that reinforces this dissonance. According to Festinger's theory of cognitive dissonance, there are three key strategies to reduce or minimize cognitive dissonance:

* To focus on supportive beliefs that outweigh the dissonance.
* To reduce the importance of the conflicting belief.
* To change the conflicting belief so it becomes consistent with other beliefs and behaviors.

It is quite difficult to change well-learned behavior because there is some pleasure connected to it. Even with non-behavioral choices, there will often be a strong impulse to choose one option over the other. This desire will cause an individual to acquire new information to reduce the dissonant thought.

Another option to reduce the dissonance is to reduce its importance. The smoker knows the health effect of the habit but may decide that a shorter life full of pleasure is better than a longer life living healthily. It needs to be noted that the effort to reduce dissonance may not change reality. A bad decision is still a bad decision no matter how much it is justified.

Leadership is associated with some charisma. There is a vast debate among scholars and practitioners whether it is better to have good leaders or charismatic ones. We can elaborate on this by looking back in ancient times. In the Greek tragedy *Oedipus Rex* by Sophocles, King Oedipus was told by a blind prophet that he would kill his father and marry his mother. In ancient Greece, prophecies were infallible and nothing could be done to change this fate. Oedipus is a well-loved king who rules his land justly, but his overly arrogant behavior condemns him to an unfortunate fate. He thinks that he can rise above the prophecy and if he does, he would be better and more powerful than the gods. To rebel against the gods was considered a very dangerous thought in those days. Oedipus was a person with *hubris*, a condition of excessive pride in oneself and exaggerated self-confidence. In other words, hubris leads to arrogance and the notion of being better than others, or in the case of Oedipus, better than the gods.

In modern-day context, hubris is often associated with a lack of humility, often with people from higher social, economic or intellectual backgrounds.

For company leaders, hubris comes gradually, usually by building a track record of success that is legal and according to the rules. As a person becomes more successful, there is even more pressure to maintain this record of accomplishment. In every organization, there are "go-to" people who have always been able to find solutions for problems and ways to remove obstacles that stand in the way of achievement and success. Hubris consumes them when they eventually have an obstacle they cannot conquer (Jennings, 2014). These individuals face the harsh reality that they have reached the limits of their abilities. In this situation, they are not driven by greed, but instead are motivated by pride and cannot admit that they are only human. Hubris causes the leader who has found his limits to cheat.

There are some characteristics of hubris that may be seen in leaders who cannot admit to failure:

- No disagreement is tolerated, as the leader will only listen to people who agree with him, and people who disagree are punished.
- Rules are for the average person and do not apply to the narcissistic leader.
- The leader fears the loss of success (e.g. a car, the executive office, high salary or prestige).
- The leader has a sense of invincibility that he can always win.
- The purpose of being a leader changes from wanting to improve the world or helping others to wanting to remain on top (Jennings, 2014).

According to Baldoni (2010), the basic cure for hubris is to welcome communication. Often leaders receive or filter the information through a small group of people rather than talking to the average people within the organization. Nevertheless, it is the duty of a leader to listen.

Most prejudicial biases are based on some sort of external marker such as sex, skin color, ethnicity, age and so forth. Yet prejudices and *biases* can be formed in a more subtle fashion as it is a human tendency to try to find the best and easiest path toward processing information and making decisions. Like electricity, humans are looking for the path of least resistance (i.e. they are looking for the easiest solution to any thought problem). This leads to a *cognitive bias*, a distortion, inaccurate judgment or illogical interpretation of the acquired information. These biases have been divided into many sub-categories and have become standard doctrine in psychology and sociology. Some of these categories include:

- Groupthink: a situation where group members begin to form quick opinions that match the group consensus, rather than critically evaluating information.
- Restraint bias: a tendency to overestimate the capacity for *impulse control* (i.e. the belief individuals have the ability to resist temptation).
- Choice-supportive bias: the tendency to give positive attributes to the choices that we have made in the past.
- False consensus bias: the tendency for people to overestimate the degree to which others share their beliefs, attitudes and behaviors, and agree with them.
- Illusionary superiority: an overestimation of our own qualities compared to others in different aspects of life (e.g. intelligence, task performance or personality traits).
- Projection bias: a prediction that one's own views will stay the same over time, but which is statistically unlikely. It is a tendency to unconsciously assume that others, or even our future self, will share the current emotional state, thoughts and values.
- Self-serving bias: the tendency to claim more responsibility for successes than failures.
- Confirmation bias: people who attempt to support a certain idea by seeking information (and people) that justifies this idea. They will also interpret the related news in a way that enhances and reinforces their attitudes.
- Omission bias: a perception that a negative outcome from an action could be worse than a negative outcome from inaction (i.e. it is better to do nothing).

Many of these biases have attributes to an umbrella bias called the *blind-spot bias* (e.g. we are unaware of our own impartiality, especially with people). Ray Dalio (2017) refers to this blind spot as the belief of being able to see a clear picture of reality. The truth is that most situations come with a wide range of perspectives. When working with people this blind spot can become even more myopic. Dalio further reiterates that all people bring a different perspective to a problem. Some people are better at seeing the big picture, while others excel at seeing details; some people are linear thinkers, while others are more lateral; some people are creative but not reliable, while others are reliable but not creative.

One shorthand to the above bias is the concept of the *should/want* theoretical framework (Tenbrunsel et al., 2007). When predicting future actions, the *should* mindset is used. When it comes to the action phase of a decision, the *want* mindset dominates and there is a need to satisfy this desire regardless of what the "should" dictates us to do. When making judgments about how people should behave, they often do not consider the environmental factors that can occur in certain situations.

The *should/want* conflict also extends to events in the past. Like the choice-supportive bias, individuals will reform memories of an event that will make themselves seem more ethical. Studies have found that individuals will reconstruct memories that are more abstract than concrete (Ross et al., 1977). For example, a witness to a woman being attacked would find legitimate excuses for not contacting the police (e.g. "I did not have my cell phone" or "I did not think she was really being attacked"). A male student that is accused of sexual misconduct will find reasons to believe that there was mutual agreement for a sexual encounter. Individuals will choose to remember those events that will protect their own self-image (i.e. they will have *selective memory*).

In the retail setting, businesses are fully aware of this *should/want* conflict in our purchases. This can be seen in the food business when we are given a choice between healthy items (what I *should* be eating) and indulgent items (what I *want* to eat, such as ice cream and pizza). We might agree on the need for a new tax (the *should* self) but decide to implement it in the far future (the *want* self prevails). An educational documentary is something we *should* be watching, but we choose to watch an action film instead (a *want* decision).

Based on our older research, it can be clearly seen that writing a set of rules decreeing "all to be good" will do little good, especially when there is a threat of losing something dear. Using Slovakia as a base, we interviewed various firms and their leaders to get a better picture of the ethical environment. The company leaders were asked directly if they have experienced any unethical or illegal practices inside or outside the business. From our findings, we can sort these issues into the following five categories and suggest solutions:

> *Everything is perfect* (approx. 25% of the responses): 44 companies addressed some sort of unethical behavior, meaning that 16 either brushed off the question with an "everything is fine" or flatly stated

that they have no ethical problems. As an example, we can use the statement of one HR manager from a telecommunications company:

> *"We did not encounter any unethical behavior in our company. We have high penalties if our employees are part of unfair or unethical behavior. In extreme cases, they can be fired".*

At the same time, the four larger control-group companies (three international, with branches all over Europe, and one local with an international market) reported no problems at all and claimed they only abided by the highest ethical standards. Remember, this control group was interviewed by us (the authors of this research). The other smaller companies were interviewed by students. As such, we might surmise that students posed less of a danger with answering such controversial questions. One company in our control group, however, did accuse another company in our control group of unethical practices. As companies get larger, there is a tendency to obfuscate and give trivial, non-damaging information (i.e. never admit to doing anything bad). This often is referred to as "CYA", which in the less vulgar definition means *cover your actions*. As the prestige of a company's duty increases (large accounting firm, high-tech company, etc.), it is less likely to admit to problems. One reason for this is that the work being produced is rather ephemeral, where the product is a service and is less tangible.

Some company representatives stated that they have a code of behavior in place and as such do not have ethical issues. As one CEO from a printing company stated:

We did not experience any unethical situations in the past. We have our own Ethical Code. We try to prevent these cases by hiring the best people. We try to support new employees so they can feel like being part of the company.

As some of the latest company scandals can attest, scandalous behavior occurs quite often and seems to be happening a bit more frequently. A one-time exercise in producing an ethical policy is a meaningless exercise if the work environment requires constant pushing at the boundaries and the naïve exploration of new frontiers (e.g. products where the information is data related) without considering all of the possible unintended consequences. It needs to be remembered that ethics is not a policy; it is behavior that is reinforced by the environment.

Internal squabbles (approx. 25% of the responses): As with any organizations dealing with large numbers of people, there is likely to be some discontent among employees. From our survey, we can find examples of alcohol use, mobbing behavior, taking credit for someone else's work, lying to cover up mistakes, disorganization, sabotaging another team's work, patriarchal behavior from foreign owners and general favoritism. For example:

We experienced unfair behavior among employees: one group in production deliberately changes the machine settings in a wrong way to spoil the performance of another group.

(CEO from an electronics company)

Several representatives admitted to intergenerational problems related to the age of employees. There were several responses indicating that the younger workers were not prepared for the work environment and displayed an arrogant attitude. Another company mentioned that older employees were unwilling to accept change. One CEO stated:

There is a sense of some unfair behavior, senior employees find the junior ones cheeky and without experience and they are not able to accept advice.

(CEO from a machinery company)

Petty theft (around 15%): Theft is always a concern for the corporation and some respondents indicated theft of non-monetary elements such as petrol for personal use, stealing of manufactured products and falsified time cards. Considering the previously mentioned study on dishonesty, petty thievery seems to be more an issue of expected benefits (free petrol, a usable item, extra salary) with low potential external cost (e.g. a penalty or getting fired). For managers, it needs to be decided how and to what extent controls are needed in theft prevention.

Unethical practices from customers, competitors and suppliers (around 24%): Companies feel that the competitors do not always play fair. This includes stealing customers and employees as well as spreading false rumors. Several respondents complained about delayed payments from customers. There were several responses related to tax issues, especially with regard to value-added tax as well as off-the-books labor. Sometimes, it is the supplier or customer that is asking for favorable tax conditions (e.g. not reporting VAT).

The anonymity of the internet provides the opportunity for rumor mongering with the intent to destroy a firm's reputation, sometimes with devastating effects. One company gave the following example:

A product created by our firm is sold through an online store where the customers can place a review on the product. One anonymous reviewer of the website's forum stated that the product was defective and full of errors that would likely to have been systemic through the whole batch run. Instead of looking into the error, the online retailer halted the sale of the item. Since our company has an extensive quality control system in place, a review of the records was able to exonerate us. As the system for negative reviews was automatic and based on good faith, there was no easy way to undo the damage from this false innuendo or to reinstate the sale of the item. A reputation, once sullied, is hard to clean.

Unethical government interference (around 10% of respondents): In a perfectly competitive world, it is assumed that there is a level playing field concerning fair competition where players are free to enter and exit the market and the rules of the game are the same for all players. But in the spirit of regional support for employment, the government, both at the national and the EU level, provides funds to companies for the purchase of new equipment. Usually these funds are given with the condition of providing local employment for a certain number of years. The problem with this approach is that the firm receiving a subsidy now has an advantage over the others that do not receive any support. Worse still, the tax subsidy is being paid in part by the firm that is not receiving support.

Normally, government bodies try to ensure that there is no conflict of interest in giving support, usually by making sure that there are no other local players in a particular market. Yet, the EU is a collection of 28 countries, so an unsupported company in one country faces challenges from subsidized companies in another country.

Another problem with arbitrary government support is that there is usually a limited number of specialized employees within a certain industry and in many cases, these employees are already employed. As such, the subsidized company has the advantage of being able to "poach" employees of other firms with the offer of higher salaries. The following anecdote illustrates the problem from the CEE region.

To support employment in a town that had high unemployment, the government gave a tax holiday to a foreign investor for a total of five years to open a factory with the agreement that they provide employment for 100 people over this time. By offering higher pay, this company found the needed specialized employees by poaching employees from other companies that had similar competencies. For the non-supported company, the brain-drain caused problems with production and added substantial risk in maintaining profitable operation. At the end of the tax holiday period, the subsidized firm continued for another two years, then declared bankruptcy as they were unable to make a profit without the gifted tax-scheme.

Despite the ineffectiveness of this type of government support, it remains popular among politicians. After all, politicians' approval ratings are greatly increased when they are able to bring a new company to an area. This is especially true during election years.

Reducing Unethical Behavior in the Business Environment

The psychology of wrongdoing suggests that it does no good to bang on about how we all must do the right thing without understanding the conditions that can drive people to do the wrong thing. As it was demonstrated from the many examples and psychological tests, we can see that human beings:

- Want to follow rules, even to the point of following the rules that are wrong (based on Milgram's experiment).
- Do not mind being a little bad, but at the same time do not want to be seen as thieves or criminals.
- Are more interested in the here and now rather than the unforeseeable future.
- Want to avoid losing money and go to great lengths to keep it once they have it.
- Are greatly influenced by the environment that surrounds them.

How to keep "the bad" in check, then? As it has been indicated at the beginning of this chapter, ethical decisions are not as simple as our own human behavior, and natural instincts can thwart our own virtuousness. There are, however, some steps that can be taken to reinforce positive ethical decisions.

Many theorists oppose the idea of being able to learn to behave ethically by just being taught about ethics. To learn our morals, we must live them. Josephson (2002) suggests that people can be led to making ethical decisions by meeting the following three conditions:

1. Decisions must consider the well-being of all affected individuals.
2. Ethical values and principles always take precedence over non-ethical ones.
3. Ethical principles may be violated only in favor of another true ethical principle.

The author further notes that in making difficult ethical decisions, it is helpful to consider the potential conflict of this decision by comparing it with our own core values, the opinion of a person who we morally respect or the effect of our decision on others. The above suggestions are rather vague. A clearer set of rules can be seen in the following questions regarding any leadership decision:

- Would I want my decisions reported on the news or in public?
- Would I want my children to know about my decision?
- Would my decision cause me to lose sleep?

It is interesting to see how appealing to people's conscience plays an important role in setting the ethical frame of mind. Josephson, however, points out that to make an ethical decision, a person must adhere to core values, and he defines them as trustworthiness, respect, responsibility, fairness, caring and citizenship.

Going back to our qualitative research, the interviewed managers proposed the following actions to reduce the unethical behavior in companies:

- Fines for employees when they do not follow internal rules (in extreme cases even the end of the employment contract).
- Having an ethical code and maintaining its strict control through daily practice and procedures.
- Introduction of an anonymous survey (or anonymous "suggestion boxes") about unethical behavior among employees.
- Open communication between leaders and their employees and business partners.
- Regular training of employees.
- Focus on new employees and their values during job interviews.

Along with these simple principles, the following concepts will provide further insights into ethical decision making.

The Conceptual Triad of Ethics in Business Based on Transparency, Accountability and Universality

It is well known that ethical lapses in an organization start from environmental conditions that are fostered by leadership. Recently, there have been many experiments that have given us more insights into how unethical decisions occur, leading to the concept of bounded ethicality; that is, people make decisions that are in accordance to their environment they find themselves in, even if it goes against their personal beliefs.

With the insights mentioned above, we developed a conceptual triad of ethics based on transparency, accountability and universality. The main goal of this concept is to decrease the environmental factors that foster selfish behavior and at the same time establish social cues that reinforce concerns for others. This concept is also forward-looking with regard to the future sustainability of the organization.

Transparency

In business, *transparency* can be characterized by the visibility or accessibility of information, especially concerning business practices. It operates in such a way that it is easy for others to see what actions are taken. It has been defined as "the perceived quality of intentionally shared information from a sender" (Schnackenberg and Tomlinson, 2014). This implies necessary exposure to *who, what, when, where* and *how*.

The anti-corruption organization Transparency International states that one of its guiding principles is "to be open, honest, and accountable in our relationships with everyone we work with, and with each other" (www.transparency.org). In terms of ethical trends, it can be said that the world is becoming more transparent as technology is destroying all former concepts of secrecy. Examples include the following:

- Tax haven countries, where it was once easy to hide money, are now under increasing scrutiny.
- Mobile phone cameras make reporters out of almost everyone, thus it is becoming increasingly dangerous to demand a bribe.
- Information asymmetry is gone. When people buy a plane ticket, a car or a vacation package, they can be reasonably sure of the true value of the product before they make a purchase since the buyer has the same information as the seller. The seller has a more difficult time keeping secret the cost of the product he offers.
- The open office concept creates environments where everyone can see everyone else at work, including management and the boss.

With these changes, new circumstances are being created where we can live in a world of no secrets. Today is a world of *metadata*, which can be defined as data about data.

Sociologists are uncertain how people will react in a world where every sin is known. Everybody does unwise things in their life and it is a part of growing up. The difference today is that those things can be recorded for perpetuity. In a world where every sin in our life is available for the world to see, who will be embraced: the sinner or the saint?

Accountability

In a world of transparency, it becomes important to have a set of measurements for *accountability*. This is more easily accomplished when there are metrics or rules to follow. It is the leader's job to create procedures that cannot be undermined by unreal expectations. Procedures or methods of operations are more important than a set of rules as they are the key to honest practice. As stated earlier, ethics rules that are meted out to employees at the beginning of employment have little value as the work environment will dictate the level of ethics in an organization. As such, the procedural approach to work is more important than any written statement of honesty.

The key to accountability is that there must be no exceptions to the procedural rule. It is, however, important that the requirements do not favor one group over another or protect the status quo. The accountability requirements should be reasonable and capable of being followed. If this is not so, cynicism will destroy not only the procedural process but also the organization that introduced them.

Requirements for compliance must be reasonable. Examples can be found in government where unreasonable regulations could lead to black marketers and *influence peddling* by corrupt officials. As such, accountability rules need to be easy to follow and made possible to accomplish in a timely manner. Time and effort are costs that are not necessarily calculated in monetary terms, yet they still take a toll on organizations and society. This problem is known as *transaction cost*, which can be defined as the cost of participating in the market. Also known as *friction cost*, it is the implicit and explicit costs associated with market transactions. These costs include commissions, tax implications, the time value of money and so forth. The main transaction problem comes with dealing with bureaucracy, and as such accountability rules should be reasonable in terms of not only time but also in terms of complexity and needed effort.

To give an example of transaction cost, we can look at the buying and renovation of property. A business may be interested in renovating an existing building for production, commerce, or for residential sale (e.g. a brownfield initiative). Many rules and steps must be taken to first legally obtain the property; second, to initiate some sort of improvement (e.g. renovation or construction); and finally, to get final approval. Transaction costs are too numerous to detail, but examples include obtaining a clear title, zoning issues, permission to build or renovate, historic preservation rules, roadway and easement permits, environmental regulations and utilities (gas, electricity, water, sewer, trash disposal, etc.). Even if the cost of all the above was zero, the myriad steps lead to *decision fatigue*, or even worse, institutional paralysis. With all of the decisions to be made, there is a calculation of risk, and the bureaucracy can make this calculation immeasurable, which can lead to making no decision at all (Brocas and Carrillo, 2003).

Lack of information leads to a *Knightian uncertainty* (i.e. a risk that is impossible to calculate). "Men in general and within limits wish to behave economically, to make their activities and their organization 'efficient' rather than wasteful" (Knight, 1941). It can create a situation where nothing happens when it should. Those involved see no solution to the problem, so they decide not to take any steps and thus avoid the uncertain result. This is the basis of the *Ellsberg paradox*, which states that people tend to avoid uncertainty and unknowns in favor of quantifiable probability (Geweke, 1992). This paradox suggests that people prefer taking risks in situations where they know the odds rather than in those where the odds are uncertain. They tend to choose a known probability over an unknown one, even if the known probability is low and the unknown probability could guarantee a desired result.

In conclusion, it can be said that accountability is a set of standards or metrics that assure proper conduct in a certain area of society. These metrics should be reasonable and achievable to the agents involved in terms of understanding, time needed to achieve the standard and the effort needed to obtain the certification for accountability.

Universality

Universality or universal ethics is the application of a rule to all. Philosopher Immanuel Kant referred to *universality* as a rule of law for all *similarly situated persons* (Green, 1992). This term suggests that all people who are at the same level of opportunity should be treated equally in the eyes of the law. The rule thus applies to all who are bounded by the ethics of the same society. There are numerous universal codes in society. One of the truly universal rules is doctors being bound by the Hippocratic Oath to "do no harm" to a patient. In business, universality would mean applying the same standards to people in a similar situation.

In order for the rule to work, all people would need to live by the same code, no matter their status or income level.

As the world is organized into countries, each with their own culture and subcultures, it is impossible to create one rule that would describe each individual as *similarly situated persons*. Each person can be identified by their nationality and with this, a different set of universal rules is developed based on that culture. There are very few truly universal codes that extend to every society of this planet (the Hippocratic Oath for doctors, treaties on certain chemicals, etc.).

Labor and business practices are areas where it would be exceptionally difficult to make a worldwide universal standard. No one would expect that a garment worker in India be paid the same as a garment worker in the European Union. Minimum and average wages and tax rates are different throughout the world.

True universality in the form of equality is not an achievable goal. There will always be inevitable performance variations, as was found in the famous Pareto distribution (e.g. the top 20% will produce 80% of the outcomes). Consider agriculture, where this distribution does often occur (20% of farmers produce 80% of food). It would be foolhardy to penalize the top producers for their perceived unfair advantage—something that did occur under some communist regimes. Instead of concentrating on outcomes, it is more important to focus on equality of opportunities.

The three rules described above form a triad of equal weight. This triad can create a system of checks and balances, as seen in Figure 2.1.

It could be conjectured that no single rule should grow in importance over the other, as it might create unintended consequences. The following hypothetical situations illustrate the point:

1. If *transparency* grows too strong, individual privacy is lost. Too much information is shared with competitors and people are excluded from the market because of past indiscretions. It is often said that good people refuse to run for political office because many details of their lives are scrutinized for indiscretions. It is important to know what needs to be known.

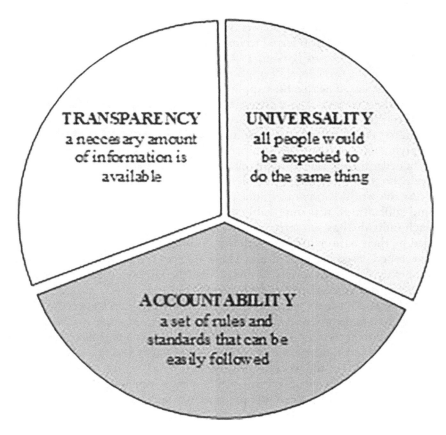

Figure 2.1 Ethical triad of ethics in business

Source: Authors.

2. If *accountability* grows too strong, the rules become too difficult to follow. Only a few people are able to understand all of the rules, which means that transparency is lost, and few have the means to follow the rules (i.e. universality is lost). Too much accountability (meaning too much bureaucracy) is often favored by big companies, as it has a way of suppressing new start-ups. This is because only big companies have the resources to navigate the bureaucratic maze.

3. If *universality* grows too strong, the rules for *similarly situated persons* would not acknowledge that, even within a society, no one truly has an equal level of opportunities. Historical injustices from the past are ignored and prejudices are assumed to be nonexistent. Accountability and transparency are lost.

Conclusion

After the horrors of two world wars, social scientists have been focusing on why people do bad things. The first significant experiment was performed by Stanley Milgram, who clearly demonstrated that the sociological need to obey authority often overrules our moral convictions.

Since the turn of the century, new research has focused more intently on the science of cheating and how it can be clearly seen that most people have the capacity to cheat a little. Since most people do not want to be considered cheaters, they refrain from cheating a lot. Even moral people find themselves in two states of mind: a business state and a moral state. Since work and business are a reality of life, the morality of the business state of mind needs to be constantly assessed.

All facets of life involve making choices based on our own thoughts, experiences and senses. Life is full of important decisions, and each individual must make order from chaos to create a reality that minimizes emotional distress (i.e. cognitive dissonance). This could lead to distortions, inaccurate judgments or illogical interpretations of acquired information (i.e. the cognitive bias) in its many forms. This bias could be summed up as the *should* self (established rules about moral action) and the *want* self (desired action that may conflict with the *should* self). As such, ethical decision making should always consider the environment surrounding and the lives of all individuals.

We also introduced the conceptual ethical triad of transparency, accountability and universality. This could be summed up by three questions: (1) Do I mind if others know what I do? (2) Do I report my actions to others? (3) Is everyone treated the same as me? Transparency works best when all actors have open accessibility to critical information and this information is readily available. Accountability is a *reasonable* and *achievable* set of standards or metrics that assure proper conduct in a certain area that is agreed upon by all agents. Universality suggests that all people who are at the same level of opportunity be treated equally in the eyes of the law. For the concept to work, each leg of the triad must be balanced without too many extremes in each area. Transparency does not mean that companies should divulge all secrets. Accountability must mean that the rules for a particular area must be achievable and not limited to a selected few. Universality must take into consideration the differences of culture, nationality and economic situations.

Bibliography

Ariely, D. (2013). *The Honest Truth About Dishonesty: How We Lie to Everyone—Especially Ourselves.* New York: Harper Perennial.

Baldoni, J. (2010). How to Recognize (and Cure) Your Own Hubris. *Harvard Business Review*, 88(3).

Bless, H., Fiedler, K. Strack, F. (2004). *Social Cognition: How Individuals Construct Social Reality.* New York: Psychology Press. Retrieved from: http://psychology.about.com/od/cindex/fl/What-Is-Cognitive-Bias.htm [Accessed 10 October 2018.]

Boardman, N.E. (2006). *Cost-Benefit Analysis: Concepts and Practice.* Upper Saddle River: Prentiss Hall.

Brocas, I., Carrillo, J.D. (2003). *The Psychology of Economic Decisions: Volume I: Rationality and Well-Being.* New York: Oxford University Press.

Corruption Perception Index 2017. Transparency International. Retrieved from: www.transparency.org/news/feature/corruption_perceptions_index_2017 [Accessed 10 October 2018.]

Dalio, R. (2017). *Principles: Life and Work.* New York: Simon and Schuster.

Doliński, D., Grzyb1, T., Folwarczny, M., Grzybała, P., Krzyszycha, K., Martynowska, K., Trojanowski, J. (2017). Would You Deliver an Electric Shock in 2015? Obedience in the Experimental Paradigm Developed by Stanley Milgram in the 50 Years Following the Original Studies. *Social Psychological and Personality Science*, 8(8), 927–933.

Festinger, L., Carlsmith, J.M. (1959). Cognitive Consequences of Forced Compliance. *Journal of Abnormal and Social Psychology*, 58, 203–210.

Geweke, J. (1992). *Decision Making Under Risk and Uncertainty: New Models and Empirical Findings.* Dordrecht: Kluwer Academic Publishers.

Giddens, A. (1991). *Modernity and Self-Identity.* Stanford, CA: Stanford University Press.

Gino, F., Ariely, D. (2011). The Dark Side of Creativity: Original Thinkers Can Be More Dishonest. *Journal of Personality and Social Psychology*, 102(3), 445–459.

Gneezy, U., Rustichini, A. (2000). A Fine Is a Price. *The Journal of Legal Studies*, 29(1), 1–17.

Green, R. (1992). *Kierkegaard and Kant: The Hidden Debt.* Albany: State University Press of New York.

Greenfield, P. (2013). The Changing Psychology of Culture from 1800 Through 2000. *Psychological Science*, 7, 1722–1731.

Jackall, R. (2010). *Moral Mazes: The World of Corporate Managers.* New York: Oxford University Press.

Jennings, M. (2014). *Business Ethics: Case Studies and Selected Readings*. Stamford: Cengage Learning.

Josephson, M. (2002). *Making Ethical Decisions*. Los Angeles: Josephson Institute of Ethics.

Knight, F. (1941). Anthropology and Economics. *Journal of Political Economics*, 49(2), 247–252.

Mazar, N., Amir, O., Ariely, D. (2008). The Dishonesty of Honest People: A Theory of Self-Concept Maintenance. *Journal of Marketing Research*, 45(6), 633–644.

Milgram, S. (1963). Behavioral Study of Obedience. *Journal of Abnormal and Social Psychology*, 67, 371–378.

Milgram, S. (1973). The Perils of Obedience. *Harper's Magazine*, 247(1483), 62–78.

Nevid, J. (2012). *Psychology: Concepts and Applications*. Boston: Jon-David Hague publishers.

Roeckelein, J. E. (2006). *Elsevier's Dictionary of Psychological Theories*. Amsterdam: Elsevier.

Ross, L., Greene, D., House, P. (1977). The False Consensus Effect: An Egocentric Bias in Social Perception and Attribution Processes. *Journal of Experimental Social Psychology*, 13(3), 279–301.

Schnackenberg, A., Tomlinson, E., (2014). Organizational Transparency: A New Perspective on Managing Trust in Organization-Stakeholder Relationships. *Journal of Management*, 40(3), 641–941.

Tenbrunsel, A., Diekmann, K., Wade-Benzoni, K., Bazerman, M. (2007). *The Ethical Mirage, Temporal Explanations as to Why We Are Not as Ethical as We Think We Are*. Harvard: Harvard Business School.

Tenbrunsel, A. E. (2005). *Conflict of Interest: Challenges and Solutions in Business, Law, Medicine, and Public Policy*. Cambridge: Cambridge University Press.

Tversky, A., Kahneman, D. (1974). Judgment Under Uncertainty: Heuristics and Biases. *Science*, New Series, 185(4157), 1124–1131.

3 Corporate Social Responsibility From the National, Community, Company and Individual Levels

Introduction

Much has been written about the need for the corporation to think about the needs of both their employees and the community in which a company is situated. It is a cliché that a company's impact on society and its employees does not end at the entrance gate. First and foremost, companies are a profit-making entity with the express intent of creating wealth for the investors. It would be overly simplistic to state that investors are hell-bent on profit, with untold riches being their main motivation. Few would want to be seen as the evil villain. Remember, the "book-of-the-self" (see Chapter 2) that individuals create through ambition is also an epitaph for remembrance. This could be called good citizenry and stewardship. This greed vs. social standing forms the basis of the well-known diametrically opposed stockholder/stakeholder models. These two fundamental models are, however, largely a reaction to the state and its influence on corporate decisions. These two models overlook the fundamental basis for societal organization: a national identity and what it means to each citizen of a nation. Even global companies are part and parcel of the nation they find themselves in. Because of this, a more holistic approach needs to be taken that goes beyond the immediate stakeholders.

We looked into how companies are dealing with externalities of production, both positive and negative. All of the corporations we observed do business on both the national and international level. To borrow an analogy from quantum physics, corporate social responsibility (CSR) is both local and global at the same time, depending on the viewpoint of the observer. Economists have long touted the benefits of globalization and to be fair, the benefits are all around us, especially in terms of availability of consumer goods.

Political turmoil throughout the world is demanding a reassessment of how we organize work (i.e. the resurgence of right-wing parties). What needs to be determined is what the role of the corporation is when considering these new demands.

CSR can also be judged on an individual level. As ordinary as it may sound, society is a collective made up of individuals. Responsibility for the collective and the individual must be shared. Without a doubt, the new digital economy is affecting behavior at the individual level as each year more of the economy is devoted to what can only be considered excess and overindulgence.

This chapter discusses the interaction of social responsibilities between the individual, state and corporate levels. In doing so, it will develop the notion of CSR that is focused on the intuitive good at all levels, but most especially the individual level.

The Role of the State in CSR

Concepts of CSR have varied over the years, but it can be said that there are two poles representing two different thoughts. The first thought is that power belongs to the entrepreneur and owners of a company. The second thought is represented by the concept that all actors involved in a corporation need to be considered and treated respectfully. At the same time, government has been both hands-on and hands-off in dealing with corporations. Throughout the history of large corporations, the thought pendulum has swung from one extreme to the other. This can be reflected in the following historical periods:

- 1800–1830, *Early industrialization*: Movement from individual artisans to mass production of standardized products and the start of a corporate model with multiple employees, each with a given competence or task.
- 1830–1880, *Mass industrialization*: The rise of corporate giants and societal control by a few oligarchs. Profit is a main motivator as well as the concept of moral superiority of a select few corporate leaders.
- 1880, *World War I rise of the unions*: The establishment of unions and collective bargaining and the beginning of minimum wages as well as safe and better working conditions.
- Between the world wars, *Strong unions and the beginning of government spending*: Power sharing between labor and management. During the 1930s, governments are called upon to stimulate the economy with spending programs for countries' infrastructures.
- After World War II, *Governmental and union influence*: Labor has powerful influence over the government. The beginning of an era of higher equality between classes. Government intervenes in the market to protect large corporations and sometimes nationalize companies. Government is called upon to protect citizens in terms of healthcare, security and general welfare.
- The 1960s, *The decade of activism and environmentalism*: The beginning of the idea that the Earth needs protection against the excesses

of corporations and society. It is also a time that addresses issues of racism and various inequalities.

- The 1970s, *The regulatory decade*: The large faceless conglomeration is seen as an entity that needed to be controlled and regulated. The large conglomerate is often considered the enemy of the public. High flirtation with socialism and government control becomes an accepted standard throughout the world.
- The 1980s, *The profit decade*: A time of reconsideration of the corporation as the enemy. It is recognized that the corporation needs to earn a proper profit for motivation.
- The 1990s, *The end of communism/the beginning of globalization*: Worldwide expansion of the supply and manufacturing chain creates a globalized market. Profit is paramount to corporate survival. Labor has lost its power to demand higher wages and benefits as labor can easily be outsourced.

The bipolar view of the corporation as friend and foe was best summed up by Winston Churchill's observation: "Some people regard private enterprise as a predatory tiger to be shot. Others look on it as a cow they can milk. Not enough people see it as a healthy horse, pulling a sturdy wagon".

The fall of the Iron Curtain left the world divided into industrial (developed) nations and developing nations without a command economy alternative, thus unlocking the creative potential of literally half of the planet. The top-down approach to steering the economy by government has been permanently disregarded. Instead, it is now seen that innovation comes from the bottom up. In other words, the government does not make a strong economy; individuals with new creative ideas do. With so much talent freed from the command economy structure, the corporation has become globalized with production, distribution and consumption not limited to one country.

Global competition cannot be viewed as a zero-sum game in which someone wins and another person loses. After all, the GDP of the world is ever growing. In the global context, though, not everyone can be a winner as there will be local jobs that are forever lost, never to return. The advantages of globalization are that it can raise living standards in developing countries by providing higher-standard manufacturing jobs. Some types of work are no longer preferred in more developed countries, so the work is outsourced to countries where there is a desire for these occupations (e.g. clothing, shoes, and textiles). Offshoring certain skill sets to new countries allows the development of higher-level skills in these countries, allowing them to move up to a higher level of value-added production. There are, however, disadvantages within the global context. International companies move their operations to countries with low pay and lay off people in the higher paying countries. When offshoring certain occupations, the standards of worker safety and benefits are lowered even when taking into consideration the different standards of living. As certain jobs are no longer performed in the developed country, these skills, especially in areas like research and development, are lost forever. Many have accused international corporations of starting a race to the bottom for the lowest production price and eventual lower living standards.

Currently, it can be said that CSR is an attempt to find a middle ground between extremes and this needs to consider from this new global context. For a modern version of CSR to be successful, it needs to consider the greatest possible good affecting the greatest possible number.

Today, it is well understood that companies are in business to make a profit for their owners, as without it no good could be accomplished. From this foundation, higher goals can be considered. Archie Carroll (Carroll and Buchholtz, 2008) saw that CSR embraced four kinds of responsibilities: economic, legal, ethical and philanthropic. For the conscientious businessperson, CSR must first be about making money. Profit, however, must be gained through legal means, thus obeying the law is paramount. Not all rules in society are specifically set out in law, thus ethical decisions that go beyond the law needs to be considered. Lastly, and dependent upon the success of the corporation, the final element is being a good corporate citizen and giving back to society. Carroll envisioned CSR as a pyramid in the following order from bottom to top: make a profit, obey the law, be ethical and be a good corporate citizen.

This pyramid should not be viewed with fixed layers or proportions. Obviously, some companies have more power to change the world for the better. Few people would argue that a chocolate company (a supplier of an indulgence) could be held to the same standard as Google (with the ability to fundamentally change the world). The pyramid also assumes that the laws are adequate. A simple way to put it is that CSR is not about how a company spends its money; it is about how a company makes its money.

Considering CSR from the Interaction of the Corporation and the Community

Economics is a science that has long been divided into two competing philosophies that could be described as an individualist approach and a collective approach. The term that is most commonly used is the shareholder and stakeholder model. The shareholder model holds that the only social responsibility that a corporation has is to make a profit. The stakeholder model believes that long-term survival of a corporation depends on the satisfaction of other people or groups that have a legitimate interest in the company. In terms of the pyramid above, it could be said that the stockholder model forms the foundation of the previous pyramid while the stakeholder model forms the top.

There is much debate about the necessity of one model over the other, with strong disagreements about each model's legitimacy. Some might consider these two models to be the yin and yang of CSR.

Nobel Prize winner Milton Friedman addressed the needs of the corporation by arguing that the corporation only has one social responsibility and that is to satisfy their owners, the shareholders (Wartick and Cochran, 1985). He went as far as to say that it was socially irresponsible for the corporation to divert time, money and attention away from maximizing profits for social or charitable causes. Friedman believed that the shareholders would not likely agree on what social causes a company should support and that social efforts would undermine market efficiency by making the company less competitive. If a company spends money on social causes, they would have less money for quality materials or hiring talented workers. Customers would find the products less desirable and choose the competitor's products. As such, spending money on social causes hurts all stakeholders. Friedman believed that the corporation could not be asked to solve societal problems, as this was something best left for governments and their representatives by making appropriate laws. If the government as the representative for all citizens in society cannot resolve social ills, how is it then that the corporation would be able to?

The stakeholder theory attempts to address the morals and values in management by identifying the interests of all groups that are necessary for the success of the company. The idea originated from Freeman (1984) with the notion of finding which groups and what actions are really important in the success of an organization. The model is based on the idea that the company exists to serve the many stakeholders who have an interest in it or who in some way may be harmed or benefited by it. These groups include employees, customers, suppliers, financiers, communities, governmental bodies, political groups, trade unions and sometimes even competitors.

There are some disagreements about who is considered a stakeholder, but we can generally divide them into two groups: primary and secondary stakeholders. The primary stakeholders are those whose participation is critical for the company's success (employees, stockholders, customers). Secondary stakeholders are those people who are affected by the company (suppliers, government, even competitors). Apart from this general definition, stakeholders need to possess three characteristics: (1) legitimacy, a legal claim to the company's activity; (2) power, the power to influence the company's decision-making process; and (3) urgency, the ability to command attention from management (Mitchell et al., 1997).

For the stakeholder model to work efficiently, all of the different groups need to interact in a way to create value, and it is the job of the corporate leader to shape these relationships. When there is a conflict between stakeholders, the executive must find ways to rethink the process. All stakeholders must be willing to accept trade-offs in order for the corporation to prosper. Grant et al. (1991) divide stakeholders into four categories:

- Supportive: high potential for cooperation/low potential threat.
- Marginal: low potential for cooperation/low potential threat.
- Non-supportive: high potential threat.
- Mixed blessing: the potential to be supportive and non-supportive.

Freeman (1984) suggests that a core competence of a manager is figuring out how the interests of the different stakeholders go in the same direction. The key question is finding out how each group is important to the business. A company can be at risk if the customers don't want or want less of its product; suppliers don't make quality parts or help to make a product more innovative; the employees don't want to be there every day using 100% of their efforts; the community is routinely ignored or the company violates local customs or laws; or if it doesn't create value or a profit for its financiers.

It is all of the individual stakeholders that create a product together; it is something that not one of them can create alone and it is important that each stakeholder group doesn't become totally self-interested. In accordance with Carroll's pyramid, the long-term existence of a corporation is dependent on the relevant stakeholders who must receive some benefit from this concern both personally and economically. Very few companies manage to pass the test of time and fewer still have remained champions in their field; Ford, General Electric, Pfizer, and Procter and Gamble are just a few examples of companies that have managed to survive for over 100 years.

Considering CSR From the Interaction of the Corporation and the State

As the CEE region was and still is the "go-to" region of Europe for new production facilities, it has provided opportunities for observation in negotiations of operational conditions. As members of the EU community, an overall rule of law, especially concerning product safety and accounting standards, has provided a certain level of transparency and accountability in these states. From our interviews, we have found that these standards are largely being upheld. The third leg of our ethics pyramid, universality, is sometimes being compromised in order to attract a large corporation to the community, that is, the Kantian rule about *similarly situated persons* (see Chapter 2) is not being applied evenly. Several of the companies we have observed were able to negotiate favorable terms for their entry into the country. This includes tax holidays, loans and infrastructure improvement. Some companies have complained that tax holidays gave the competition an unfair advantage. Part of this competition is for the limited talent in a country where the company with a tax benefit has an advantage over other companies. This is especially true in manufacturing where many blue-collar workers can work across a wide range of jobs (e.g. heavy equipment operator, welder, electrician).

Infrastructure, especially in the forms of highways, is a large factor that is indirectly violating the notion of universality among players. According to Camagni (2002), transport infrastructure is the competitive advantage that many businesses look for when deciding on where to invest. Cushman and Wakefield's 20th Annual European Cities Monitor (EUR, 2009) found that international links and connections to other major economic centers is the third most important criterion for determining the location of investment. The CEE region is considerably behind Western European nations in terms of highway construction.

Spatial evidence of regional inequality of infrastructure can be found in roadway construction, specifically four-lane highways. This basic necessity for prosperity and the lack of balance can be seen in any highway map from the Central European region. Some notable missing links include the following:

- There is only one east/west four-lane highway link across Poland extending to the Ukrainian border, and none to Belarus.
- There is only one east/west four-lane highway link from Hungary to Romania.
- In Slovakia, there is no major highway connecting the two largest cities (the capital Bratislava in the west and Košice in the east). In 2018, not a single kilometer of highways was built here.
- There are no north-south links between Poland, the Czech Republic, Slovakia and Hungary.

The level of development in the Germanic countries (Germany, Austria, Switzerland) is much greater than the Visegrad nations. The extreme eastern regions of the Visegrad nations have even fewer connections to the inter-European grid, with only two four-lane east/west links and no continuous north/south link—a huge visual sign of the lesser status of the region. With tension in Russia, Belarus, Ukraine and Moldova, the economic push east has slowed considerably, adding to negative outlooks.

The corporate need for infrastructure and the government's ability to provide it are unwittingly creating regional winners and losers. The study *Growing and Shrinking Regions in Europe* (2013) by the German Federal Institute for Research on Building, Urban Affairs, and Spatial Development paints a very clear and disturbing picture, at least for Europe:

- City regions are growing, in Central and Eastern Europe as well.
- Half of Europeans live in shrinking regions.
- Shrinking regions exist in nearly all countries.

The result is an expectation of further imbalances between the growing and shrinking areas. As infrastructural investment is seen as a duty of the government, corporations are not seen as being responsible, yet this is dodging the responsibility of causation, especially if the corporation is a recipient of a tax holiday or a government loan. By not building highways, the state is indirectly disadvantaging some regions. If tax and financial incentives are to be used by the government to entice businesses, they logically should be used to reduce regional disparities. As for highways, this should be a high priority for the EU. After all, highways do not stop at a country's border.

What CSR Means to the Company and the Community

From our research, we can find that companies fully understand the perception of CSR especially in terms of stakeholder support. Many companies do have initiatives designed to promote the company as being a good corporate citizen. As such, we find the companies of the CEE region to be fully in line with the concept of stakeholder CSR. This is rather unsurprising as, during socialism, the companies held a high social role in the community. Most all of the company representatives we interviewed feel a deep connection with the local community and the corporation is careful to nurture a positive image. Corporate leaders fully understand the need to have an image of benevolence.

The digital era has added a new layer of complexity to the notion of universality in terms of competition and also regional stability. It is assumed that all firms must keep reinventing themselves in order to stay relevant. Not doing so means that today's corporate leaders can become yesterday's horse and carriage in a heartbeat. This is Schumpeter's notion of creative destruction, that is, the process of innovation where new products (and firms) replace old, outdated ones. This is standard dogma as the corporation and its competitors are seen to have the same universal rules and privileges.

New research from the OECD (Andrews et al., 2015) suggests that Schumpeter's model is breaking down as frontier firms are growing much faster than laggard firms. Andrews et al. define the frontier firm as companies in the top 5% of their industry with laggards being the remaining 95%. They found that frontier firms tend to be global and part of a multinational group and use other global frontier firms to provide benchmarks. What this means is that the gap that frontier firms have between frontier firms in other nations is shrinking while the gap between a frontier firm and a laggard firm within a nation is growing. The established notion that a market challenger may one day unseat the market leader becomes questionable. This is especially true in services. The use of digital innovations by the frontier firms can lead to an incredibly fast scaling-up of networks and lowering of marginal costs which means that the competition is overwhelmed with little time or resources to react. The productivity gains made by these firms stay at the frontier and do not trickle down to the rest of the economy. In the global context, a country can have a competitive frontier-leading firm that can take on the world. On the other hand, the countryside will be littered with national laggard firms that have no place in this modern modern landscape.

There is little consensus as to what should be done about this. Should government support the laggards or should frontier companies give away their trade secrets? One thing is quite evident: the losers are crying foul at the voter box. In Europe, England and the United States, marginalized people are voting for a dose of anarchy in hopes of shaking up the established order. There is little reason for people to engage in a protest vote other than a desire to get back at leaders that are not listening to them. Corporate leaders in frontier firms are playing by the rules of the game defined by society, but are still creating conditions where many are not benefiting and this is very often geographically situated (i.e. some areas grow stronger while others continue to decline).

CSR Between the Corporation and the Individual

Classical economic theory suggests that man seeks to maximize his utility while firms seek to maximize profit. What has been forgotten is that the needs of mankind are as much rooted in the past (historical institutions, national traits) as for future aspirations (modernity). This suggests that corporations must also consider other, more humanistic needs. Individuals strive to complete their "life story" as mentioned in the previous chapter (see Giddens, 1991, Chapter 2) by choosing options that will leave them with a respectable legacy. All individuals in society are looking to find the best alternative for themselves and this desire can be expressed in terms of both material attainment and societal status.

The single largest purchase in an individual's life is a house, and for the CEE region, homeownership is of high importance (most CEE countries have homeownership rates over 90%). According to the *State of Housing in the EU* by the EU Urban Agenda Housing Partnership (2017), housing has become a problem due to the following:

- Housing has become the highest expenditure for Europeans and prices remain stable at a high level, hitting the poor disproportionally harder.
- House prices are growing faster than income in most member states, while inequality and housing exclusion are mutually reinforcing.
- The territorial divide is alarming, as finding adequate and affordable housing in places where job opportunities are is increasingly hard.
- As the level of housing construction is still low, the major cities especially face a structural housing shortage.
- The political response to Europe's housing challenge remains poor.

For many larger firms, the importance of infrastructure exacerbates this problem. For management and corporate leaders, the decision to move to where housing is not readily available becomes ethically questionable, especially when a corporation seeks government funding. Even if a company is compensating their own employees fairly in a high-priced region, a knock-on effect can cause negative externalities for other firms. Consider the following scenario:

- A well-established global company wants to set up shop in a new country, creating many high-paying jobs and raising the general competency of the area. The company chooses to locate in an area that is already well established with infrastructure and economic activities.
- Because of the higher pay and the status of the company, it is able to attract workers from other companies. The low-profile laggard companies suffer.
- Still unable to find enough local employees, the company asks newer workers to migrate to a community where housing is in short supply. This increases costs for all locally. Established residents of the community are reluctant to approve of more housing and infrastructural spending and are happy with the status quo (after all, they are also enjoying the appreciation of home equity values). Other workers decide on making long commutes.
- One solution is to set up dormitories on the company's facilities, where workers can live temporarily. The dormitories come with privacy restrictions. People, mostly men, get to see their families only during off days.
- The prestige and large presence of the company give it clout to demand further infrastructure improvements from the government, even before basic improvements elsewhere have yet to be started.

Even with the above negative externalities, the company is still seen as upholding the concept of good corporate stewardship. In the eyes of the corporate leader, it seems truly benevolent.

In the research we have conducted with university students over the past ten years, we have been able to define the expectations of work among the newer generation with over 1,000 respondents. This evaluation was made from an assessment of essays of future expectations (where do I see myself in ten years?) and making choices between work and living options presented in a binary form (choosing between two possibilities). We have found that:

- Students overwhelmingly wish to avoid a move to a large metropolitan area.
- Houses are preferred overwhelmingly over flats, with bungalows being the most popular style.

- Students almost unanimously see themselves in some sort of desk job behind a computer without any consideration of other options.
- Students will choose a desk job over a blue-collar job even when the pay is one-third less.
- Female students overwhelmingly would choose a white-collar husband over a blue-collar husband even when he is paid one-third less.
- A change that has occurred recently is that younger students have a lower desire to go to another country for work opportunities.

For the new generation, there is a well-bounded definition of what work should be, and for most, a job in production does not create a good narrative to go into the book-of-the-self. The corporate leader would do well to increase the perception of work in production and stress the outcome of this work as being stable, rewarding and helping with the individual's legacy.

The digital economy has added to the uncertainty of long-term stability as companies can now quickly move and adapt to new environments often more quickly than people can. There is much cynicism among the young generation about companies having any long-term loyalty to their employees. As such, CSR between the corporation and employee must include long-term commitments to employees, and more importantly, a pathway to success that is defined by the individual and guided by leaders.

Collective Responsibility vs. Individual Responsibility

A main concept of Kantian theory is that individuals take responsibility for their actions and do not transfer these consequences to somebody else. This is a rather simple notion to follow on a personal level as one's own actions have direct causes and effects on others. Like Adam Smith, Immanuel Kant lived in a time when basic survival was a challenge. People could not dream of a world with so much interconnection. It is this interconnection that has made life far more purposeful by allowing us to create the tools to overcome its challenges. Wars, famine and disease, though still in existence, have been tamed to such a point that human toil can now focus on pursuits other than basic survival. Now a new concern is replacing the older ones. This can best be described as "too much of a good thing". We can refer to these good things as indulgences or engaging in activities more often than what is good for you.

In the past indulgence had its limits, with alcohol and tobacco being a main concern. Shopping was functional rather than recreational. Hobbies were recreational rather than habitual. Few people had time or money to be so singularly dedicated to any addictive behavior, especially negative behavior.

There is a growing area of the economy that is predisposed to the usurpation of individual responsibility. To put it bluntly, there are many economic agents that are prospering from addiction in its many forms. The big question is what is the responsibility of the corporation in regard to individualistic negative externalities?

Society and corporations have largely come to terms with alcohol/ tobacco addiction, as there are many controls placed on their consumption and sale (e.g. taxes, warning labels, rules of sale). In psychological terms, addictive behavior can be traced to brain chemistry, specifically dopamine. This neurotransmitter was found by Schultz (1998) to be a chemical reward for meeting the goals of an anticipated action. With this reward mechanism, an action can be habituated, a basic tool needed for learning. Dopamine is a short-term experience with a need and a desire for more and higher levels of release. According to Lustig (2017), the corporation has learned to "hack" into this dopamine hit, presenting a growing list of problems such as obesity, consumer debt and, above all, the use of internet devices in its many forms. Few today could even consider purposely leaving home without the ubiquitous smartphone. For most individuals, a day does not go by without connecting to the internet. Food companies have gone from providing the basic staples to supplying added value processing and an abdication of the cooking responsibility to the food company. As such, sugar has become a common food additive.

All of the above has the risk of too much moralizing and chasing imaginary enemies. Few would want to turn their backs on these modern conveniences in a Luddite quest for a more nostalgic time, yet there are several major concerns that cannot be swept under the carpet of individualistic responsibility. Today's parents are constantly facing the threats posed by the smartphone, the internet and food issues aimed at their children. Bad actors who disseminate fake news, inflame hatred, supply pornography and so forth have a platform that can reach millions with few limits. It needs to be asked if corporations have a responsibility to limit activities that are overly destructive to society, the collective, especially when it becomes all too apparent their products are facilitating societal and individual problems. What is an acceptable level of depravity when it comes to free speech?

It would be hard to argue that firms should assume the obligation for individual responsibilities, and few would relish living in a nanny state of government-imposed rules on commerce seen as vices. On the other hand, it would be hard to call a corporation socially responsible if the end result is too many customers facing too many abhorrent issues. This is especially true when the customer is a child.

Psychologist Timothy Leary (1983) famously encouraged a previous generation to *tune in, turn on, drop out*. In order to meet the responsibilities of today's world, the inverse of Leary's pronouncement may be more appropriate—to *tune out, turn off, drop back in.*

Conclusion

In this chapter, the interaction of social responsibility was explored between the corporation and the state, the community and the individual. We also discussed the issue of individual versus collective responsibility. From our interviews, we have found corporations to be engaged in the community and doing their best to be seen a positive light. Globalization has added a layer of complexity to CSR as a company could be doing all the right things and still be contributing to negative externalities. We see a need for more open dialogue and cooperation between the state, corporate and individual levels. Instead of focusing on legal obligations, attention should turn to what is intuitively right. With a focus on what could be considered an intuitive good, it would be easier to come to agreements between all three levels. Consider the following examples:

- Food industry: Individuals are free to purchase their desires, but the amount of sugar and fat could be clearly and understandably marked on packaging.
- Car industry: Cars should be marketed on their actual efficiency and emissions, judged on real-world conditions rather than laboratory conditions.
- Children: Companies need to be careful with supplying and marketing products that could be unhealthy to the body and the minds of children and not engage in the unscrupulous collection of their data.
- All parties need to consider the individuals and regions that are being left behind, keeping in mind the principles of universality, that is, equally situated people should have the same opportunities; the underprivileged need to be helped.

The above examples are all instinctive in theory but are often overlooked in attempts to achieve greater short-term profit. Global companies have a special obligation to the nations they reside in. As frontier companies operating on the global level are pulling further away from their challengers, some are losing their sense of national obligation as their focus is myopically on other global competitors. Too many governments see the frontier firms as "white knights" and gift these "savior" companies with infrastructure improvements and tax subsidies, yet the trickling-down of technology is limited as the speed of the accumulative advantage has accelerated. Laggard firms and declining regions are truly at a disadvantage.

A common theme throughout this book is the notion that individuals attempt to create a legacy that can be described in the book-of-the-self.

One yardstick for the success of an individual is the intergenerational comparison: am I better off than my parents when they were my age? This a hard comparison now that generations can be divided between pre- and post-internet. For Central Europe, where this research is focused, the generational differences are starker with the socialism/capitalism divide. In our gadget-driven world, it is hard to imagine going back to a time of corded phones, limited TV and information gathered from books in libraries. On the other hand, it becomes harder for the younger generation to imagine affording a house or even worse, affording children. These are the real canaries in the coal mine and call into question the long-term viability of some nations. CSR is more than just doing some good things for the immediate stakeholder; it is also a holistic interaction between all levels of society. The greater good is one where all parties can agree on what is considered fundamentally right. This is especially true at the level of the single individual, as this level wields the least amount of power.

Case Study 1 The CEE Cultures in Transition

The Nature of Economic Transformation

The macroeconomic factors of life in Central and Eastern Europe before the transition process began may be summarized as follows (Grayson and Bodily, 1996):

- Because of the unfavorable economic legacies left by the respective communist regimes, the post-communist governments had to adopt restrictive economic policies which caused recessions in the domestic markets; the recessions most unfavorably impacted companies such as those selling home improvement products or other postponable consumer goods.
- The collapse of the communist regimes coincided somewhat with cyclical recessions in Western Europe and North America; the Soviet bloc markets collapsed in 1991.
- In addition to the recessions in Western Europe, export possibilities were harmed by the tariffs and quotas erected by the European Union (EU), especially in industries where CEE countries had spare capacity, such as agricultural products, steel and textiles.
- Successive devaluations of domestic currencies, vis-à-vis US dollars or German marks, raised the prices of imported inputs; for

domestic producers, the degree and timing of the devaluations added to already existing uncertainty, and for foreign joint ventures, partners' devaluations worsened their income statements.

- As the target countries reduced their tariffs and quotas in an effort to liberalize, foreign companies entered the markets, causing giant problems for domestic companies.

It has been a long time since the fall of socialism and it would be folly to continue to blame today's pathologies on a government system that has long vanished, yet it did provide a steep learning curve to the rule of law as rules were quite negotiable. In terms of ethical decision making, everything was possible and everything could be illegal. A common saying from the period of socialism was "If you don't steal, you are stealing from your family". The archaic rules of socialism led to the creation of a shadow economy along with the official one, while in this unofficial economy transactions occurred through bartering, illegal payments and favoritism.

The transition to capitalism did not occur overnight, nor was it without its share of problems. For business, the transformative period (1989–2005) was a time of destruction of capital stock and lost economic activities. The culture differences (described in Table 3.1) influenced the transition period in Vysegrad countries.

In the case of Slovakia, there were three significant waves of seismic shock: first, the failure of socialism (followed by the Velvet revolution in 1989); second, the partitioning of Czechoslovakia (and later creation of Slovakia in 1993); and third, the crony-capitalist period of Vladimír Mečiar (1992–1998). During this period of chaos, there was no ability to adequately address ethical issues as day-to-day survival was the main concern. During this time, factories faced disorganization as they lost their old customers, and even if they found new customers, they lost their old suppliers (Schnitzer, 2005). This period lasted longer than expected and led many to the notion that continuous decline was inevitable. This reflexive response set the condition for overlooking tangible progress in unexpected areas.

Cynicism corrupts on a mental level. As soon as people feel that they have no power to change the system, they learn to just live with it and do nothing about it. Yet from the turn of the century, CEE countries have managed to establish working ethical rules, especially in business.

As Silver (2012) states, "it is important to separate the signal from the noise" with observations. Many are quick to discount the advances

Table 3.1 The cultural differences of four Visegrad countries prior to entry to EU before 2004

Czech Republic	Slovakia	Hungary	Poland
Quick liberalization and privatization. Creation of the "Czech management approach". Foreign experts and investors are despised. Management orientation on technologies, autocratic leadership styles. Little emphasis on the employees. Professional management, a bit overrated.	Legacy of an agrarian society. Middle management very cost concerned. Little risk-taking in business. Undervalued own capabilities. High power distance index in companies. Low market orientation. Strong masculinity-gender problems.	Strong innovation culture. Active entre-preneurship, mostly in SMEs. New opportunities are highly welcomed, based on informal contacts. Networking and relationships help with job promotion. High individualism and self-confidence.	Individualism, discipline and loyalty to old principles. Strong preferences for formal structures. Presence of both "old" and "young" management. Zero correlation between age of organization and management style.

Source: Authors.

in Central Europe because of the very "noisy" governments that seem to be mired in a continuous state of corruption and a reversion to nationalist sentiments. Consider the corruption index from Transparency International in Table 3.2.

Compared to their Western European counterparts, Central Europe still has low expectations from their governments and in the case of Hungary, it is in decline. One possible reason for the higher perception of corruption is that some of the governmental institutional structures are still dealing with a certain level of corruption, nepotism and self-interested indulgence.

Though there is still a perception of high levels of corruption in Central Europe, there is a sense of positive change in business that can be reflected in the GDP growth rate (see Table 3.3). Despite the perception of a less than ethical climate, the region is experiencing dynamic growth led by the multi-national companies that have located there.

Table 3.2 Perception of the corruption index

Corruption Perception Index for the Past Five Years*

Country	2016 Score	2015 Score	2014 Score	2013 Score	2012 Score
Hungary	48	51	54	54	55
Slovakia	51	51	50	47	46
Poland	62	63	61	60	58
Czech Republic	55	56	51	48	49
Germany	81	81	79	78	79
France	69	70	69	71	71

* Score ranking from 1–100, with 100 being very clean.

Source: Transparency International, www.transparency.org/news/feature/corruption_perceptions_index_2017.

Table 3.3 The GDP per capita growth in % between 2011 and 2018

	2011	2012	2013	2014	2015	2016	2017	2018 Forecast
Croatia	–0.3	–2.2	–1.1	–0.5	1.6	2.9	2.8	2.6
Czech Republic	–	–0.8	–0.48	2.72	5.31	2.59	4.29	2.6
Estonia	7.9	4.7	1.8	3.1	1.6	2.1	4.9	3.7
Hungary	2.0	–1.1	2.4	4.3	3.4	2.2	4.0	4.1
Latvia	8.3	5.3	3.7	3.1	3.6	2.8	4.5	3.5
Lithuania	8.5	5.2	4.6	3.9	2.4	2.3	3.8	3.3
Poland	5.0	1.6	1.3	3.3	4.0	2.9	4.6	4.2
Slovakia	2.7	1.5	1.4	2.5	3.7	3.2	3.4	3.3
Slovenia	0.4	2.9	1.2	3.0	2.2	2.6	5.0	2.2

Source: World Bank website database, https://data.worldbank.org/country/.

One could draw a comparison between Central Europe as a place for business and Las Vegas and the state of Nevada, a place where gambling was always legal. After some fits and starts, the first casino, the Flamingo, proved to be a profitable business for the Mafia, drawing other mafiosi to join. As no one would really want to gamble at a crooked casino, rules for business were established to keep the industry respectable. Eventually, the criminal element faded away and Las Vegas became legitimate operating under the regulations of the state. Likewise, investors would not want to come to a Central

European country if the rules were "compromised", so order was eventually established from the disorder of the transition period of the 1990s.

High Power Distance Culture, Masculinity and Particularism in Central European Culture

Old habits and old perceptions die hard, and even harder among the older generations—visions from their youth are viewed through tinted glasses. For some in Western Europe and the United States, Central Europe is still seen as that "land behind the Iron Curtain", painted in a cold-gray color, pockmarked with smokestack industries. This political divide harks back to an even colder time of dreadful battles and the unspeakable inhumanities of World War II. The not-so-old generation sees Central Europe as a place of Slavic languages with the oddity of Hungarian thrown in. This language divide is decidedly westward— habitants of this region are expected to learn English, German or French, but students in Western Europe have no expectation to learn Central European languages. Thus, Western homogeneity of culture becomes an expectation.

Cultural homogeneity cannot be taken for granted. There are significant differences between these regions. Consider the Hofstede cultural dimension (2018), which rates each country in the world by the following six dimensions:

- *Power distance*: The view of power relationships between superior/ subordinates.
- *Individualism*: The degree which a society acts as a group (collectivism) or as individuals (individualism), that is, the emphasis on "I" vs. "we".
- *Uncertainty avoidance*: The degree upon which people embrace or avoid the unexpected, the unknown, or stray away from the status quo.
- *Masculine vs. feminine*: The degree of societies' preference for "masculine" achievement, heroism and assertiveness vs. the "feminine" traits like modesty, caring for the less able and quality of life.
- *Long-term vs. short-term orientation*: The degree to which society associates the past with current and future conditions; for example, long-term oriented countries are likely to have continuing development.

- *Indulgence vs. restraint:* The degree that society allows for relatively free gratification of basic human desires related to the enjoyment of life (i.e. having fun).

By using the Hofstede cultural dimension insight index, we find that Central Europe is a hodgepodge with no uniform characteristics in cultural dimension except one. Compared to Germany and France, the indulgence factor is approximately 30% lower. This gives credence to the concept of "work before play".

Central Europe has succeeded in transitioning to a developed economy that can be considered business friendly. Ironically, this transition has faltered in the states of the former USSR, not including the Baltic States.

City and Town Development and Its Impact on the Corporation

Using the country that was Czechoslovakia (CSSR) as an example, we can find a classic sociological study of national economic experimentation especially during the 40-year period of one-party (communist) rule. As such, its history was shaped by non-market and unofficial market norms. This is especially true with town and urban development. Consider the following:

- Socialist policies restricted migration to the larger towns as there was a desire to have a balanced population and industrial distribution by fiat (Gawdiak, 1989).
- In an attempt to equalize wealth among citizens, great efforts were made to increase opportunities in the Slovak territory to match their Czech counterparts. By 1980, income in the Slovak territory was 80% of that of the Czech Republic, a major economic accomplishment (Gawdiak, 1989).
- Income differentials (less educated blue-collar workers vs. highly educated white-collar workers) were the lowest of any country in Central/Eastern Europe. This meant that there was a large population that could comfortably be considered middle-class (Gawdiak, 1989).
- There was a general unspoken treaty between the ruling KSČ political party and the populace that political acquiescence would,

unlike some other socialist countries, guarantee relative material security (Gawdiak, 1989).

All of the above favored relative prosperous small-town communities, creating a considerable amount of stable residential property. In other words, during the socialist era in the Slovak territory, small towns meant large homes and relatively large plots of land while larger cities meant "brutalist" tower blocks.

Corporate leaders need to understand that the attachment to the land and the home is of de facto high importance to Central Europeans and the need to supply this utility could be seen as paramount. In short, homeownership in the CEE is an expectation. This is not as true of Western European countries.

Bibliography

Andrews, D., Cruscuolo, C., Gal, P. (2015). *Frontier Firms, Technology Diffusion and Public Policy: Micro Evidence from OECD Countries*. OECD 2015. Retrieved from: www.oecd.org/eco/growth/Frontier-Firms-Technology-Diffusion-and-Public-Policy-Micro-Evidence-from-OECD-Countries.pdf [Accessed 10 October 2018.]

Camagni, R. (2002). On the Concept of Territorial Competitiveness: Sound or Misleading? *Sage Journals*, 39(13), 2395–2411.

Carroll, A.B., Buchholtz, A.K. (2008). *Business and Society: Ethics and Stakeholders Management*. Mason: Cengage Learning.

Corruption Perception Index 2017. Transparency International. Retrieved from: www.transparency.org/news/feature/corruption_perceptions_index_2017 [Accessed 10 October 2018.]

Cushman and Wakefield 20th annual European Cities Monitor (EUR, 2009). Retrieved from: http://europe-re.com/cushman-wakefield-20th-annual-european-cities-monitor-eur-2/40379 [Accessed 19 October 2018.]

Freeman, R E. (1984). *Strategic Management: A Stakeholder Approach*. Boston: Pitman.

Gawdiak, I. (1989). *Czechoslovakia: A Country Study*. Washington, DC: Federal Research Division, Library of Congress, Retrieved from: www.loc.gov/item/88600487/ [Accessed 7 July 2017.]

Grant, T., Nix, T., Whitehead, J., Blair, J. (1991). Strategies for Assessing and Managing Organizational Stakeholders. *Academy of Management Executive*, 5(2), 61–75.

Grayson, L.E., Bodily, S.E. (1996). *Integration Into the World Economy: Companies in Transition in the Czech Republic, Slovakia, and Hungary*. International institute for applied systems analysis, Laxenburg. Retrieved from: http://pure.iiasa.ac.at/id/eprint/4765/1/RR-96-019.pdf [Accessed 19 October 2018.]

Growing and shrinking regions in Europe, German Federal Institute for Research on Building, Urban Affairs, and Spatial Development, 2013. Retrieved from: www.bbr.bund.de/BBSR/EN/SpatialDevelopment/SpatialDevelopmentEurope/ AnalysesSpatialDevelopment/Projects/growing_shrinking/growing_shrinking. html [Accessed 10 June 2018.]

Hofstede, G. H. (2018). *Hofstede Insights.* Retrieved from: www.hofstede-insights.com/product/compare-countries/ [Accessed 19 October 2018.]

Leary, T. (1983). *Flashbacks.* Los Angeles: G.P. Putnam's Sons.

Lustig, R. (2017). *The Hacking of the American Mind: The Science Behind the Corporate Takeover of Our Bodies and Brains.* New York: Penguin Publishing.

Mitchell, R., Bradley, R., Wood, D. (1997). Towards a Theory of Stakeholder Identification and Salience: Defining the Principles of Who and What Really Counts. *Academic Management Review,* 22(4), 853–856.

Schnitzer, M. (2005). Disorganization and Financial Collapse. *European Economic Review,* 49(2), 387–408.

Schultz, W. (1998). Predictive Reward Signal of Dopamine Neurons. *Journal of Neurophysiology,* 80(1), 1–27.

Silver, N. (2012). *The Signal and the Noise: Why So Many Predictions Fail—But Some Don't.* New York: Penguin Books.

State of Housing in the EU. (2017). *Housing Europe.* Retrieved from: www. housingeurope.eu/resource-1000/the-state-of-housing-in-the-eu-2017 [Accessed 29 October 2018.]

Wartick, S., Cochran, P. (1985). The Evolution of the Corporate Social Performance Model. *Academy of Management Review,* 10(4), 758–769.

Part II

Complexity View on Leadership

4 The Concept of the Leadership Approach Based on the System and Relational Theory

Introduction

Based on our studies of everyday work and leadership, we argue that there is a complicated interplay between external influences and historical events on the one hand and performance expectations and the perceived need to exercise leadership in organizations on the other hand. Leadership in the context of all events and developments is vital for individuals and the entire organization. By understanding the impact of all those external and internal events on the people, it is possible to develop a vision of the organization as a system. If we take a Darwinian approach that "the system with the greatest flexibility has the highest chance of success", then the leadership role is to create such a system in the organization.

The new era of organizations and several emerging views of the process and relational context of leadership are crucial for the development of a modified leadership model. The initial focus presented in this chapter is to explore leading as a process and as an approach that focuses on a better understanding of what is happening in the organization's external and internal world.

Leaders are expected to understand the organization as a system and perform their leadership actions as a process that emphasizes building relations within an organization ecosystem. Such a process-relational leadership model may inspire higher individual performance, change organizational settings, form effective workplace relationships and create a sense of strategic direction.

This approach emphasizes the social and metacognitive processes where critical thinking, emotional intelligence, trust, a creation of interactions and networks are essential tasks for leaders. This is also where transparency and interpersonal relations become crucial elements of the organizational environment.

Current Organizational and Leaders' Challenges

Curphy and Hogan (2012) divide leaders into two categories: successful and productive leaders. The successful leaders are focusing their efforts on making contact, lobbying, developing relations with executives and searching projects that are taking up too much attention. On the other hand, they are spending very little time being in personal contact with their subordinates, finding out what motivates them and giving too little emphasis on building high performing teams. Productive leaders have different characteristics. They focus on making productive relationships with their subordinates via their development and motivation. They are searching to implement projects which make their organizations more competitive. They spend less time with corporate politics and lobbying. Nevertheless, only one-third of leaders are in the productive category. One of the reasons is that organizations are not clear about the leadership process and are not able to explicitly define what they expect from their leaders.

This justifies our aim and entire research effort to frame the new leadership concept upon two parameters: process and relations. We believe that the combination of these two elements can develop human resources, establish teamwork (which is essential for any change) and enhance organizational well-being. We also recognize that people in any organization are most often their own best experts on what they are doing, that their strengths and capabilities are the most powerful catalysts for change and that they will be affected by change. Such thinking has focused our work on designing a new leadership concept which proposes that leadership should be seen not only as a position of authority but also as an emergent, interactive, dynamic, complex form of interplay. It results in collective actions and changes when heterogeneous agents interact in networks in ways that produce new patterns of behavior or new modes of operation.

When we use grounded theory to analyze how organizations are dealing with current challenges, an absolute contradiction occurs. Even though respondents acknowledge the importance to focus on innovation and establish new leadership approaches oriented more on people, in some organizations the traditional approach still exists. The system view in most organizations is missing. Therefore, leaders are struggling to combine two dimensions, that is, innovation/change process and people focus.

Unpredictable External and Internal Challenges

Two principal categories were identified through the various answers to this issue. The first category is addressing the external environment, which has rather broad meaning. *Macroeconomic uncertainty* is identified as the critical category reflecting external challenges. The majority of the interviewed respondents operate not only in the CEE region but also within the EU as well as worldwide. Macroeconomic uncertainty addresses changes in legislation, relationships with suppliers and market challenges. Even though the businesses of the research participants have growth potential, leaders are aware of intense competition from Asia. Many companies within the CEE region benefit from being part of the large EU market, but on the other hand, some of the EU policies significantly impact the companies' costs and products.

The second category identified is referring to internal challenges. The respondents realized that changes are numerous and complex. Complexity features are clear from the selective codes which characterize current business issues, such as:

- Strategy is changing faster.
- Technology is one of the most frequent generators of innovation and change.
- A new way of leading and motivating the diverse labor force is needed.

When we look into more details of the initial coding outcomes for the last code, "new way of leading and motivating the diverse human resources", especially when it refers to generation Z (which is entering the labor market), leaders realize the necessity to change their approach. They have admitted that adequately skilled and qualified staff represents a considerable asset for the further development of the business. Currently, the structure and the quality of human resources is changing due to a more diverse workforce, technically skilled labor is becoming a scarcity, and continued life learning possibilities are one of the key staff and talent development strategies in many organizations.

A new type of relationship between employees and employer has been suggested. It has been underlined as the most crucial approach of today's leaders to developing people for higher performance while at the same time enabling their satisfaction and loyalty.

The role of new technologies (e.g. social networking and virtual collaboration) in the leadership process will be analyzed in Chapter 8.

The Organizational Focus on Innovation and Human Resources

Various opinions have been put forward to explain what companies should do to sustain their business. From all the responses one key category has appeared: *to succeed and maintain the competitive advantage, companies inevitably need to invest in innovation and people.* It is interesting that such an interconnected relation between two aspects (innovation and people) can jointly contribute to the success of the organization. When we implement the back and forth approach we can see how these two sides were elaborated and how they are interrelated. The organizations we studied acknowledge that research, innovation and organizational change contribute significantly to a competitive advantage. To keep the speed in innovation, respondents stated that organizations need to have enough qualified people who can actively participate in business. Critical challenges for the organizations are not only the scarcity of technically skilled people but also the involvement and creativity of those people.

The change in leaders' approaches has been acknowledged and several important recommendations have been proposed by respondents:

- New technologies and any innovation as a result of R&D activities have to be incorporated into the formulation of new strategies.
- Change from a production-based businesses toward an R&D-focused company is feasible through creating internal innovative potential.
- A goal-oriented approach needs to be implemented through the whole organizational hierarchy.

Nevertheless, in most organizations there are still traditional methods in place. New strategies are mostly formulated using the conventional concept (new products and services balanced with the proper price and cost structure); competitiveness is acquired through reducing costs; adjusting the price and adequate range of products and further growth is planned purely through incremental changes in product or service development and/or entering new markets.

Investments in new technology, research and development are often considered to be a matter of having financial resources. In contrast, investment into people has been defined more broadly by the respondents; for instance, some of them claimed that (1) motivation should be an issue for each manager from top to bottom, (2) establishment of open communication is helpful to knowledge sharing and (3) it also initiates employee's active participation.

However, there is a lack of a systematic approach for bringing together these two overlapping issues (innovation and people) in the respondents' organizations. The primary interest of the researched organizations is still focused more on technological and product changes rather than seeing organizations as living systems. It is a primary task of a company's highest leader to develop the human potential from within the company in order to deal with internal and external challenges.

Leaders' Approach to Challenges

The responses to this issue were the richest. We obtained a considerable variety of views, and line-by-line coding prompted us to study each line of data and gain a conceptual handle on them. The researched organizations were all very concerned with the urgent need to *improve the strategic decision-making process*, and to react internally to all challenges coming from the external environment. The coding process defined two categories as the main tasks of leaders in the researched organizations. The first focus stressed by the researched participants was the entire process of strategic decision making and how to make employees a part of the participation process. Rapid growth of a company often requires implementing the process management approach, which links organizational and personal goals. The assessment and appraising of those goals on a regular basis was underlined as a fundamental prerequisite for performance improvement by the respondents.

The second category was defined as the *people-oriented focus*, which has a short-term operational dimension and long-term strategic dimension.

The short-term operational dimension is connected with the need to build an *effective and open communication system* across the company, which is an important tool for reliable information exchange. This is linked with another leader's function which enhances the development of *critical thinking skills* at the managerial level and also among the employees. Leaders are expected to encourage employees to provide reasonable explanations and arguments that help them to build their confidence and responsibility. This refers to an urgent need which was repeated through several interviews: to develop highly capable employees who can be an essential part of the system of successorship.

The long-term strategic dimension of this category was defined as *specialization and diversity of the workforce*. This encompasses future trends and requirements for new specializations and different job positions, which have to be implemented into personal development and training plans at all managerial levels. The dimensions of diversity and its effects on a company's performance will be analyzed in Chapter 7.

Leaders' Support for the Development of People

The coding process revealed an exciting finding. No matter what the position (top or middle manager) and what function the leader had within the organization, they all admitted that only proactive employees could enhance any innovation that contributes to organizational success. To develop such an employee who will actively participate in the organizational processes, internal coaching becomes an efficient tool in personal development and retraining.

> *We have a special meeting with each employee. By using coaching, we identify his/her strengths and further development needs.*
> (Talent and Organizational Development Manager,
> automotive industry)

This category was analyzed through our sequence of codes as well, as it occurred in a few autonomous answers to the formulated research question. The implementation of an internal coaching tool is closely related to leaders' different attitudes toward employees. The researched participants acknowledged that human resources is very diverse nowadays and to select a suitable employee for further development by coaching isn't a simple task.

One of the suggestions for this challenge is the implementation of a project team structure. In order to manage change and enhance innovation, working in teams within the project organizational structure could be a suitable pathway.

On the other hand, respondents stress that every innovation requires specific expertise which needs to be developed, and has its complexity features. They saw the benefits of providing coaching support to every employee, but they admitted that coaching skills have to be learned first by the leader and then incorporated into everyday interactions with subordinates.

If we compare the results provided by the grounded theory method with the various survey outcomes presented in Chapter 1 related to leadership challenges and new tasks, many of the same issues have occurred. The most significant driving forces have been identified and formulated as follows: (1) balancing the pressure to digitalize organizational processes with the necessity to develop talent and well-structured human resources, (2) managing organizational complexity and (3) enhancing work diversity as the crucial source for innovation and change.

Systemic and Complexity View on the Leadership Process

The systemic view is a fundamental attitude or philosophy of leaders with an understanding of the organizational processes, and thus fosters changes which result in external and internal influences. Leaders are expected to be able to develop such procedures and practices inside of the organization where all employees work and solve problems, share their knowledge and experiences and engage in continuous improvement. That requires an understanding of systems theory that is applied by leaders.

According to Daft et al. (2010), a system is defined as a set of interrelated parts that function as a whole to achieve a common purpose. The fundamental system theory of organizations consists of five components: inputs, a transformation process, outputs, feedback and the environment. Those are defined as follows:

1. Inputs are the material, human, financial or information resources used to produce goods and services.
2. The transformation process is management's use of production technology to change inputs into outputs.
3. Outputs include the organization's products and services.
4. Feedback is knowledge of results that influence the selection of contributions during the next cycle of the process.
5. The environment surrounding the organization includes social, political and economic forces.

Organizations are described as an open system and an essential part of a bigger system that can be an industry, specific market or another important enterprise (other stakeholders). Any system is characterized by its dynamism, complexity and requirement to be flexible to reflect changes in the external environment. Due to the internet revolution, the organization started to be seen as an ecosystem rather than a monolithic entity that follows the standard organizational pattern. In the corporate ecosystem, relationships and interactions matter. Humans interact with processes, which associate with technologies, applications and various infrastructures that have a significant effect on the system as a whole.

In an organizational environment where change creates uncertainty and unpredictability, it is almost impossible to expect one person, a leader, to have overwhelming knowledge of everything and decide what needs to be done, and meanwhile develop strategy and vision. Yet leaders are expected to effectively guide all processes and relations within the organizational ecosystem to maintain stability and interconnections between an organization and its environment.

Other authors put provide the characteristics of the organization as a system. For instance, Zavadsky et al. (2012) define the systemic approach as the complexity of thinking, problem solving and related actions where everything is considered in both external as well as internal interrelations and connections.

Other authors, such as Sakal and Jerz (2006), elaborate more on system theory and state that the system approach has two main functions in the organization:

1. It provides a better and deeper understanding about relations between the actors within the systems, their behavior and new features.
2. It increases the effectiveness of the system and its functions.

The fundamental view on organizations as a system is presented by Senge (1990) in his book *The Fifth Discipline: The Art and Practice of the Learning Organizations*, where he described system thinking as the ability of leaders to integrate all knowledge and understanding of all facts into a more profound and more complex understanding of the world around the organization.

Giddens (1984) adds to system theory by stating that when studying a system, whether either social or economic, both the structure and the agents within the structure need to be examined together (Cole, 2013).

Organizational theory has shifted from the traditional type toward post-industrial types. The conventional view in the last century was provided by Uhl-Bien et al. (2007), where leadership models have been products of a top-down bureaucratic paradigm. These models are eminently useful for an economy premised on physical production but are not well suited for post-industrial organizations in the time of a knowledge-oriented economy. Post-industrial organizations can be characterized as complex adaptive systems. They are complex because they are the result of multiple interconnecting relationships, so the way they respond to their environment has the effect of creating new connections and thus increasing their complexity. They are adaptive in the sense that they develop to the forces of change in environments and technologies while retaining the coherence of their purpose (Collier and Esteban, 1999).

The current digital era is characterized as a world of global networks, rapid and continuous change, shifting demographics, environmental challenges and innovative technologies. This current dynamism pushes organizations to be flexible with many variable parts of their internal systems. In addition, it is accompanied by more complicated processes and decisions and increasing pressure to analyze a massive amount of data and information. The final results are often surprisingly negative. Very often the leaders themselves, with good intentions, complicate things even more. Leaders and their employees in organizations must be well informed on how to cope with these dynamic challenges and be able to understand the potential impact on their processes, products, services, stakeholders and the environment.

Leaders influence and design the system as an organized collection of actions. Such systems are critical to individuals within the team and the work they produce. This, in turn, makes the entire organization more effective. Because of their importance, systems need to be clear, purposeful and consistent.

We raised a reflective question for managers as follows: "Do I design simple and clear systems?" The implementation of the Critical Reflection Analysis (CRA), which is described fully in Appendix II, helped to develop reflection skills among respondents. Even though the responses are presented by their percentages in Figure 4.1, a detailed explanation and discussion on how to evaluate and reflect their ability to simplify things for their employees were conducted with each manager. This also led to figuring out what the expected standard value of the leader's competence should be and what impact this capability makes on overall organizational performance.

The standard value of a leader's capability was proposed to be 62 points (scoring in the interval "good"). The group we researched suggested this competence's weight should be 5, as far as its impact on organizational and individual performance.

The researched group of managers scored on average 49 points, the individual minimum score was 10, and the maximum score was 95. The majority of managers reflected their ability to create simple systems in a "good" zone; however, a significant number (20.8%) remain in the indecisive area and a surprising 9.1% of managers scored in the "bad" interval. This gap between the suggested standard value of 62 points and average of 49 points opens the door for questioning on how this competence

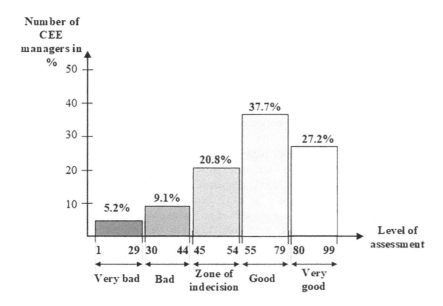

Figure 4.1 Designing simple and clear systems
Source: Authors.

can be enhanced. More important is the discussion of the impact of this capability on the more diverse structure of the employees. For them, all processes have to be constructed in a rather simple form, thus assuring their understanding and accomplishment in standardized quality.

However, there is a theoretical debate among scholars on whether the task of designing the systems belongs to leaders or managers. Our researched leaders admitted that all work in the organization is process based. There is a sequence of different actions performed at all hierarchical levels. Nevertheless, leading the people through the organizational system requires an understanding of all processes, how they are interrelated and what output is offered to various stakeholders. One of the responses explains the view of practitioners on the role of leadership:

> *Leaders need to understand how the production is functioning, what the customers' needs are and what are the current trends and latest technologies. Then it has to be converted into the strategic goals and the leader then leads people to accomplish them.*

In order to lead processes and people across the organization successfully toward better results and the achievement of strategic goals, a strong emphasis is given to establishing a flow of information between units, departments and individuals across the entire organization. Specific fundamental information is expected to be provided and gathered on a continuous basis to individuals, departments, SBUs (strategic business units) and within the whole organization. This flow of information is a two-way process, from leaders to people and vice versa. This information flow represents the inputs and outputs to the examined system (Theodoulides in Raguz et al., 2016).

In previous chapters, especially regarding topics related to ethics and corporate responsibility, fundamental systems dilemmas have been raised. For example, high enhancement for innovation can end with a worse solution which does not correspond to organizational values. Effective leaders need to understand the impacts and influences within systems dynamics as the solution for better and meaningful outcomes. Leaders are expected to identify the size and character of the system and work with information flow from all aspects of the system. The leaders transform those systems for positive results, which give benefits within the broadest environment (i.e. internal and external ones).

The most common organizational system consists of three main elements: the closer and wider environments, the organizational unit and individuals. To clarify the content and character of the organizational system and its interconnections within the external and internal environment, fundamental questions need to be raised:

- Within the inner circle: what are our (department, SBU, organizational and individual) goals? Aren't those goals in conflict? What is the primary purpose of our/my facility? How does our/my team support the results of the whole organization? Who counts on the output of our/my work?
- Within the outer circle: who are our/my stakeholders and what are their expectations related to our organization's outcomes? What is our/my contribution to the broader society? How do our/my outputs improve someone's quality of life?

The answers to the aforementioned questions guide the leadership process and the leader's actions to focus on the impact as well as on people who are contributing to the results of the organization's performance. It can help them to make their focus broader on several systems including societal, economic, environmental and so forth.

The approach which reflects the interrelations and how they influence the people's actions is called the *big picture* or the *helicopter view*.

The concept of the "big picture" can be described as a complex organizational ecosystem. The leaders are required to create such a system for their employees or subordinates and help them to have a clear understanding of what their tasks, roles and contributions within the system (inside and outside the organization) are.

The big picture concept of the organizational system consists of five main elements:

1. *Structure*, a network of formal and informal interconnections between organizational units.
2. *Processes and infrastructure*, which include core technology/tasks, primary logistics for the venture, vital elements of its business model and value chain.
3. *Culture*, the subsystem including relations, values, behavior, standards, procedures and strategies.
4. *People*, their feelings, expectations, skills and attitudes.
5. *Overall assessment—performance*, a set of agreed goals and measures.

Hence, we can highlight the core features of systems theory and its implementation to leadership. The system approach to leadership discusses the leaders' determination and ability to factor in their leadership activities to the external environment and relationships with and among all elements. The system theory clarifies the thought on the complexity and dynamism of the environment and provides a framework for building ideas. If it is applied to complex social systems, it fosters a better understanding of wholeness, relations, pattern, processes and content. In a leader's work, this ability is called upon to create a shared vision or a common purpose. Developing a shared vision requires time for reflection, sharing, seeing things from all perspectives and creating networks. Leaders, together with their followers, can achieve a sense of purpose when they see and understand what they do, why they do it and how it impacts the success of the organization. The necessary task for each leader is to share the big picture with everyone to make sure that all people in the organization become aware of their contributions to overall organizational performance. The leader's ability to understand the concept of the big picture together with the ability to design a simple system is crucial in a dynamic and ever-changing organizational environment.

In our research, we focused on assessing leaders' ability to understand the concept of the big picture. Again, the Critical Reflection Analysis was implemented to assess and evaluate the managers' understanding of the concept of the big picture and its five elements. The standard level of the leaders' capability was represented by a value of 77 points. The researched managers saw the impact of this criterion on overall performance rather high. They agreed to nominate its weight level at 9 out of a maximum of 10.

The leader's awareness of the organization as a system where goals, processes, relations and networks scored the highest results; for instance, the individual maximum value was 99 and the minimum personal value was 23. All scores in the five intervals are presented in Figure 4.2. The average score was calculated and resulted in the highest value of 59 points among all examined competences.

This ability is considered to be the most crucial to be performed by leaders to maintain success. The highest percentage of managers (40.2%) saw their ability to understand the big picture concept at the "very good" level. On the other hand, a significant number (16.9% of respondents) saw their ability as "very bad".

We offer insights into the complexity issue and how it can be applied to the leadership process. The complexity of a dynamic system is constituted by the intricate relationships between all components and leadership, and also it is based on the complex interaction between leader and followers.

Complexity science suggests a different paradigm for leadership—one that frames leadership as a complex interactive dynamism from which adaptive outcomes such as learning, innovation and change emerge.

Lichtenstein and Plowman (2009) introduced the complex view that reframes leadership by focusing on the dynamic interactions between all individuals, explaining how those interactions can, under certain conditions, produce new outcomes. They also identify the role of agents or internal partners across the organization which contributes to the development of the process network. In complex systems, mutual influence

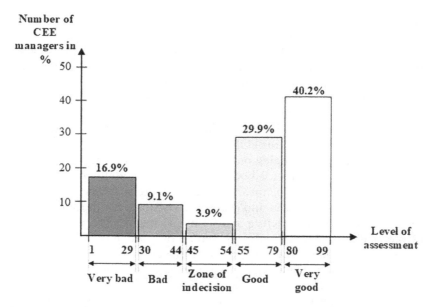

Figure 4.2 Understanding of the "big picture" concept
Source: Authors.

between partners is necessary for survival. All agents are in constant interaction, exchanging information, learning and adapting their behavior in locally coherent ways. Every contact and every exchange of information presents an opportunity for influence, which reflects a particular act of leadership.

Complexity has become a crucial ability of leaders to understand what is happening within an organizational system. A complex system is not constituted merely by the sum of its components, but also by the intricate relationships between these components (Cilliers and Greyvenstein, 2012).

An outstanding contribution is made by Drucker (1999, 2001) by promoting the interactionist method that defines the value of complexity approaches to leadership. His interactionist frameworks highlight identifiable organizing principles that cause directional flows which occur between leaders and followers and have an impact on organizational performance.

Our research findings back up Drucker's assumption that managing complexity is considered an essential leadership skill.

> *The leader should watch the market and competition and understand what is going on. Then to be able to inform internal people and guide them.*
>
> *Be a good example, explain the interconnections and create conditions for knowledge sharing across the organization are the key expectations on what leaders should do.*

Hence, we can summarize that implementing complexity builds the space between individuals and it reflects the network of relations at the formal as well as informal levels. Such organizational interactions are explained through various social exchanges between leaders and followers. Successful change demands that everyone has time to think and reflect on what they're doing. This is an essential attribute of the learning process which results from thinking that is disciplined, logical, creative or innovative as required by the situation. To assess a leader's competence, the question "Do I think about what is going on?" was asked to our researched group of managers. Since managers see this competence as having a rather significant impact, this competence weight was represented by a value of 7 out of a maximum 10. The standard expected level of the leader's ability to reflect was agreed to be 67 points.

As presented in Figure 4.3, 75.3% of managers scored very high in the top two levels (good and very good). None of the respondents scored in the "very bad" range. The average result of this ability was 54. The individual minimum value was 41, and the individual maximum value was 93.

The leader's role is described by Osborn et al. (2002), who explain that leadership is not only presented as an incremental influence of an

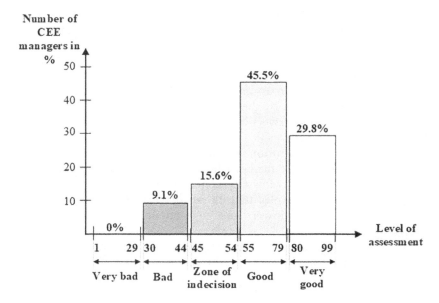

Figure 4.3 Complexity and reflective view
Source: Authors.

executive toward subordinates but more importantly, it is an additional collective influence of leaders in and around the system. Leadership connects individual behavior with organizational context.

The view of leadership that is appropriate for post-industrial organizations in situations of rapid change is presented as the systematic approach by leaders. It combines both a relational and a process approach based on influencing, coalition building and bringing together different people with their diverse capabilities and competencies.

Since the systematic leadership approach involves all members of the organization, the emergent outcome of such leadership is to create links between purpose, actions and various results to produce a "common good". Although leadership is a crucial factor for organizations to deal with a complex competitive landscape which is primarily driven by globalization and technological revolution, there is little explicit discussion on how the leading process could be of help to meet these new challenges.

To address these shortcomings, a new leadership framework reflecting a fast-changing and complex system is studied further. System thinking is at the root of effective problem solving and the ability to create functional teams in the organization. The ability to think systemically, practically and concretely is probably the most definitive sign of maturity in a leader's behavior.

The notion of the systemic leadership approach does not require the abandonment of the distinction between leaders and followers. Leadership and followership may have varying concerns for new expectations and the role for both leaders and followers. The notion of a systemic view on leadership is deeply relational, and it fosters the followership and leader-follower relationships at the center of system leadership capacity (Krantz and Gilmore, 1990).

In the complex and fast-paced external and internal environment of every organization, people seek out others they can count on. They want to work with people they can trust and who have what it takes to address and overcome daily challenges. The leading process is a part of various dynamic systems which are characterized by complexity, interactions and influencing the flow of relations. All of these attributes are based on social and interpersonal interaction, reflection and trust that make the leading process dependent on the quality of connections and a reflection of various types of relationships in the organization.

The Relational Perspective of Leadership

The concept of relationship-oriented behavior appeared in earlier studies on leadership where a meaningful, considerate and supportive approach was examined by Stogdill and Coons (1957) or where leadership behavior focused on developing high-quality, trusting work relationships was studied by Graen and Scandura (1987) and later continued by Graen and Uhl-Bien (1995).

In recently developed discourse, the term "relational" focuses on viewing leadership and the organization as human social constructions that emanate from rich connections and interdependences of organizations and their members. In contrast to traditional leadership theories which consider relationships from the standpoint of individuals as independent, discrete entities, a relational perspective starts with processes and not persons, and views individuals, leadership and other relational realities as a critical element in organizational processes (Hosking et al., 1995; Bradbury and Lichtenstein, 2000).

Traditional leadership assumes that (1) individuals have their knowledge in their minds, (2) the mind's content and expertise of individuals are properties of entities to which they have access and (3) these entities can be distinguished from other entities (people) and the environment. This view approaches relationship-based leadership by focusing on individuals (i.e. leaders and followers) and their perceptions, intentions, behaviors, personalities, expectations and evaluations relative to their relationships with one another (Uhl-Bien, 2003). Hence, leadership uses social relations to interact with individuals to achieve individual knowledge about and influence over both other people and groups.

The new relational perspective is explained by Hosking et al. (1995) who view knowledge as socially constructed and socially distributed, not as the source built or accumulated and stored by individuals. Relational orientation means that an organizational phenomenon exists in inter-dependent relationships and intersubjective meaning. Knowing occurs between several subjects or phenomena simultaneously, and thus multi-ple meanings and various constructs continuously emerge. From this new perspective, knowing is a process of relating that is a constructive, ongo-ing process of making sense. We elaborate more on the "knowing" pro-cess as having two additional processes of leading-following presented in Figure 5.5.

Leadership based on the relational perspective does not focus on identifying attributes of individuals involved in leadership behaviors or exchanges but rather on the social construction processes by which understandings of leadership emerges in the content of those processes.

Relationships appear to be a key to a new view of leadership compar-ing traditional authority, superiority or the dominance sides of leader-ship. Even though relationships are core topics in leadership literature (e.g. Marion and Uhl-Bien, 2001; Brown and Gioia, 2002; Pearce and Conger, 2003), there is little study and research to find out how to form, develop and lead those relationships. Moreover, the investigation into relational dynamics of the leading process has not yet been given detailed study.

The relational perspective has developed a conceptual framework for understanding the role of relationships in the process of leadership. The broad content of relations has been identified by Todeva (2006): needs (incentives and preferences), resources and capabilities, behavior and activities, cognition, affection and trust, identity, roles and status, con-tent (bonds, links), farming and value.

Social relationships are driven by the basic need to communicate, to learn, to integrate with society or the organizational system and to express oneself. These relationships are generally driven by the necessity of actors to access specific resources, information or knowledge, to engage in the process of decision making and problem solving, to contribute to a joint performance or project or to do work together with another actor.

The behavior and choices of actors within a relationship are trig-gered by specific individual incentives, motives or social preferences that are framed within established relationships, and by leaders who to develop them.

The relational focus is not restricted to a single or even a small set of formal or informal leaders. It is based on its active and robust form and functions as a dynamic system embedding the leading process and environmental and organizational aspects. Leadership has been defined as a complex system which is not constituted merely by the sum of its components but also by the intricate relationships between the elements.

Drucker (2001) was a pioneer in this interactionist method, where leadership is based on the complex interaction between a leader and his or her followers. The value of this complexity approach to leadership is to understand the organizational systems and principles as well as to focus on the human beings behind all these processes. This interactionist and relations-based framework enables us to move beyond the simplistic views of leadership as a top-down influence, where followers, process and context appear secondary (Fairhurts, 2011; Marion and Uhl-Bien, 2001; Osborn and Hunt, 2007).

A new relational perspective is provided by Uhl-Bien (2006), later advanced by adding new features and implementation of relations into leadership (Uhl-Bien and Ospina, 2012), where they both share a view that leadership is co-created in relational interactions with followers and is dynamic, developing and changing over time.

A relational view recognizes leadership as a phenomenon generated in the interactions among people acting with the aim to produce leadership outcomes (Fairhurts, 2011; Hosking and Morley, 1988).

This relational process occurs inside or outside a formal leadership role and interaction has been studied through a characteristic or behavioral style of an individual leader (Yukl, 2010; Avolio and Bass, 1991). This approach has limitations since it provides little guidance on the context of the leader-follower relationship and shows the interaction as a top-down individual process.

The relational orientation of the leadership is primarily defined by the leading-following process. Studying relational orientation in leadership requires identifying specific interactions through various processes between leaders and followers. They influence one another, which also reflects their mutual interest. This is a modified approach which relates to identifying and building the bottom-up interactions that are crucial to fostering innovation, learning and adaptation in an organization.

The specific findings on "What is the role of leadership in supporting innovation?" from our research show rather high expectations of leaders and their direct role in enhancing people to be innovative. For instance:

- Formulate goals and guide employees toward their fulfillment.
- Express the purpose of innovation, evaluate the benefits and then inspire.
- A leader should be the initiator of change.
- Be able to critically scan organizational processes and identify the problems which have to be improved.
- Provide constant support and motivation to people.

Several partial research outcomes were stressing the importance of the established communication between leader and followers. It sounds so fundamental to communicate, but is it performed effectively? The responses we received highlighted specific actions of how leaders should communicate. For instance:

> *Listen to their people and encourage them to talk freely.*
> *To establish regular two-way communication flow.*
> *By avoiding criticism, people will trust their leaders and feel secure to make mistakes when trying new things.*

The question "Do I share information and knowledge with my subordinates or colleagues?" aimed to reflect how well leaders distribute information and the necessary knowledge that might be important to followers to understand critical processes and the purpose of their work. It also represents the most fundamental element of effective communication between leaders and their followers. Our respondents agreed to weight this competence with the value of 6 out of 10. Sharing information and knowledge with their subordinates and colleagues was assessed as the third most important leadership ability with an average value of 52 points. Shown in Figure 4.4, 77% of the managers we researched scored on the two best levels: "good" and "very good". The individual minimum score was 15 and the maximum was 95.

When we summarize the results of the managers' reflection on their leadership competencies and actions, primary attention to the interaction

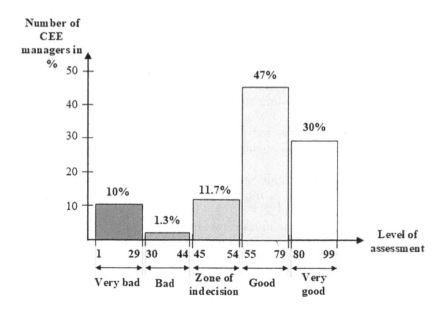

Figure 4.4 Sharing information and knowledge

Source: Authors.

between leadership and followership needs to be studied. Referring to Kelley (1992), while leaders contribute a maximum of 20% to organizational success, followers contribute an estimated 80% to the success of the organization. He conceptualizes followership concerning the behaviors that are associated with positive results of the following process, and he characterizes followership behavior on two dimensions: the first dimension is independent critical thinking. Followers who engage in independent critical thinking analyze the information given to them, evaluate situations and actions and make judgments independent of the political consequences of decisions (Kelley, 1992; Latour and Rast, 2004). These followers are innovative and creative; they voluntarily analyze information and provide constructive feedback. If leaders intend to develop critical thinking in their followers, they need to establish a continuous flow of information. Research findings have shown that sharing information and knowledge is essential in order to start the learning process. Moreover, research shows that understanding the concept of the "big picture" together with reflecting on what is happening across the entire organization are essential leadership actions.

The second dimension of followership is active engagement (Kelley, 1992). Followers who are actively engaged take initiative, assume ownership and actively participate in performing their job. These individuals understand responsibilities beyond their minimum job requirements and exert considerable effort to accomplish goals (Kahn, 1990; Romano, 1995; Rothbard, 2001). Individuals who demonstrate active engagement go above and beyond expectations, proactively participate in activities and provide high-quality work results. Therefore, the effective leadership process emphasizes developing followers high in both critical thinking and learning skills.

These key aspects together with our research results constitute the path toward the development of the Reflective Leadership concept, which is presented in the next chapter.

Conclusion

Part I presented the various literature on the fundamental understanding of the role of leaders in a changing environment. Chapter 4 opened Part II and started the discussion on what current leadership challenges are, how managers are addressing them and how they are coping with their leadership tasks in the digital era. It has also explored how the main challenge "to establish the balance between the focus on digitalization and focus on human resources" influences leadership actions.

The organization has been described as a system that reflects on what is happening in the external as well as the internal environment. The interrelations between the two worlds affect the performance of the organization as well as the employees' understanding about their contribution.

This causes certain complexities, which starts to underline the two main dimensions of leadership (process and relations). These dimensions are continuously overlapping in the everyday work of any leader and also impact the relationship between leaders and followers. To identify more carefully what information is crucial to be provided by leaders to the followers, the "big picture" concept was described. The understanding of this concept was researched among managers in the CEE region. The assessment and evaluation of the results were conducted using the Critical Reflection Analysis, of which a detailed description is provided in Appendix II. The respondents showed the highest average scores in leadership competence in understanding the "big picture" concept; the second highest average scores in their ability to cope with "complexity and reflecting what is going on"; and third highest average scores in "sharing the information with others". The intention was to identify the vital leading actions which reflect the process and relations dimensions, as they are the main elements of the proposed Reflective Leadership concept in the next chapter.

Bibliography

Avolio, B. J., Bass, B. M. (1991). *The Full Range of Leadership Development. Basic and Advanced Manuals*. Binghamton, NY: Bass, Avolio & Associates.

Bradbury, H., Lichtenstein, B. (2000). Relationality in Organizational Research: Exploring the Space Between. *Organizational Science*, 11(5), 551–564.

Brown, M. E., Gioia, D. A. (2002). Making Things Click: Distributive Leadership in an Online Division of an Off-line Organization. *The Leadership Quarterly*, 13(4), 397–419.

Cilliers, F., Greyvenstein, H. (2012). The Impact of Silo Mentality on Team Identity: An Organizational Case Study. *SA Journal of Industrial Psychology*, 38(2), 1–9.

Cole, D. (2013). *Academic Writing: In Search for the Lost Narrative*. Brno: CAL-SALC Review.

Collier, J., Esteban, R. (1999). Governance in the Participative Organization: Freedom, Creativity and Ethics. *Journal of Business Ethics*, 21, 173–188.

Curphy, G., Hogan, R. (2012). *The Rocket Model: Practical Advice for Building High Performing Teams*. Oklahoma: Hohan Press.

Daft, R. L., Kendrick, M., Vershinina, N. (2010). *Management*. Andover: South-Western/Cengage Learning.

Drucker, P. F. (1999). *Management Challenges for the 21st Century*. Oxford: Butterworth-Heinemann.

Drucker, P. F. (2001). *The Essential Drucker*. Praha: Management Press.

Fairhurts, G. T. (2011). *The Power of Framing: Creating the Language of Leadership*. San Francisco: Jossey-Bass.

Giddens, A. (1984). *The Constitution of Society: Outline of the Theory of Structuration*. Los Angeles: University of California Press.

Graen, G. B., Scandura, T. (1987). Toward the Psychology of Dyadic Organizing. *Research in Organizational Behavior*, 9, 175–208.

Graen, G. B., Uhl-Bien, M. (1995). Relationship—Based Approach to Leadership: Applying a Multi-Level Multi-Domain Perspective. *The Leadership Quarterly*, 6(2), 219–247.

Hosking, D., Dachler, P., Gergen, K. (1995). Management and Organization: Relational Alternatives to Individualism. *Organization Studies*, 18(2), 339–340.

Hosking, D., Morley, I. E. (1988). The Skills of Leadership. In Hunt, J. G., Baglia, R., Schriesheim, C. (eds.), *Emerging Leadership Vistas*. Lexington, MA: Arlington Heights.

Kahn, W. A. (1990). Psychological Conditions of Personal Engagement and Disengagement at Work. *Academy of Management Journal*, 33, 692–724.

Kelley, R. E. (1992). *The Power of Followership: How to Create Leaders People Want to Follow, and Followers Who Lead Themselves*. New York: Doubleday.

Krantz, J., Gilmore, T. N. (1990). The splitting of leadership and management as a social defense. *Human Relations*, 43(2), 183–204.

Latour, S. M., Rast, V. J. (2004). Dynamic followership. *Air & Space Power Journal*, 18(4), 102–110.

Lichtenstein, B., Plowman, D. (2009). The Leadership of Emergence: A Complex Systems Leadership Theory of Emergence at Successive Organizational Levels. *The Leadership Quarterly*, 20(4), 617–630.

Marion, R., Uhl-Bien, M. (2001). Leadership in Complex Organizations. *The Leadership Quarterly*, 12(4), 389–418.

Osborn, R. et al. (2002). Toward a Contextual Theory of Leadership. *The Leadership Quarterly*, 13(6), 797–812.

Osborn, R. N., Hunt, J. (2007). Leadership and Choice of Order: Complexity and Hierarchical Perspectives Near the Edge of Chaos. *The Leadership Quarterly*, 18, 319–340.

Pearce, C. L., Conger, J. A. (2003). *Shared Leadership: Reframing the Hows and Whys of Leadership*. Thousand Oaks, CA: Sage.

Raguz, I. V., et al. (2016). *Neostrategic Management. An International Perspective on Trends and Challenges*. Switzerland: Springer.

Romano, C. (1995). A Star Is Made. *Management Review*, 84(2), 1–6.

Rothbard, N. P. (2001). Enriching or Depleting? The Dynamics of Engagement in Work and Family Roles. *Administrative Science Quarterly*, 46, 655–684.

Sakal, P., Jerz, V. (2006). *Operačná analýza v praxi manažéra 2*. [Operational analysis in managerial practice 2.] Trnava: Tripsoft.

Senge, P. (1990). *The Fifth Discipline: The Art and Practice of the Learning Organization*. Praha: Management Press.

Stogdill, R. M., Coons, A. E. (1957). *Leader Behavior: Its Description and Measurement*. Columbus: Ohio State University Press.

Todeva, E. (2006). *Business Networks: Strategy and Structure*. Oxon: Routledge.

Uhl-Bien, M. (2003). Relationship Development as a Key Ingredient for Leadership Development. In Murphy, S., Riggio, R. (eds.), *The Future of Leadership Development*. New Jersey: Lawrence Erlbaum Assoc. Inc. Publishers.

Uhl-Bien, M. (2006). Relational Leadership Theory: Exploring the Social Processes of Leadership and Organizing. *Leadership Quarterly*, 17(6), 654–676.

Uhl-Bien, M., Marion, R., McKelvey, B. (2007). Complexity Leadership Theory: Shifting Leadership from the Industrial Age to the Information Era. *The Leadership Quarterly*, 18, 298–318.

Uhl-Bien, M., Ospina, S. (2012). *Advancing Relational Leadership Research: A Dialogue Among Perspectives*. Charlotte, NC: Information Age.

Yukl, G. A. (2010). *Leadership in Organizations*. New York: Pearson.

Zavadsky, J., et al. (2012). *Management III. Systemic Approach Towards Management and Auditing of Organizations*. Bratislava: Iura Edition.

5 Designing the Concept of Reflective Leadership

Introduction

This chapter emphasizes a deeper understanding of the chosen topics and examines the relations between studied themes and the research insights that lead to developing the Reflective Leadership concept. The framework starts with the two fundamental concepts which are Leading-Following (Figure 1.1) and the already proposed big picture concept in Chapter 4. These two concepts weave between well-established theoretical approaches and new emergent frameworks that contribute to the process-relational worldview on leadership.

Despite the differences in theoretical approaches, there are deep similarities between the behavior of leaders, the strategic content of leadership and the interactions across the organization. One of these common issues is that the leading function is a continuous process cycle with two main features, that is, support and people-oriented leaders' behavior. Managers at the corporate level confirm that leadership actions are more like social processes, which are difficult to be quantified.

Drawing on some of the world's famous thinkers such as Kotter, Hammel and Goleman on leadership issues, we seek to withdraw the most important lessons from the study of organizational needs on leadership and to address a few critical questions that leaders face nowadays. Embracing this leadership theory background enables us to develop a new leadership concept and change the way how to lead organizations. A deeper investigation into leadership practices and a search of what leaders should actually do was conducted and implemented within a new concept. Another aspect of leadership practices that we address in this chapter is the emergence of interactions between leaders and subordinates and how to facilitate those relations in the organization. This are based on the philosophy of critical thinking, reflection and elements of building the relationship.

Thus, the framework of the Reflective Leadership concept aims to provide a better understanding of organizational contexts and relationships, based on stronger social interactions between actors. Particular focus is given to several processes which form a new leading approach and which describe how interrelations between actors can be established.

The Main Pillars of the Leading Process Framework

The sociological view perceives the organization as a collective actor comprising individuals, bound with formal and informal ties, and carrying subjective views, intentions, evaluations and decision-making power embedded in culture and institutional norms. Within organizations, existing inter-firm relationships are explained with various social exchange and cognitive theories (Monge and Contractor, 2003).

We have embarked on a twofold approach within our research. We have used the code analysis to interpret the answers to the question: "what is the main leadership challenge in leading digital era organizations?" This lead to formulation of a demand of a new leadership approach. From this newly established approach a new leadership category emerges.

> *The leadership challenge in the digital era is to enhance continuous innovation and change flow in all organizational processes and inspire human resources to take a proactive role within those processes.*

The social interaction between two actors (leaders and followers) presented by the Leading-Following process aims to convert crucial challenges from the external environment into internal organizational actions. The key distinguishing features of this leading process are as follows. First, the interaction between leaders and followers is established through effective communication. Each individual has his or her own way of performing, understanding of what is happening around and fulfilling different work duties and incentives. Effective communication prevents misunderstandings and confusion about different expectations on the leader's side and employee's side. It helps recognize different points of view, clarify the most necessary information and ensure that everyone is "on track". Using various tools and techniques to communicate constructively in order to reach the envisioned goals becomes one of the crucial tasks for a leader.

Second, the Leading-Following process is based on relationships. As the core characteristics of leadership based on relational perspective have already been defined in Chapter 4, the focus here is to identify how to form, develop and lead those relationships.

Third, the fundamental difference between the leader and manager has at its core a nature of trust. Covey (2006) states that "people in organizations do not listen to leaders, they watch them". When obedience, power and results are gained just by listening and fulfilling orders, that's the sign of control and the presence of a good manager. There is a significant shift in the organizational system from an ideology of control and managerial efficiency to one of consulting, participation, involvement and intervening of followers. This involves developing interactions and relations in terms of mutual trust with well-defined capabilities and knowledge.

Research has shown that in the digital era, human resources is influenced by the strong impact of ICT, both negatively and positively. The implementation of ICT across all organizational operations reduces costs and simplifies the work. Digitalization is considered to be the engine for future successful performance. It also seems to be the solution to cope with the lack of skilled labor and to deal with a structural gap occurring in some professions. Internal communication is also happening via ICT tools (intranet, social media, digital channels), thus reducing face-to-face interactions in many organizations. Labor starts to lack interpersonal skills (this has already been researched and identified in the new generations Y and Z). Less attention and resources are given to development and human resources than to investment in the latest technologies. The effort given to balance between the focus on digitalization and on human resources has been identified by many leaders as their current role in several of our researched companies. This is accompanied by the two new generations entering the labor market seeing the leaders as teachers, mentors and coaches.

To find out what the fundamental pillars to construct the new leadership concept are, we have merged some of the reviewed literature on the subject of learning that relates to communication and then linked it with our research findings. Three main pillars have been identified, and those are presented in Figure 5.1: critical thinking, reflection and feedback. They are elaborated in more detail next, as they all contribute to the creation of a new process of leading that can satisfy the new era's organizational needs.

Critical Thinking

Critical thinking has recently gained attention as a desirable employee characteristic. Critical thinking can improve useful outcomes of employees in various organizational situations and events. It is a necessary skill not only for trustworthy and efficient leaders but also to help develop active followers.

As Dowd and Bolus (1998) stress, critical thinking can improve useful outcomes of employees in various organizational situations and events. It can also improve performance through continuous learning (Yeo, 2007; Dundis and Benson, 2003; Kurubacak, 2007). It becomes a core feature when constructing Critical Reflective Analysis as a main research method implemented in the research strategy, as it is presented in the introduction of this book as well as in Appendices I–III.

Paul et al. (1997) mentioned that critical thinking was first mentioned by the Greek philosopher Socrates 2,500 years ago when he established

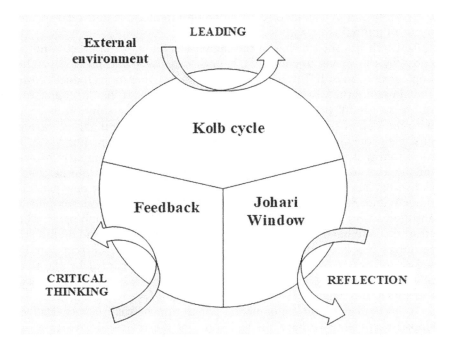

Figure 5.1 The main pillars of the new leading concept
Source: Authors.

the importance of asking deep questions that probe profound thinking before we accept ideas as worthy of belief.

Many definitions related to critical thinking are concerned with achieving this kind of thinking among scholars. It is true that the development of critical thinking in the education environment has become highly researched and discussed. The literature has listed a number of definitions for critical thinking though some of them define it in general terms.

For instance, Facione (1990) understands critical thinking to be purposeful and self-regulatory judgment which results in interpretation, analysis, evaluation and inference, as well as an explanation of the evidential, conceptual, methodological and/or contextual consideration upon which that judgment is based on.

Critical thinking is unique and purposeful in that the thinker systematically imposes purposes, criteria and intellectual standards, and assesses the thought, taking charge of its construction while assessing the effectiveness of the thought according to those purposes, criteria and standards (Paul et al., 1997).

Many authors underline the evaluation and assessment of the functions of critical thinking as a crucial component of any mental process (Petress, 1984; Cottrell, 2005).

Since we have already emphasized a systems approach to leadership, the task to exploring a problem, question or situation has the main goal of integrating all available information about an issue and this can be undertaken only when the critical thinking ability is in place (Warnick and Inch, 1994). The ability to understand the contents from a rigorous and complex review can be provided by the critical thinking process (Natale and Ricci, 2006).

The role of critical thinking in the leadership process can be summarized and described as follows:

1. Identifying other people's position.
2. Evaluating the evidence for alternative points of view.
3. Weighing the opposing arguments and evidence fairly.
4. Being able to read between the lines, seeing behind the surface.
5. Recognizing the techniques used to make a certain position more appealing than others.
6. Reflecting on issues in a structured way, bringing logic and insight to bear.
7. Drawing conclusions.
8. Presenting a point of view in a structured, clear, well-reasoned way.

From all these views we can summarize that the conditions of critical thinking in organizations encourages the individual to explore and investigate assumptions and biases and also review arguments and propositions of decision makers for their applicability to various problems and situations. Dynamic two-way discussions between leaders and followers based on critical thinking result in more effective decisions and accompanying innovations and improvements in organizational performance.

The most successful leaders have been characterized as perpetual learners. The explanation for this is that knowing how to lead people is a skill that can be learned; the leader's work is under the influence of continuous changes and new situations which, now more than ever, requires new and creative decision-making skills; and the final argument is that a good leader coaches their followers toward higher performance results and self-realization.

Reflection as a Process of Social Interactions

Reflection and self-discovery are essential means to critically evaluating relationships in the internal organizational environment as well as the impact of the external environment of the organizational processes.

Reflection is defined as a cognitive process in which people attempt to increase their awareness of personal experiences and therefore their ability to learn from them (Gordon Hullfish and Smith, 1961; Gray, 2007).

Hall (2002) states that reflection aims to intensify the cognitive elaboration of experimental data that leads to necessary behavioral changes. This view is not accompanied by a critical understanding of what the mechanisms are that show an impact on economic results and behavioral choices.

Dualism in any reflection process has been identified by Anseel et al. (2009). They suggest that reflection as a dual process model of information processing and the depth of elaboration of complex data influences learning and behavioral outcomes. This has been further advanced with reflection interventions which may be instrumental in helping employees to switch their mode of knowledge (data or information) processing from automatic to conscious, leading to better learning from experience and thus enhancing their performance.

From our point of view, reflection in the process of leading is a careful thought which can be designed as a cycle with critical consideration of all processes that make impacts on the organization's results as well as on individuals' performance and behavior (Theodoulides and Jahn, 2013).

Strange and Mumford (2005) investigate the role of reflection in the process of vision formation by leaders. They found that reflection led to better vision formation only when leaders were exposed to external as well as internal information on appropriate models. The process of vision and strategy creation is collective work and information flows from the top down and also from the bottom up. The establishment of such effective information flow relates to the development of social interactions and network relationships between the leader and other actors in the organizational system. Although the relational theory in leadership has already been discussed in Chapter 4, there are other contributions related to the creation of relationships that have not been incorporated sufficiently into the current stream of research on leadership. These approaches extend the concepts and multi-theoretical base in the analysis of social interactions in which relations, feedback, trust and motivation play an important role.

Helping people better understand their relationship with oneself and others has been studied by two American psychologists, Joseph Luft and Harrington Ingham (1955), who developed the Johari window model. The Johari window model is a simple and useful tool for illustrating and improving self-awareness and mutual understanding between individuals in a group. This model can also be used to assess and improve a group's relationship with other groups, reflect the level of communication and establish a feedback process.

It also illustrates the process of giving and receiving information, which is elaborated on further regarding the importance of social interactions.

The model can be seen as a communication tool through which leaders give and receive information about themselves and others (individuals or group). The information flow between leader and followers is discussed further by describing what is going on in four quadrants.

The first quadrant, called "Open", is characterized by the free and open exchange of information between all members; their behavior is public and available to everyone. Individuals share more information, particularly personally relevant information.

The aim in any group should always be to develop the "open area" for every person because when we work in this area with others, we are at our most effective and productive and the group is at its most productive too. The open free area, or "the arena", can be seen as space where good communication and cooperation occur, free from distractions, mistrust, confusion, conflict and misunderstanding.

Established team members logically tend to have larger open areas than new team members. New team members start with relatively small open areas because relatively little knowledge about the new team member is shared. The size of the open area can be expanded horizontally into the blind space by seeking and actively listening to feedback from other group members. This process is known as "feedback solicitation". Other group members can help a team member expand their open area by offering feedback, in a sensitive way of course. The size of the open area can also be expanded vertically downward into the hidden or avoided space by the person's disclosure of information and feelings about him/herself to the group and group members. Also, group members can help people expand their open area into the hidden area by asking about themselves.

Leaders can play an important role in facilitating feedback and disclosure among group members and indirectly give feedback to individuals about their own blind areas. Leaders also have a big responsibility to promote a culture and expectation for open, honest, positive, helpful, constructive, sensitive communications and sharing of knowledge throughout their organization. Top performing groups, departments, companies and organizations always tend to have a culture of open positive communication, so encouraging the positive development of the "open area" or "open self" for everyone is a simple yet fundamental aspect of effective leadership.

The second quadrant, called the "Blind Spot", is what is known about a person by others in the group, but unknown by the person him/herself. By seeking or soliciting feedback from others, the aim should be to reduce this area and thereby to increase the open area (to increase self-awareness). This blind area is not an effective or productive space for individuals or groups. A blind area could also include issues that others are deliberately withholding from a person. Whoever begins to participate in the group is not aware of the information which is communicated to the group. The people in the group learn this information from verbal cues, mannerisms, the way things are said or the style in which we relate to others. Leaders and group members can take some responsibility for helping an individual to reduce their blind area and in turn increase the open area by giving sensitive feedback and encouraging disclosure. Leaders can promote a climate of non-evaluated feedback and group response to individual disclosure, which reduces fear and therefore encourages both processes to happen. The extent to which an individual seeks feedback and the issues on which feedback is sought must always be at the individual's own discretion. The process of soliciting serious and deep feedback relates to the process of "self-actualization" described in several motivation models (e.g. Maslow's Hierarchy of Needs).

Quadrant three, the "Façade" or "Hidden Area", is what is known to ourselves but kept hidden from, and therefore unknown, to others. This hidden or avoided self-represented information, feelings and anything that a person knows about himself is not revealed or is kept hidden from others. It's natural for very personal and private information and feelings to remain hidden; indeed, certain information, feelings and experiences have no bearing on work and so can and should remain hidden. However, typically, a lot of hidden information is not very personal; it is work- or performance-related, and so is better positioned in the open area.

Relevant hidden information and feelings should be moved into the open area through the process of "disclosure". The aim should be to disclose and expose relevant information and feelings (hence the Johari window terminology "self-disclosure" and "exposure process"), thus increasing the open area. By telling others how we feel and other information about ourselves, we reduce the hidden area and increase the open area, which enables better understanding, cooperation, trust, team-working effectiveness and productivity. Reducing hidden areas also reduces the potential for confusion, misunderstanding and poor communication, which all distract from and undermine team effectiveness.

Organizational culture and working atmosphere have a major influence on group members' preparedness to disclose their hidden selves. Most people fear judgment or vulnerability and therefore hold back hidden information and feelings that if moved into the open area (i.e. known by the group as well) would enhance mutual understanding, and thereby improve group awareness, enabling better individual performance and group effectiveness.

The extent to which an individual discloses personal feelings and information, and the issues which are disclosed and to whom, depends on the level of trust. Leaders create an environment where people make disclosures at a pace and depth, they are personally comfortable with.

The fourth and last quadrant, called the "Unknown", contains information, feelings, latent abilities, aptitudes and experiences that are unknown to the self and unknown to others in the group. These unknown issues take a variety of forms: they can be feelings, behaviors, attitudes, capabilities and aptitudes which can be quite close to the surface and which can be positive and useful, or they can be deeper aspects of one's personality, influencing one's behavior to various degrees.

Whether unknown "discovered" knowledge moves into the hidden, blind or open area depends on who discovers it and what they do with the knowledge, notably whether it is given as feedback or disclosed. Providing people with the opportunity to try new things, with no great pressure to succeed, is often a useful way to discover unknown abilities, and thereby reduce the unknown area.

These four quadrants should be viewed with full knowledge of the cognitive bias that is laid out in Chapter 2 (understanding cognitive biases in the business decision-making process). The desire to reduce cognitive dissonance can lead to avoidance of addressing the unknown, within our self and with others. Humans, in general, are reluctant to explore or share in the weakness of ourselves and others. Giving and receiving feedback is hard.

Leaders can help by creating an environment that encourages self-discovery and to promote the processes of self-discovery, constructive observation and feedback among team members. It is a widely accepted industrial fact that the majority of staff in any organization are at any time working well within their potential. Creating a culture, climate and expectation for self-discovery helps people to fulfill more of their potential and thereby to achieve more and to contribute more to organizational performance.

Mutual understanding and orientation between leaders and actors are framed by continuous communication and exchange of information. Mutual understanding of the situations, processes and other organizational issues establishes a platform where motives, drivers and incentives are modified under interactions between leaders and actors. This is an ongoing social exchange which is composed under the reflection process. It comprises individual resources, skills and capabilities of the actors that are used in all organizational processes and the expected outcomes and results within the organizational system.

Kolb's learning cycle (1984) develops the traditional model of the learning process based on experience. The learning cycle consists of four main parts as described in Figure 5.2. His traditional model has been modified by implementing the reflection as an important tool for developing the Reflective Leadership concept.

The development of the learning environment, where people are led and motivated to learn, has a huge impact on every organization. The most effective learning processes are those which are supported through social interactions that occur, directly by doing the work, not in the classroom, and are those where the intuition, reflection, creativity and experience is present (Kokavcova, 2011).

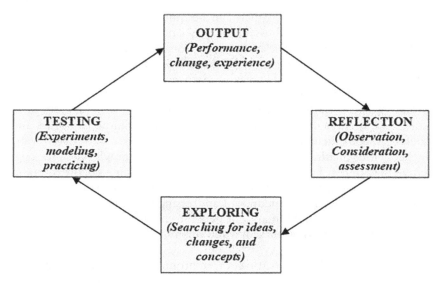

Figure 5.2 Learning process based on the reflection
Source: Theodoulides and Jahn (2013) on the basis of Kolb (1984).

A summary of the most key examples of ways for leaders to enhance organizational learning has been elaborated and presented as follows:

- Encourage people to question traditional methods and look for innovative new approaches that will be more effective.
- Articulate an inspiring vision to gain support for innovative changes from members of the organization.
- Foster and facilitate the acquisition of skills needed for collective learning by individuals and teams.
- Strengthen values consistent with learning from experience and openness to new knowledge.
- Enhance social networks that facilitate knowledge sharing, collaborative development of creative ideas and the acquisition of political support for innovations.
- Help people to develop their critical thinking skills in order to be able to make their own decisions and judgments.
- Provide and assist employees with the complexity view and to understand its implication for individuals, teams and the entire organization.
- Encourage teams to conduct after-activity reviews to identify effective and ineffective processes and provide suggestions for improvement.

- Develop measures of collective learning and knowledge diffusion to assess how well it is accomplished and give support for learning how to learn.
- Develop, implement and support programs and systems that will foster and reward the discovery of new knowledge and its diffusion and application in the organization.

The previously discussed and studied theories and models, such as Johari window, reflection cycle and critical thinking, all have the same core element, which is feedback. Feedback is an essential and crucial part of any effective information exchange as well as the building of relationships.

Process of Feedback

One of the most valuable things a leader can provide followers is feedback. Their understanding of organizational goals, awareness on how their performance may impact the overall fulfillment of the aims, and what evaluation and assessment will be conducted are the fundamental elements of feedback. The two new generations Y and Z are expected to receive feedback from supervisors on an everyday basis. Research results show that giving and receiving feedback was not an essential expectation of generation X that became important for the two new generations.

Ellis and Davidi (2005) understand after-event reviews as organizational learning procedures that give leaders and employees an opportunity to systematically analyze their work and behavior as well as to evaluate the contribution of various components to performance outcomes. Another similar view of feedback is presented by Astrom and Murray (2008), who see feedback as a reactive tool, usually an error before corrective actions are taken.

The main objective of feedback is to provide people with information which enables them to understand how they worked and how effective their behavior was. This explains the instructional and motivational functions of feedback for those who receive it.

The process of giving and receiving feedback is one of the most important concepts in the leading process. Employees need to receive feedback in order to be able to perform their tasks according to the standards (instructional function), but they are also encouraged to increase the expectations of their work (motivational function). It can be seen as a communication cycle in which the main aim is to exchange information about the individual or collective performance shared with those in a position to improve situations.

In order to develop an effective feedback process, hard data are combined with qualitative assessment and evaluation of performance.

The information provided via feedback tells others how their behavior affects others, how they feel, and what they perceive (feedback and self-disclosure). As Armstrong (2006, p. 236) says, "feedback should be based on facts, not subjective judgments"; the systemic collection of data on job performance derived from a variety of sources has to be organized by leaders and used efficiently when providing feedback to employees.

In Figure 5.3 we present the managers' abilities to understand the importance to evaluate process and progress in quantitative or qualitative ways.

This research question was ranked by the managers we studied with the highest impact weight of 10 points. The reason for this is the managers' core preference for traditional procedures when they motivate their employees. In most companies, rewards based on financial and nonfinancial tools are framed in accordance to the ability to measure fulfillment of goals, standards and quality of performance, and/or evaluating the results by quantifiable methods. But how can we assess and evaluate attitude, behavior, effort or any open-minded approach, which are essential prerequisites to foster an innovative environment? How can people know whether their effort and partial performance results are in accordance with strategic goals and if they are a good way to reach their individual targets? How do managers know whether everyone understands what their roles and contributions are within overall organizational

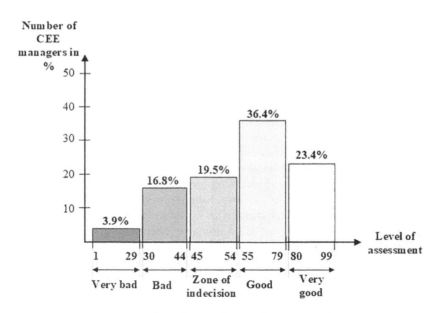

Figure 5.3 Quantitative and qualitative forms of process evaluation

Source: Authors.

performance? The most frequent answer is feedback. This instrument is a fundamental tool in a leader's set of tools and methods to be used when guiding, leading and motivating people. In many situations feedback is presented as a solution for improving individual performance, explaining what has to be done or just assessing the results.

Feedback is a cyclical element of communication, allowing systematical connections between sender and receiver, and also controls the perception of shared information. Various types of relationships are made through this kind of communication.

But that is a very simplified understanding of what feedback is all about and what can be obtained by implementing this tool correctly and effectively. Feedback is a two-way communication instrument. It is a two-stage process: giving and receiving the feedback. This means that when trying to discover external environmental opportunities, leaders are encouraged to ask for feedback not only from customers and partners, but more importantly to encourage their subordinates to give them feedback.

> *We have in place an on-line feedback instrument and also a 360-degree feedback process which is mainly focused on the development of the soft skills. Managers are giving feedback to their team and also to individual employees. At the present, we would like to implement the other side of the feedback process which means that the manager will ask for feedback.*
>
> (Talent manager in the automotive industry)

In Figure 5.4 the awareness of the continuous process of giving and receiving feedback among the leaders we interviewed is shown. The results reached the lowest measurements among all of the reflective questions we raised. First, managers valued leader's competence at 79 points and its impact on the organizational performance was given a weight of 8. The average value of all responses was only 44, where the individual minimum was 15 and the maximum value was 88. Compared to previous results, the highest number of responses occurred in the indecisive zone (33.7%) and shifted toward the left in the zone of "bad" and "very bad". Even though 39% of managers evaluated their effort in providing and receiving feedback in the "good" zone, only a small number of managers (6.5%) reflect their ability in the "very good" zone.

Implementing reflection within the feedback process can yield stronger performance increments than feedback alone. Reflection without feedback is inefficient and reflection enhances feedback interventions. A number of authors have researched the strategies which create an organizational environment that is supportive to the employees' development through the feedback process (London and Smither, 2002; Yukl and McDonald, 2003; Levy and Williams, 2004).

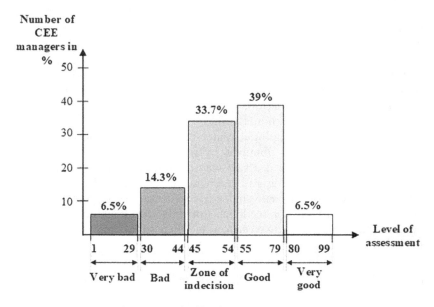

Figure 5.4 Giving and receiving feedback
Source: Authors.

Implementing feedback into the leading process is one of the most important prerequisites to develop the process-relational approach in leadership in organizations. Feedback is as an essential part of reflective communication as is critical thinking of what has been already discussed previously. It is conducted through social interactions and developing relations between all actors in an organization. It will also contribute to the concept of the Reflective Leadership Model, which requires a deeper understanding of critical thinking within all processes and relationships in an organization.

Reflection seems to be a particularly useful strategy for organizations to enhance feedback as two-way processes (i.e. providing feedback as well as receiving feedback). These two-way processes also represent a learning strategy and in the organizational context it is applied to after-event reviews.

Through the feedback process, we see ourselves as others see us. Through feedback, other people also learn how we see them, as shown in the Johari window model. The Johari window model is an example of increasing the open area by reducing the blind area, which would normally be achieved through the process of asking for and then receiving feedback. The open area can also be developed through the process of disclosure, which reduces the hidden area. The unknown area can be reduced in different ways: by others' observation (which increases the blind area), by self-discovery (which increases the hidden area) or by mutual enlightenment—typically via group experiences and discussion— which increases the open area as the unknown area is reduced. Discovery through sensitive communication, active listening, and experience will reduce the unknown area, transferring in part to the blind, hidden areas, depending on who knows what, or better still if known by the person and others, to the open free area.

A team which understands itself, that is, each person having a strong mutual understanding with the team, is far more effective than a team which does not understand each other, that is, whose members are largely hidden, blind and/or unknown in other areas. Team members and leaders should always be striving to increase their open free areas and to reduce their blind, hidden and unknown areas.

Feedback is also a reflection of others, usually in terms of compliance with standards, goals, and expectations of their work to be performed.

At the heart of providing feedback is an understanding of what can be achieved and what others' strengths and capabilities are that match organizational goals and strategies. Feedback, by its nature, is about sharing information in order to discover what can be improved and how a new quality of relations could be developed. The process of feedback becomes a social interaction and provides effective results when it is compared to goals or standards and the expectations that are discussed.

Whitmore (2009) states that feedback is a tool which evaluates reality, proposals or ideas about improvement and thus helps with real learning and an increase in performance.

Providing feedback on a regular basis can create the important precondition for the development of employees and also improve all processes within the organization. Certain basic steps are proposed when implementing the feedback process with leading actions:

- All processes can be established by giving and receiving feedback across the organization that include transparent assessment and evaluation procedures.
- This can be a first step in changing the inefficiency process in the entire organization.
- It is crucial to explain to people the meaning and reasons for implementing the feedback process as a tool for communication and mutual discovery of areas for potential change.
- The feedback process needs to include both harmonized a structure and a set of procedures in order to provide functional information for assessment and evaluation.
- Understanding and learning how it is used could provide a motivating tool for helping and developing capable work from labor.

In the process of providing and receiving feedback, emphasis is given to establishing the environment for open communication and leading people to express their ideas and opinions freely. That can be assured by raising simple questions, such as: "What makes you do the task this way?" "What other suggestions do you have?" "How can we achieve this goal?" "What obstacles do you envision?"

Leaders tend to receive feedback in their year-end reviews, which is often conducted as part of a 360-degree feedback program, and they are confronted with specific views on their leadership style, communication approach and interpersonal skills. They may also realize the employees' concerns about strategies, key decisions and organizational objectives. Since any feedback process is usually conducted at the end of a certain process or time period, information that leads to corrections and improvements is obtained too late. This phenomenon has been observed in a number of case studies conducted over three years and brought our attention to incorporating the process of feedback into the Critical Reflective Analysis method and later into the new Reflective Leadership Model. The implementation of feedback into the reflection process and making it a fundamental part of any social interaction will establish a tendency to conduct feedback continuously, thus contributing to strategic advice and to a number of quality improvements in the organization. A motivational function of feedback enhances good relations between leaders and employees, reduces uncertainty and increases trust in leaders and in the organization.

The Pathway Toward Reflective Leadership

The discussion of what impact leadership has for the organization operating in an uncertain and frequently changing environment starts in Goleman's concept of emotional intelligence (1995). His emphasis is given on identifying the leadership role in strategy formulation and its implementation. A challenge for leaders is to create an organizational environment where everyone contributes to a strategic architecture, where people continually learn, seek opportunities and support change.

One of the greatest challenges for leadership at all levels in organizations is how to create the type of conditions that combine achieving high results with a favorable level of good relations and learning. Leaders can directly encourage and facilitate the performance of their teams by what they say and do, and they can directly influence it by modifying and improving all organizational processes and systems.

The relations between leaders and followers have already been presented by the concept of Learning-Following in Chapter 1. The "knowing" phase highlights for leaders the importance of knowledge and information-based creation, a process of knowledge sharing and exchange.

Nonaka (1998) introduced the concept of "Ba" as a space for dynamic conversion of knowledge and for emerging relationships. Ba is a shared space for emerging relationships. Four different types of Ba have been defined:

1. Originating Ba is a world in which individuals share their feelings, emotions, experiences and mental models.
2. Interacting Ba is a space in which knowledge converts to results where the key factors are dialogue and metaphors.
3. Cyber Ba represents a space for monologue where explicit knowledge combines with the existing experience.
4. Exercising Ba facilitates the conversion of explicit to tacit knowledge; it relates to in-practice training or active involvement in various managerial processes.

All types of Ba have one feature in common—knowledge is embedded in Ba and it is acquired on the basis of an individual's experiences or as a reflection on other people's experiences. For any individual to participate in Ba means being involved in processes, constructive dialogues and adapting to practices. A number of theories and studies trying to define the organizational conditions enabling knowledge creation are rooted at this point. Since social validity makes knowledge creation a delicate process, the relationships among individuals in Ba positively influence the synthesis and advancement of organizational knowledge. Knowledge creation becomes more effective when the relationships show a high degree of interest in others, mutual trust, active empathy, available support, indulgent judgment and courage (von Krogh et al., 2006).

The main purpose of this Ba theory of creating organizational knowledge is to determine conditions enabling new knowledge creation and thus developing innovation and improving learning (Nonaka, 1998).

Such quality relationships with high interest from both leaders and followers give priority to the creation, transfer and exchange of knowledge.

The growing importance of the knowing phase is linked with the socio-technological approach which is based on five components: structure, task, technology, people and the environment (Coakes et al., 2002). The collaboration, exchange of knowledge and experiences are influenced by the specific type of leadership, usage of technologies and existing culture in the organization. All these key features were determined and described through the systemic approach presented by the "big picture" concept. In such a network structure, there is an increasing interest in understanding how the social context in which people are embedded in the organization influences their behavior and performance together with evidence suggesting that knowledge transfer is facilitated by intensive interactions of organizational actors.

The continuous learning process stresses the importance of learning together and expanding the leaders' and followers' capacity to create desired outcomes. As Senge (1990) states, high-quality products and services that exceed expectations characterize this mutual learning process. This is related to organizational learning where the core aspect is represented by collective learning by all members of the organization.

The learning stage in the first Leading-Following sequence has brought the importance of raising questions, seeking feedback, being curious, reflecting on what worked and what didn't into the relationship between leaders and followers.

Yukl (2009) defines the process of learning as discovering relevant new knowledge, diffusing this knowledge to people in the organization who need it and applying the knowledge to improve internal processes and external adaptation.

Leadership has a strong influence on developing collective learning in teams and organizations. One of the greatest challenges for leadership at all levels in organizations is how to create the type of conditions that encourage, facilitate and sustain a favorable level of innovation and collective learning. Leaders can directly encourage and facilitate collective learning by what they say and do, they can indirectly influence it by implementing or modifying relevant programs, systems and structures (Yukl and Lepsinger, 2004).

Ancona et al. (1999) stress the new networked learning paradigm as radically different from traditional ways. It is described as a joint learning process which is goal-driven and intrinsically motivating, empowering teams and diversity. This creates a network of alliances with suppliers, clients, partners and even competitors that are innovative and global.

Employees learn to critically evaluate situations, make a decision, take a risk and develop thinking in teams. The team context creates an opportunity for team members to distribute their attention, search for information and pool their collective knowledge via information exchange. Moreover, the collective search and information exchange process lies at the core of effective collective learning (Latham and Locke, 2007; Ellis and Davidi, 2005; Gibson and Vermeulen, 2003). Teams are empowered with committed leaders at strategic and personal levels that constantly strive to experiment, improve, innovate and produce high-performance results.

The social and political impact of technology is creating a new generation of people who possess a new and legitimate challenge to the way leaders act and think. Considering the changing societal values, this challenge is part of a legacy where one generation questions another concerning the expectations of work commitments as well as a suitable leadership approach.

Watson (2010) argues that the technology age urges the shift from old notions of leaders as heroes toward more reflective, collaborative and authentic leadership. The integrated approach to the task of reforming and modernizing the leadership process is needed.

The diversity of the workplace and the continuous changes in both the external as well as internal environment fosters a focus on opportunities rather than problems with the dialogue crossing issues and cultural boundaries and establishing collaborative communities across the world. The main work for leaders is now about people: listening to them, enabling them to develop and involving them in most of the organizational processes. We have already presented the previous research and business practices, mainly from large organizations. This has shown the myth that leadership is about performance and fulfillment of external measures. This approach puts more emphasis on how leadership looks and often favors a more extroverted style. The consequence of a performance-led approach is that it negates the power of reflection and the integrity of a value-led approach. Measurable tasks, scorecards and performance models are constructed as quantitative results of any performance and rarely point out any insights on how the results were accomplished, what the learning outcomes are and how to understand others and oneself.

Already discussed in this chapter, the bottom-up approach in leadership (which was elaborated on through a few reflective techniques such as the Johari window), feedback and critical thinking enhance the development of the inside-out approach to leadership which was presented as a Leading-Following Model (Figure 1.1). Through this approach, leaders find ways to build their own understanding as well as help other people get familiar with the organizational context and thus contribute to overall organizational success. If leaders and followers are indeed influenced by their joint interactions, they cannot be successful without building relationships. The process of relational interactions such as knowing and learning are also fundamental actions (i.e. actions involving leading and following run in both directions, from top down and bottom up). We propose a modified model, Leading-Following-Knowing-Learning (Figure 5.5), where the key leadership processes are implemented through relations with other people.

The interaction sequence for the leading phase suggests providing space and direction, as the knowing phases are related to gathering all knowledge, information and data from both a top-down as well as bottom-up direction. The following phase includes inspiring and engaging other people, together with interaction on how people respond to the leading phase. The learning phase represents the collective learning outcome for both leaders and followers. This social interaction develops meaningful interplay between all processes and constructs effective relationships among all agents engaged in leadership.

The implementation of reflection based on critical thinking was a valuable asset to develop the process-relational based perspectives of

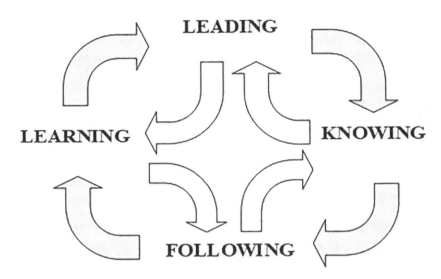

Figure 5.5 Leading-Knowing-Following-Learning Model (LKFL Model)
Source: Authors.

leadership. The Critical Reflection Analysis was used in our studies and research conducted in various organizations.

To suggest such a new approach, we compare the process-relational perspective of leadership to the system-control perspective. The system-control approach is characterized by rigid goals, rather formal and structured relations between supervisors and subordinates and it represents what used to be called the "outside-in" approach to leadership. This approach to leadership has few obstacles for successful use in the diverse and fast-changing organizational environment.

The assessment and evaluation of all processes conducted in organizations by leaders and understanding the importance of relationships with actors in the organization have the biggest influence on the framing of the effective leading process. The next section presents the Reflective Leadership concept that emerges from our extensive qualitative research.

The Framework of the Reflective Leadership Model

Leading people's performance in an unstable and frequently changing external as well as internal environment, where changes in the team and performed tasks occur frequently, has strengthened the shift from traditional approaches toward a more complex leadership process.

Our analyses, both conceptual and reflective, showed that the process-relational based approach to leadership emphasizes establishing the balance between the organizational internal world and various externalities. If we see the organizational ecosystem as a living element, to keep the balance between the achievement of strategic goals and focusing on the relationship network with all stakeholders, then this is the leader's task. In this view, leaders bring into focus these two interrelated environments by exercising several key processes.

Referring to a variety of discussed approaches and theories in previous chapters, we can highlight that the process-relational-based leadership concept connects the main functions of:

- *Strategic planning and strategy implementation* (a process of formulation strategy and setting up strategic goals, vision and missions reflecting challenges and externalities).
- *Understanding the organization as a wider ecosystem* (setting up and communicating goals with various stakeholders in order to establish well-performed networks and relations).
- *Formulation of common purpose with meaning and engagement of people through commonly shared values.*
- *Evaluation and assessment* (impacts communities, society, customers, clients and employees).
- *Providing continuous support and development of a diverse workforce* (performing constructive two-way feedback, coaching and establishing information flow, both inside and outside).

The inside-out approach, reflection, use of critical evaluation and assessment done by executives are the key means to understand the move toward Reflective Leadership. It is framed as a dialectical process, a conversation that has to go in two ways, not just one. Since questioning is the best tool to start the dialogue and reflect our own and others' ways of understanding and actions, critical questions were constructed (see Appendix I).

The multidisciplinary view on leadership, through the variety of theories, tools and models such as the Ethical Triad (Figure 2.1), the big picture and the Learning-Knowing-Following-Learning Model (Figure 5.5), together with results of analyses used in our qualitative research, grounded theory and Critical Reflection Analysis, all contribute to the design of the Reflective Leadership Model, which is presented in Figure 5.6. During our research, we have examined a number of specific actions or processes leaders and their organizations undertake regularly in order to enhance the likelihood of future success.

The key processes and questions that help to build important relations are suggested as follows:

The process of involving (engagement) focuses on encouraging debate and the exchange of different views. Differences of perception (e.g. about the significance of facts, goals, methods or values) are

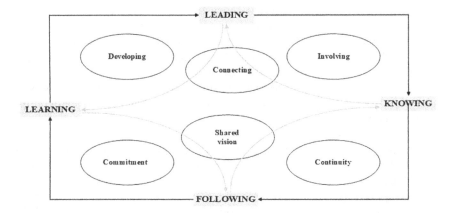

Figure 5.6 Reflective Leadership Model
Source: Authors.

supported through open discussion. We believe that diversity of personality and acknowledgment of differences is critical to healthy team function while team homogeneity is a weakness and can cause problems by overlooking important considerations in any process. The diverse team might be difficult to manage and various conflicts could occur; nevertheless, it is a source of innovation and further development.

Do I/Do we communicate clearly? Do I/we accept mistakes? Do I/ we acknowledge different opinions and feelings? Do I/we give and receive feedback?

The process of continuity (knowing) reflects the importance of the past, the present and the future. The past needs to be analyzed, and we need to critically reflect and respect what worked. Not all team members have to act identically. Some may follow rules while others need a degree of flexibility and creativity; some will reflect on the past while others will be encouraged or expected to pioneer a new or different way of working. Continuity demands respect for differences through time and recognizes that decisions may affect people well into the future.

Do I/Do we share information and knowledge? Do I/we acknowledge the past? Do I/we respect the work of others? Do I/we know how the team works? Do I/we respect difference?

The process of commitment makes sure that all processes are clear to everyone. It results from the actions which set up specific goals, parameters and measurements of progress or completion of tasks. It is a combination of confidence in and enthusiasm about individual performance. This will be increased if potential negatives and uncertainties are communicated and placed in clear perspective. In this process, the balance between what information is needed and what is crucial for our performance brings a continuous dilemma to leaders' decision making.

> *Do I/we participate meaningfully? Do I/we know what actions are required? Do I/we realize what the impact is of those actions inside and outside of the organization? Do I/we notice and acknowledge progress and improvements? Do I/we evaluate processes both quantitatively and qualitatively? Do I/we seek consensus?*

The *process of connecting* stresses that a good process can build relationships. People gain a sense of identity from their relationships with others. Each process should foster social relationships where trust, reciprocity and shared values are built. It is important to identify the values that are implied in what may seem to be a simple technological or organizational adjustment. With any change or innovation in order to be ethical, it is necessary to consider the purpose, the manner and also the results on every possible social and economic impact on the internal as well as the external environment of the organization.

> *Do I/we act ethically? Do I/we expect some unpopular decisions? Do I/we understand the stakeholders' needs? Do I/we set a good example? Do I/we value social relationships? Do I/we respect others in a wider circle? Do I/we take the initiative?*

The *process of developing* explains that a good process will value, support and develop the potential for learning that each individual brings. Learning is a key tool to improve self-awareness through all interactions. Creative and original thought, and informal as well as formal learning and practice development, will be encouraged. Reflection is the key ingredient that turns individual or team action into further development.

> *Do I/we understand how the team learns? Do I/we learn from mistakes? Do I/we welcome new ideas? Do I/we think about what is going on? Do I/we think beyond just doing things? Do I/we notice and develop strengths?*

The *process of making a shared vision* concentrates on sharing the big picture with everyone. It means that all actors involved in a process has a clear picture of where the organization is taking them. This picture is called a shared vision or a common purpose. Developing a shared vision requires time for reflection, sharing things from all perspectives and creating networks. There are certain rules and standards introduced in compliance with ethical behavior and in accordance with CSR policy and guidelines.

> *Do I/we act to reflect our shared vision? Do I/we act in connection with others? Do I/we design simple and clear systems? Do I/we clarify standards? Do I/we understand the big picture? Do I/we value contact with others?*

Many leaders say that leading people as well as delivering results is hard work. Working with both dimensions and combining them effectively is extremely difficult. Therefore, these main steps can offer advice on how to perform the complexity of this proposed model and to focus on both process and relations.

Every day we witness the alarming disconnect between thinking about leadership from a historical perspective and the life experiences of a new generation of young people and many other people who are working under a certain type of leadership. They are often dissatisfied with leadership approaches or behavior. Sometimes they excuse the leaders by saying "a good leader has to be born", which starts the argument about whether effective leadership can be developed and learned. Our conducted research and discussions with a number of executives challenged our study to reflect assumptions about leadership within the new technology and innovation era. The emphasis on both process and relations and a description of the interactions between these two elements shaped the concept of Reflective Leadership, which can be a suitable model for the new generation of employees working in a technology-driven environment.

Given the complexity and uncertainty that surrounds most organizations, the next chapter will assess the Reflective Leadership concept in the process of directing change. Attention is given mainly to examples of how leadership can focus on enhancement and guidance of people to create and accept change.

Conclusion

The digital era and emerging views on the system and relational perspectives of leadership are crucial for the development of the Reflective Leadership concept. The initial focus presented in this chapter is exploring the leading process that can reflect the key features of the new era of organizations, where technology and a diverse workforce are the main focus. Such a leading concept can be implemented by leaders in all hierarchal levels, across various sectors and in any region or country.

Referring to researchers' comments that more qualitative data focused on senior leaders is needed in order to understand better the scope of organizational transformation and the associated processes and practices of leadership (Gordon and Yukl, 2004; Beck, 2014), we have conducted extensive qualitative research. The research strategy, philosophy and methodology are described in the introduction as well as in more detail in Appendixes I and II.

The design of the Reflective Leadership concept starts with the two concepts in the previous chapter (Leading-Following and the big picture). These two concepts weave between well-established theoretical approaches and new emergent frameworks that contribute to the process-relational view on leadership. In spite of the differences in conceptual apparatus across many theories, there are deep similarities between the behavior of leaders, the strategic content of leadership and the interrelations within an organizational ecosystem. One of these common issues is that the leading function is a continuous process cycle where the main leaders' task is to bring together organizational goals with individual ones in order to be in line with the organizational strategy and vision.

Case Study 2 Generational Changes in the Workforce Within the Socioeconomic and Political Context

The Characteristics of Different Generations

Since three or sometimes even four generations are performing collectively, the topic related to differences among those generations gained the interest of many scholars and practitioners. Differences between generations can affect the way the managers manage and build teams, deal with innovation, recruit, motivate and develop people.

Deloitte's review (2010) points out those socioeconomic and political events which drove societal transformation, influenced attitudes, habits and values. Global companies often oversimplify their view of a homogeneous workforce worldwide. The different generations and their labels are often seen as universal with people in all countries sharing the same experiences. Though there may be some overlaps, the experiences in each country are quite different. Many of the terms and stereotypes of the generations from Western countries are well known, with monikers like baby boomers and generations X, Y, and Z. These terms are not so fitting for the CEE region. With a lack of descriptive terms of the generations, we have put forth our own terms that would be fitting to this region (see Table 5.1). It is at this point that we need to differentiate between EU countries and non-EU countries

Table 5.1 Timeline and typology of generations

Birth	Western Terms for the Generations	CE Counterparts
Born 1946–1964	Late baby boomers	Socialist generation
Born 1965–1980	Generation X	Go-west generation
Born 1981–2000	Millennials or Generation Y	Transition generation
Born after 2000	Generation Z, iGen or Centennials	The tethered generation

Source: Authors.

in the eastern sphere. Attitudes toward work in those countries are likely to differ from the EU nations and so there are generational differences. As such, we are only focusing on Central Europe (CE) and member states of the EU.

Special attention was given to the most recent generation in our observation over the last 10 years. This generation can be defined by the 3Cs of communication, control and contact. The main feature of this generation is their virtual life with each member having at least one social network account constraining their connection and contacts mainly to the digital world. This profoundly differentiates them from previous generations.

Recently there were several surveys conducted by consulting groups such as Deloitte (2017) and Price Waterhouse Coopers (2018) in order to define the new working habits and what managers' responses to those challenges are. These secondary findings are confronted by our primary data. We have examined the generations in the CE region in two ways. First, we interviewed leaders of companies to get an assessment of what each generation is like. For generations Y and Z (the transition and tethered generations of CE), we conducted an in-class survey for the past ten years to assess generation behavioral changes. This research was conducted from the perspective of the "book-of-the-self" that all individuals are attempting to write (i.e. what choices will I make in order to have a meaningful life). Another aim was to find out what their learning habits are.

In the next section, we will briefly summarize the historical background that has shaped those four generations (socialist, go-west, transition and tethered generations) that are all present in the working environment in the CEE. We will also examine current generational attitudes in regard to life and work. Finally, the different leadership approaches toward them will be proposed as the result of our survey, conducted among the respondents from new generation Z.

The Socialist Generation (Boomers)

This group was raised under socialism and started their working lives in a socialist system. The options were limited in this generation and once your path in life was set, there were little options to change. It was the common worker who was glorified, as the laboring class was seen to be the dogged foot-soldier in society and was thus awarded a high status. A job was something that was held for life. A university education was limited to a select few and the quality of education was quite high. There were very limited opportunities to travel outside of the country with the possible exception of neighboring socialist countries or to Yugoslavia.

On the positive side, flats were given to people for free, but with no ownership rights. Many people were able to build their own house in a "do-it-yourself" way. For those living in a flat, a garden cottage could easily be obtainable. After the collapse of communism in 1989, the flats could be bought and converted to personal ownership for very little money. In larger cities, this means average workers were basically given their own flats for absurdly low prices.

Only in former Czechoslovakia was there a relatively functional society with, from the perspective of a socialist country, fewer shortages and deprivations than the other socialist nations (Poland, Romania, East Germany).

The socialist generation is a product of post-war communism and embraces more collectivist working styles. Managers have found these workers to be the easiest to work with in terms of responsibility and dedication. For the most part, these workers are not looking for high salaries or promotion. They are rather looking to finish their working lives and enter into retirement. These workers, for the most part, do what is asked, finish their work and go home. For this generation, homes are paid off and kids are grown and on their own. They can be said to be looking forward to a life without work. On the other hand, due to some facts (for instance that this generation is still capable of work), the retirement age is gradually getting higher and higher, and there is a lack of skills, mainly in manual professions (e.g. plumbers, carpenters, electricians, etc.). As such, the demand for elderly skilled labor is increasing.

Go-West Generation (Generation X)

Unlike their Western counterparts, this generation was born during a time of rising birth-rates (i.e. a second baby boom) in the CEE. In the case of Romania, there was a forced governmental attempt to increase birth-rates under the leadership of Nicolae Ceauşescu.

Similarly, in Czechoslovakia, the period between the years 1970 and 1979 had high population growth and this generation was called "Husak's children", after the leader of Czechoslovakia.

The impact of Prague Spring in 1968 and the Velvet Revolution in 1989 directly influenced the attitude of generation X. This generation is mainly focused on compensation and career development opportunities. This group entered the workforce when conditions were at their worst in the CE region as the command economy was replaced by a market economy. During this time, mass unemployment ensued with many enterprises going out of business. For the new workers entering into the workforce, leaving the country was wise, if not the only, avenue for success. If one was to stay in their own country, the only real options were to head to the capital cities (Warsaw, Prague, Budapest, Bratislava, etc.).

Working in base level jobs in a Western country, however, was seen very positively as it could lead to immigration to a better country where the pay was much higher than in the home country (e.g. a taxi driver could earn twice the salary of a doctor in the home country). Like the previous generation, this group, for the most part, was able to obtain housing that was commensurate to their wages.

This is the generation of hard knocks. The employment situation was dire in CE countries during the 1990s and getting to Western countries for work was not an easy affair. The workers from this generation are well regarded. Due to the hard times during the 1990s, this generation put off having children to later in life, leading to a smaller future generation and a baby-bust. A large number of managers in the top managerial hierarchy in many local subsidiaries of multinationals are from this generation. The managers face difficulties in dealing with different work attitudes represented by generations Y and Z, who favor work-life balance and flexibility. The managers from generation X believe that whoever wants to live better should work harder. Many of them are considered to be "workaholics" and they are considered to be the most experienced. They are goal-oriented people. Leaders from this generation tend to use a more authoritarian leadership style.

The Transition Generation (Millennials)

This generation has some childhood memories of socialism but came to adulthood during the transitional period where the rule of law, especially for commerce, was ambiguous. Their pay is still low when compared to Western countries. From the turn of the century, there was a steady trickle of foreign firms setting up companies in Central Europe. The best jobs in these companies go to people with good language and computer skills. As such, it is still seen as a good idea to go abroad to earn money and then to come back to Central Europe with both a small reserve of cash and heightened working skills such as speaking in a foreign language.

In 2004, the Czech Republic, Estonia, Hungary, Latvia, Lithuania, Poland, Slovakia and Slovenia became members of the EU. At the same time, the United Kingdom opened their labor market to workers from the EU. They had expected only a few thousand workers but instead received 20 times their original estimate. In 2007 alone, 112,000 immigrants went to the UK to find work (Salt, 2015).

With the ability to go abroad without visas or to move to one of the capital cities in CE, this generation has had an easier time finding a job and gaining experience. A common practice for this generation is to work in England while living minimally and to come back to CE with money to buy property and obtain a position in a local company. This generation became attuned to the unequal pay levels in CE and is less happy to be earning so little. This pay problem is exacerbated by the rise in home prices as many are getting priced out of the market or have to settle for less. Unlike the two previous generations, home acquisition has become a concern and there is a feeling of frustration at having to work harder and still not having enough. They deal with a constant paradox in the work environment: work less while having a flexible work time and work-life balance but on the other hand, within two to three years after university, move to a managerial position. They often rotate between jobs and even unrelated professional fields.

They are relationship-oriented people that could be seen as having little respect for authority, but the leadership approach is very important. The leaders from this generation are using a more partici-patory leadership style.

The Tethered Generation

This youngest generation shares a common trait that is similar all around the world: possession of the ubiquitous smartphone that allows anytime/anywhere connectivity to the internet as well as to their parents and peers. This generation has never known a time with-out the internet. The negative externality of the smartphone and its portable internet capability does not lie specifically within this gen-eration, as it is the parents that are often initiating contact with their children. This is the age of the helicopter and the lawnmower parent. A helicopter parent is a parent who pays extremely close attention to a child's experiences and problems, especially with schools and extra-curricular activities. The lawnmower parent clears a path of all obstacles so that their children never have to deal with any problems by themselves. Parents are clearly more involved in their children's lives than in previous generations and this generation is tethered to their peers, parents and the instant gratification of on-demand infor-mation and entertainment.

This generation is more risk averse than previous generations as they are delaying or forgoing traditional age-related responsibilities and rites of passage. Like their Western counterparts, this generation is less involved in negative risky behaviors such as alcohol, drugs and sexual experimentation. In CE counties, this generation is learning to drive earlier than in the previous generation. This means that the automobile is a still a growing utility in this region.

This is the first generation that is entering the workforce where the unemployment rate is relatively low and jobs are relatively plentiful. At the same time, other countries are not as welcoming as before with immigration (e.g. Brexit). Currency stabilization has also lessened the appeal of going abroad to work.

This generation is less willing to go abroad to earn their stripes, as Brexit has taken away the welcome mat for foreign workers in the UK and jobs are readily available in the home country. This is a genera-tion that has had less demand placed upon them in terms of responsi-bilities. They are not expected to go to another country to work (unlike the go-west and transitional generations) and they are not expected to pick their lifelong fate at an early age (unlike the socialist generation).

This is the first generation which has been born with ICT. Even though their parents are from generation X, this generation is very different due to the strong impact of digitalization. They are quick to search for information, and are sometimes overwhelmed with it and struggle to critically assess it. They are extremely skilled in relations and building networks across geographic locations. By using ICT tools, they are more inclined to raise questions and search for different opinions, preferably through social media. Environmental issues, ethical and social responsibility became topics of their interest.

Multitasking jobs, continuous flow of various challenges and impulses for learning new things are the main motivating factors for this generation. They prefer to be led by managers who use various digital media in leading teams, thus enabling them to share global views and to provide some kind of intellectual incentive.

What Are the Learning and Training Expectations of Generation Z?

In addition to those outside factors, CEOs are also concerned about how to attract and retain qualified employees with the skills they need and a new set of expectations brought by younger employees for what they want from their employers. Price Waterhouse Coopers' (2018) latest survey drew as many as 86% of respondents who were "extremely" or "somewhat" concerned about the availability of key skills. Looking more closely at what skills they worry about, 62% of CEOs from the CEE region find it "very" or "somewhat" difficult to recruit digital talent, compared with 50% globally. This is reflected by the many multinationals that have discovered the CEE region's strengths in good education in the hard sciences and having the highest proportions in the world of IT and technology specialists per capita. But this has been gradually decreasing since investments in education in most CEE countries is below the OECD average.

Research shows that while companies and their managers in the CEE still rely on traditional forms of learning and training, there is a strong need to look at the methods successful global players are using to better attract and develop digital talent in a new generation.

A survey was conducted in 2017 among 100 representatives of generation Z at Matej Bel University in Slovakia. The aim was to find out how they see their development and what their preferences are as far as the methods, techniques and sources for learning are concerned. The key findings provided by the secondary research of the new generation Z which is now entering the labor market were also examined and compared with the primary data.

The respondents were asked to highlight the *major source* of new thoughts, aspirations, and ideas of practical experience. Surprisingly, they valued social networks, publications and the internet as the least significant sources for their learning. Additional sources for new ideas were considered through various contacts with people: people with experience in a specific area, work with various colleagues, groups of experts and people who can inspire them. Since generation Z has been characterized as the "smartest generation", keen on communication and discussion in groups, searching for an opinion from various people and making decisions collectively, this matches up with our research findings.

This also correlates with the question examining what type of learning approach the young generation considers the most important. *Learning by practice, continuous feedback and learning from more experienced colleagues* came out as the most significant for their learning path. Coaching and lifelong learning were ranked as other types of learning. On the other hand, on-line education was the least preferable way of learning.

The preferred ways of performance are contradictory to all previous findings. The most preferable form of performance was *teamwork* where listening to others and giving constant feedback to others was specifically addressed. On the other hand, willingness to ask questions ranked as the least popular action.

Throughout our academic and practical experiences, we had observed that the term "feedback" is rather misunderstood, not only in education but also in the business environment. The results of this survey showed that feedback is known neither as the tool to carry out two-way communication nor as the process for improvements. Of the respondents, 51.85% considered feedback as the way "to express my own opinion".

The three most important skills for their future success in practice were underlined and ranked from the most to least important by young people, as follows: In first place, there were interpersonal skills focused on communication, presentation and assertiveness, followed by entrepreneurship and creative thinking with the same scores, and in the third position were language skills.

Motivation is considered a rather hard job for every manager since companies offer unified social programs where various benefits are included. However, each employee has his or her own needs and incentives which motivate them to perform and to be satisfied. Our research results show that the most significant factors the young generation is looking for in a future job are "working with other generations and constant learning".

The broader question related to generation Z expectations of their leaders in future jobs was formulated when key leadership actions were stated. The respondents ranked those expectations from the most significant to the least. Leaders should:

1. Understand employees' strengths and use them appropriately when formulating their work assignments.
2. Stimulate people's creativity and be the source of inspiration.
3. Provide regular and constructive feedback in order to improve performance.
4. Have concerns about people's feelings and workplace relations that can make an impact on employees' performance.
5. Identify employees' views on key organizational issues.
6. Form strategic goals and then communicate them to employees.
7. Flexibly respond to changing environments and lead people to cope with it.
8. Behave and act in accordance with the organization's values.

Conclusion

Referring to the recent indexes for cultural dimensions provided by Hofstede, individualism is increasing, and not only in CEE countries where collectivism was the main feature for socialistic economies and social processes. The growth in individualism has been linked with economic growth, prosperous economies and rising trends in every developed economy. How to link that to recent preferences to be a part of a group, of a team, where relationships, collaboration and people are the crucial elements for ideas, aspirations and learning? How is that possible when the digitalization and implementation of the latest technologies are key challenges for every business? As the tethered generation (generation Z) is well versed in digital knowledge, they lack the traditional knowledge of the organization of the socialist generation (baby boomers) and the older go-west generation (generation X). We can conclude that intergenerational teams would provide the best continuity for an organization. In other words, it is of absolute importance to transfer the knowledge of the older generation to the younger generation before they retire.

The conclusion can be formulated that leaders need to emphasize technology and digital skills alongside strengthening the soft skills in their organizations. Today's young generation is looking for employment where they can see purpose and fulfillment and have the opportunity to be actively involved in organizational life. Companies are urged to invest in leadership which can follow the current trends in developing, leading and retaining a capable workforce if they want to be successful in the competitive environment.

Bibliography

20th CEO Survey 2017. PwC. Retrieved from: www.pwc.com/gx/en/ceo-survey/2017/pwc-ceo-20th-survey-report-2017.pdf [Accessed 5 September 2018.]

Ancona, D., et al. (1999). *Organizational Behavior and Processes.* Boston: South—Western College Publishing.

Anseel, F., Lievens, F., Schollaert, E. (2009). Reflection as a Strategy to Enhance Task Performance After Feedback. *Organizational Behavior and Human Decision Processes*, 110, 23–35.

Armstrong, M. (2006). A *Handbook of Management Technique: A Comprehensive Guide to Achieving Managerial Excellence and Improved Decision-Making.* London: Kogan Page Ltd.

Astrom, K. J., Murray, R. M. (2008). *Feedback Systems: An Introduction for Scientists and Engineers.* Princeton, NJ: Princeton University Press.

Beck, C. D. (2014). Antecedents of Servant Leadership: A Mixed Methods Study. *Journal of Leadership and Organizational Studies*, 21(3), 299–314.

Coakes, E., Willis, D., Clarke, S. (2002). *Knowledge Management in the Sociotechnical World.* London: Springer.

Cottrell, S. (2005). *Critical Thinking Skills: Developing Effective Analysis and Argument.* New York: Palgrave Macmillan.

Covey, S. M. R. (2006). *The Speed of Trust. The One Thing That Changes Everything.* Praha: Management Press.

Dowd, S. B., Bolus, N. E. (1998). Stress Resulting from Change and Restructuring: A Cognitive Approach. *Family and Community Health*, 21(2), 70–78.

Dundis, S., Benson, S. (2003). Building More Effective Virtual Teams: An Examination of Task Variable in Online Group Problem-Solving. *International Journal on E-Learning*, 2(4), 24–38.

Ellis, S., Davidi, I. (2005). After-Event Reviews: Drawing Lessons from Successful and Failed Experience. *Journal of Applied Psychology*, 90, 857–871.

Facione, P. A. (1990). *Critical Thinking: A Statement of Expert Consensus for Purposes of Educational Assessment and Instruction.* California: California Academic Press.

Gibson, C., Vermeulen, F. (2003). A Healthy Divide: Subteams as Stimulus for Team Learning Behaviour. *Administrative Science Quarterly*, 48, 202–239.

Goleman, D. (1995). *Emotional Intelligence.* Praha: Columbus.

Gordon Hullfish, H., Smith, P. G. (1961). Reflective Thinking: The Method of Education. In Anseel, F., Lievens, F., Schollaert, E. (eds.), Reflection as a strategy to enhance task performance after feedback. *Organizational Behavior and Human Decision Process*, 110, 23–35.

Gordon, A., Yukl, G. A. (2004). The Future of Leadership Research: Challenges and Opportunities. *German Journal of Human Resource Research*, 18(3), 359–365.

Gray, D. E. (2007). Facilitating Management Learning: Developing Critical Reflection Through Reflective Tools. *Management Learning*, 38, 495–517.

Hall, D. T. (2002). *Careers in and Out of Organizations.* Thousand Oaks, CA: Sage.

Kolb, D. A. (1984). *Experimental Learning.* Englewood Cliffs, NJ: Prentice Hall.

Kokavcova, D. (2011). *New Paradigm of Knowledge Management.* Bratislava: Iura Edition.

Kurubacak, G. (2007). Building Knowledge Networks Through Project-Based On-line Learning: A Study of Developing Critical Thinking Skills via Reusable Learning Objects. *Computers in Human Behavior*, 23(6), 2668–2695.

Land of the clear-eyed realists. Price Waterhouse Coopers 21st CEO Survey. (2018). Retrieved from: www.pwc.pl/en/publikacje/2018/ceo-survey-2018-cee.html [Accessed 5 September 2018.]

Latham, J. R., Locke, E. A. (2007). New Developments in and Directions for Goal Setting Research. *European Psychologist*, 12, 290–230.

Levy, P. E., Williams, J. R. (2004). The Social Context of Performance Appraisal: A Review and Framework for the Future. *Journal of Management*, 30, 881–905.

London, M., Smither, J. W. (2002). Feedback Orientation, Feedback Culture, and the Longitudinal Performance Management Process. *Human Resource Management Review*, 12, 81–100.

Luft, J., Ingham, H. (1955). The Johari Window, a Graphic Model of Interpersonal Awareness. *Proceedings of the Western Training Laboratory in Group Development.* Los Angeles: University of California.

Monge, P., Contractor, N. (2003). *Theories of Communication Networks.* New York: Oxford University Press.

Natale, S., Ricci, F. (2006). Critical Thinking in Organizations. *Team Performance Management*, 12(7/8), 272–277.

Nonaka, I. (1998). The Concept of "Ba": Building a Foundation for Knowledge Creation. *California Management Review*, 40(3), 40–53.

Paul, R., Elder, L., Bartell, T. (1997). *Teacher Preparation for Instruction in Critical Thinking: Research Findings and Policy Recommendations.* Sacramento, CA: Commission on teacher credentialing.

Petress, K. (1984). Critical Thinking: An Extended Definition. *Education*, 124(3), 461.

Salt, J. (2015). *International Migration and the United Kingdom.* Report of the United Kingdom, SOPEMI Correspondent to OECD. Retrieved from: www.geog.ucl.ac.uk/research/research-centres/migration-research-unit/pdfs/Sop10_final_2112.pdf [Accessed 5 September 2018.]

Senge, P. (1990). *Fifth Discipline: Theory and Practice of Learning Organization.* Praha: Management Press.

Strange, J. M., Mumford, M. D. (2005). The Origins of Vision: Effects of Reflection, Models, and Analysis. *Leadership Quarterly*, 16(1), 121–148.

Talking about whose generation. (2010). Deloitte Review, 6/2010. Retrieved from: https://www2.deloitte.com/content/dam/insights/us/articles/talking-about-whose-generation-ages-and-attitudes-among-the-global-workforce/US_deloittereview_Talking_ About_Whose_Generation_Jan10.pdf [Accessed 5 September 2018.]

The 2017 Deloitte Millennial Survey. Deloitte. Retrieved from: https://www2.deloitte.com/content/dam/Deloitte/global/Documents/About-Deloitte/gx-deloitte-millennial-survey-2017-executive-summary.pdf [Accessed 5 September 2018.]

Theodoulides, L., Jahn, P. (2013). *Reflective Method: Tool for Organizational Learning.* Bratislava: Iura Edition.

Von Krogh, G., Voelpel, K., Nonaka, I. (2006). *Enabling Knowledge Creation: How to Unlock the Mystery of Tacit Knowledge and Release the Power of Innovation.* Oxford: Oxford University Press.

Yeo, R.K. (2007). (Re) Viewing Problem-Based Learning: An Exploratory Study on Perceptions of Its Applicability to the Workplace. *Journal of Managerial Psychology*, 22(4), 369–391.

Yukl, G. A. (2009). Leading Organizational Learning: Reflections on Theory and Research. *The Leadership Quarterly*, 20(1), 49–53.

Yukl, G. A., McDonald, R. A. (2003). Effects of Multisource Feedback and a Feedback Facilitator on the Influence Behavior of Mangers Towards Subordinates. In Seifert, C. F. (ed.), *Journal of Applied Psychology*, 88(3), 36–47.

Yukl, G. A., Lepsinger, R. (2004). *Flexible Leadership.* San Francisco: Jossey-Bass.

Warnick, B., Inch, E. (1994). *Critical Thinking and Communication.* New York: Palgrave Macmillan.

Watson, S. (2010). *Reflective Leadership.* Retrieved from: www.trainingjournal.com/ [Accessed 14 March 2018.]

Whitmore, J. (2009). *Coaching for Performance. GROWing Human Potential and Purpose.* London: Nicolas Brealey Publishing.

Part III

Focus on Change and Innovation

6 Bridging the Process of Leading With Change and Innovation

Introduction

This chapter examines the process of forming and implementing change as one of the fundamental prerequisites to enhance any innovation in an organization. An overview will be given of key leadership theories which focus on change, creativity and innovation followed by a critical assessment of leadership as a central element of managing change.

As the business environment becomes more complex and is continuously changing, organizations need to be more flexible and alert. The dynamic external environment is a significant driver of change and innovation. Organizations can thrive in this environment if leaders and followers identify emerging patterns and seize opportunities presented by these external changes. Technology, economic conditions, labor conditions, social and cultural diversity have made significant influences on leadership in recent times where most organizations function under the high turbulence and uncertainty of their environment.

The main focus will be the *source of innovation and change* in organizations and consequently the *type of these changes and improvements* proposed by employees. The leading process focused on planning and implementing changes is defined. The research findings illustrate the main tasks of leadership that appear crucial to deal with the change continuum, emphasizing innovation and people as well as managing organizational complexity.

This section provides insights on how to implement the concept of Reflective Leadership in the process of leading change which can form an innovative environment in the organization.

The Need for Organizational Change

The managers we researched identified the significance and necessity of organizational change as one of their major challenges. One emerging insight highlights the idea that leading and changing organizations appears to be more difficult to achieve yet, in this innovation-driven era, it has become quite important. On the other hand, it has been pointed out by our respondents that radical changes have become a highly complex topic. It is rather difficult to understand their broad impact and almost impossible to deal with them systematically.

The famous author John Kotter (2014) discusses the issue of change in his most recent articles, stating that change and innovation are closely related and overlapping. He said that creating a culture of innovation cannot happen in the existing organizational environment if there is no willingness for taking risks, supporting creative thinking and acknowledging that there are various sources of innovation and change.

However, several authors (Kinicki and Fugate, 2012; Moorhead and Griffin, 2012; Eriksson-Zetterquist et al., 2011) identify the external and internal forces of change. These points of view are supported by facts and evidence of what the warning signals are that significantly pressure the organization to innovate. There were two groups of sources for change and improvements identified within the organizational ecosystem: the first group is represented by various external impulses coming from customers, business partners, the parent company or headquarters; and ideas gathered at international trade fairs and conferences.

The second group relates to internal sources of improvements which are provided by both senior employees who already have a more complex view as well as by junior employees who are searching for "smart solutions", mainly related to the implementation of various ICT forms.

When we observe the sources of changes, we can refer to the analysis of Dess et al. (2008) related to environmental scanning. This represents the essential activity of leaders and their teams of gathering information about trends in the external environment, which is mostly related to:

1. Stakeholder analysis: an assessment of the expectations, wants and needs of all parties that have an interest or stake in the organization.
2. Competitors' activities: knowledge of their products and services, methodologies through benchmarking and other information-gathering approaches.
3. Demographic changes: changes in age, ethnic composition, growth or decline of the population.
4. Social and lifestyle changes: women in the workforce, health and fitness awareness, erosion of educational standards, concern for the environment.
5. Technological changes: advances in and use of all forms of technology.
6. Economic changes: stock market indices, budget deficits, consumer spending patterns, inflation and interest rates, trade deficits and unemployment rates.
7. Legislative/regulatory and political changes: changes in criminal laws, environmental protection laws, deregulation, antitrust enforcement, laws protecting human rights and employment.

8. Global changes: economic alliances, economic development, changes in consumer tastes and preferences, international markets, and poverty and disease rates.

Hickman (2016) adds that the executive leadership team uses information from environmental scans to determine the organization's opportunities and threats along with its strengths and weakness. Based on this analysis, the managers identify the core competencies in the organization and evaluate whether there is a need for any change in the internal process.

Internal processes also require the introduction of change, which is painful to their employees and challenging to design and implement effectively. All members of the organization are caught up in change initiatives, and they are considered to be agents of change.

Change can take different forms in organizations. Several authors have introduced two essential perspectives of change. The first perspective of change sees the need for continuous improvement, and the second one describes change as a radical, system-wide effort (Hamel, 2000; Handy, 1989; Kanter, 1983; Burns, 1978).

The studying of incremental and radical changes is rather broad and general. We aimed to identify the specific features of change, its planning process as well as its implementation. We use more precise typology provided by Armstrong (2006), and in the cases we studied we observed examples of seven different types of changes: incremental, transformational, strategic, organizational, systems and processes, cultural and behavioral. In all of our case studies, we describe in more detail what specific change was formed and implemented based on interviewing top executives. A detailed description of all implemented changes has been developed. For instance:

1. Incremental: gradual change that happens in small steps, steady and progressive adaptation to new processes, systems or procedures (e.g. new distribution, marketing activities, redesign of the location, implementation of legislation changes, web presentation, etc.).
2. Transformational: ensures that the organization can develop and implement significant change programs that strategically respond to new demands, and may involve radical changes to the structure, culture and processes of the organization (e.g. mergers and acquisitions).
3. Strategic: concerned with broad, long-term and organization-wide issues, moving to a future state based on the strategic vision and scope (e.g. strategic partnerships, expansion into new markets, product diversification, franchising, licensing).
4. Organizational: changing the way the organization is functioning and how it is structured (e.g. changes in organizational structure, new positions, development and training of staff, job rotation).

5. Systems and processes: impacts working arrangements and practices (e.g. ICT implementation, new technology introduced, quality processes, logistics, product and process improvement).
6. Cultural: change in existing corporate culture; usually involves developing a more appropriate set of values that influence behavior and ensuring that employees live the values (e.g. setting up new values, fostering the responsibility and decision-making process, improving the working environment).
7. Behavioral: encouraging employees to be more effective by shaping and/or modifying the way in which they carry out their work (e.g. changes in managerial and employees' attitudes toward work).

The initial research on the process of planning and implementing change started in 2013 with the primary goal of identifying the specific types of change and highlighting the positive and negative impacts of the process of leading the change. An analysis of 123 case studies was conducted in 2013, 2014 and 2015 (using the same number of companies each year, 41, to evaluate trends). Various sectors were addressed as well different-sized enterprises. In 2013, there were 22 SMEs and 19 large companies from different industries: production (24), hospitality (4), financial (4), IT and telecommunication (5) and trading and other services (4).

In 2014, there were 21 SMEs and 20 big organizations with more than 500 employees in various industries: production (23), hospitality (5), financial (3), trade/shop (3), ICT (1), public sector (4) and others (2).

In 2015, the number of SMEs we researched that implemented some change increased to 29 organizations. The number of big companies observed decreased to 12. The following sectors were covered: production (12), services including the hospitality sector (11), financial (1), trading (7), ICT (4) and public sector (5). The broader variety within industries corresponds to the increased number of SMEs since hospitality, ICT and trading are the most common sectors among these types of organizations in the targeted region.

In Figure 6.1 the observed trends during the period from 2013 to 2015 and the typology of different changes is presented.

In the researched companies there were 55 changes implemented in 2013, followed by an increase of 15% with 63 changes in 2014 and an increasing of 38% in 2015, with 87 changes in total.

It has been observed that there are some interrelations between two fundamentally different types of change efforts: incremental and radical changes. In practice, there is often a scenario where small, incremental change is just the beginning of revolutionary and transformational change in the near future.

The critical milestone in our research strategy was achieved by the creation of the CRA method and its implementation in research in 2014 and 2015. This enables us to measure the importance of specific types of change for

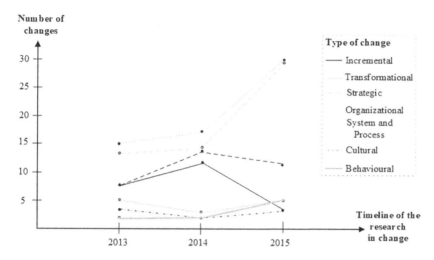

Figure 6.1 Typology and number of changes in 2013–2015
Source: Authors.

an organization's performance as well as evaluating the impact or improvement that the change caused. These outcomes are presented in Table 6.1 where types, number of changes and average improvement are provided. Every kind of change has a different level of importance. The information has been calculated as the average number gathered from all cases.

Since the number of observed organizations each year was 41, it seems that on average two changes were implemented per organization. The implementation of organizational changes increased most significantly, by 107%. The system and process type of change had the second highest increase, by 76%. This can be explained by the close relationship and mutual influence between these two types of changes. In some cases, system and process changes simultaneously enhance change in organizational design that could reflect the complex character of any change in the organization. Moreover, the highest results of achieved improvements were obtained in both years (2014, 2015) through behavioral changes and also through system and process changes.

A significant reduction appeared in the implementation of incremental changes in 2015. One of the reasons might be the growing importance of more complexity and a more systematic approach toward changes. Another explanation for the lower number of incremental changes relates to the origin of these changes. For example, a change in location or implementation of new legislation are not considered to be changes for many organizations, rather they are necessary reactions to various events happening in the external environment.

Table 6.1 Typology and results of the change implementation process

Type of Change	2014			2015			No. of Changes 2014/2015
	No. of Changes	Average Importance	Average Improvement (in scores)	No. of Changes	Average Importance	Average Improvement (in scores)	
Incremental	12	7.8	14.6	3	7.3	22.5	−9
Transformational	3	9.5	12	5	8.5	9.5	+2
Strategic	13	7.9	19.5	12	8.0	11.4	−1
Organizational	14	8.0	19	29	7.8	11.1	+15
System and process	17	8.4	25.6	30	7.7	18.2	+13
Cultural	2	6	19	3	8.25	12	+1
Behavioral	2	6.5	27.5	5	7.6	26.4	+3
Total	63			87			+24

Source: Authors.

Because the research was conducted over three years, the trend showing dynamism in the process of implementing changes and their importance for companies is visible. As presented in Figure 6.1, a significant increase occurred between 2014 and 2015 in system and process changes, which can reflect the impact of technology development and implementation of ICT in organizational processes. Organizational changes were very much linked to systems and processes, from designing new or modifying existing organizational structures, reduction of specific functions or creation of new job positions.

On the other hand, in the last year of our research, the highest average improvements (26.4 points) were obtained when behavioral changes were implemented. Contrary to this, the total number of behavioral changes (5) in each observed period was the second smallest. Cultural changes in both periods were the least implemented, followed by transformational changes.

Planning and implementation of this type of change requires more extensive preparation, and it is linked with the involvement of human resources and organizational culture. These types of changes are always associated with high resistance and proper action from leadership and are inevitable.

When we examined radical changes in our studied organizations, certain misunderstandings among the leaders occurred in the sense of how we should define radical change. Jarvenpaa and Stoddard's (1998) description of radical changes is those which rapidly unfold and alter underlying assumptions, business practices, culture and organizational structure. Our identified changes comply with this definition. However, there is a high level of identity crises, disorders and ambiguity associated with radical change. Again, it is somewhat debatable whether change in organizational structure could be considered radical. These changes are widespread; in most cases, they refer to small improvements in the existing corporate design or changing the authority in the current organizational chart. In other cases, such a change is influenced by the advancement of information technology; organizations generate more information and it circulates faster. Consequently, employees can respond more quickly to problems so that the organization can be more flexible to demands from other organizations, customers and competitors (Moorhead and Griffin, 2012).

Except for incremental changes, any other implemented changes have not increased improvements in 2015 compared to 2014. The expected improvements were assessed and evaluated by managers using the Critical Reflective Analysis matrix (see Appendix III). We discovered that the scope and importance of these changes and their implementation influence the whole organization and that leaders underestimated it. A reason for this, presented through the reflections of the leaders, was that when they were planning and implementing changes, their attention was given more to the content of the change rather than to working with their people to explain to them the purpose and meaning of the change and to understand their emotions. Managers' responses are a bit contradictory regarding how vital each type of change is to the overall performance of their organization (using a scale from 1 to 10). In 2014, the managers considered the most important type of change to be transformational change (9.5), followed by the system and process (8.5); the least importance was given to behavioral (6.5) and cultural (6.0) changes. In 2015 the differences between change importance were smaller. For instance, the significance of transformational changes was ranked 8.5 and cultural changes 8.25. All changes were considered and respondents gave them almost the same ranking of importance, from 7.3 to 8.5.

If we reflect on these results along with the individual improvements and increased number of changes in 2015, we can conclude that the importance of all types of changes for organizations has increased, but on the other hand, the expected improvements did not have better results.

Based on the Critical Reflection Analysis results that reflect the process and outcomes of change implementation, we can draw the following key findings and conclusions:

- Change is a fundamental necessity to succeed and provides continuing improvements to the organization.
- There is a growing trend to implement more complex system changes that are interrelated and create the "change continuum" paradigm.
- Successful implementation of more complex and systematic changes depends on an appropriate leading process with a strong focus on change actors.

The implementation of change is composed of both the attributes of a process that is developed as step-by-step actions and relations between leader and followers. Synthesis of the previously discussed research findings brought us to examine the specific leaders' understandings of *what* their role is and *how* they can develop human potential.

The father of change management, Harvard professor John Kotter, claims that the central issue around change is never strategy, structure, culture or systems. He sees the core of this matter in changing the behavior of people. Behavioral change happens mostly by speaking to people's feelings, and that is considered to be the core task for leaders (Beerel, 2009).

Organizations today are encouraged to adapt and change to an unprecedented degree: leaders need to make decisions more quickly, and employees are required to be more flexible and able to accept new opportunities.

Any change is associated with the people's fear and resistance to change even in situations where crisis or beneficial innovations are justified. There are multiple reasons to be resistant to change, as identified by Yukl (2009):

1. Lack of trust: distrust of the people who propose the change.
2. The belief that change is unnecessary: satisfaction with the status quo and no clear evidence of severe problems with the current way of doing things.
3. A belief that change is not feasible: a view that the change is unlikely to succeed, too tricky or likely to fail, like some previous efforts.
4. Economic threats: fear that the change may benefit the organization but result in personal loss of income, benefits or job security.
5. Relative high costs: the concern that the cost of change may be higher than the benefits due to injury of resources already invested in the current approach or loss of performance as employees learn the new procedures and debug the new system.
6. Fear of personal failure: organizational members' reluctance to abandon known skills or expertise and their insecurity about mastering new ways of doing things.
7. Loss of status and power: fear of shifts in power for individuals or subunits that may result in loss of status in the organization.
8. A threat to values and ideals: resistance to change that appears incompatible with personal values or strongly held values embedded in the organization's culture.
9. Resentment of interference: the opposition of individuals to perceived control, manipulation or forced change by others in situations where they have no choice or voice in the transition.

These issues related to resistance to change and coping with the whole process of change adoption by employees are the tasks for leaders. Based on our findings, because of the importance leaders placed on cultural (6.0) and behavioral (6.5) changes, it can be concluded that they do not consider the resistance of employees as an essential priority.

From our discussions and reflection analysis conducted with managers, several reasons were identified why some changes did not deliver the expected results or why improvements did not reach the expected level:

- Overestimation of the people's understanding of the content of change.
- Too much emphasis given to the content of change rather than to people's emotions.
- Lack of discussion about the expected impacts on current people's position or work.
- Previous negative experience with unsuccessful change implementation.
- Lack of cooperation between departments across the organization.

The Process of Leading Change

The interaction between the types of changes and the need for a process-relational-based leadership approach is shown in Figure 6.2. In the case

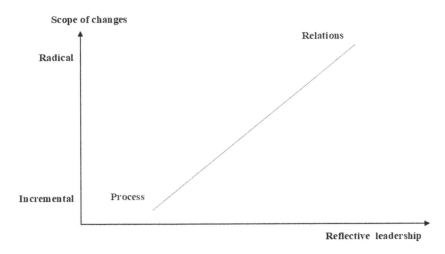

Figure 6.2 Linkage between changes and process-relational approach
Source: Authors.

of incremental changes, more emphasis is given to establishing and implementing new processes quickly (e.g. use of anew ICT software or tool), improvement of existing processes to make them more efficient or substituting existing products or services. The importance of understanding the social impacts and relational aspects grows when implementing radical changes (e.g. any adaptation or organizational change).

The system view of organizations makes assumptions that the organizational systems which are most alert to signals from the external environment and thus manage to change in reply to those signals are most the likely to survive. Many such demands from the external environment foster significant changes in internal organizational operations, which are considered to be radical, usually referred to as structural changes or a system-wide rearrangement of task division and authority and reporting relationships. Structural changes are divided into two main types, technological and adaptive change. Adaptive change is related to the change of values, culture and behavior; therefore, it requires leadership action to minimize resistance to change and increase general understanding and involvement among employees.

The process of leading change consists of two parts: the process of forming change and the process of change implementation. The qualitative research conducted in 2013–2015 enables us to observe what managers do well regarding planning and implementing any change successfully. The research findings are presented in Table 6.2, where key pros and cons in the process of designing change have been highlighted.

Table 6.2 Process of planning change

Pros	Cons and Barriers
• Supportive management which persuades about the need for change. • Awareness of the change necessity among the management at every hierarchical level. • Visibility of management support within specific actions such as delegating competencies, assigning responsible persons, allocating financial resources, incorporating change into the strategic plan, elaborating the guidelines for change assessment and using ICT in the development of the communication flow. • Breaking down complex transformational change into partial plans and specific projects. • Using and learning from best practices from the external and internal environment. • Developing and following the general guidelines and procedures where step-by-step actions, responsibilities and competencies within the organization are addressed. • Analysis of the external and internal environment conducted by the team (which consists of experts from different disciplines). • Defining key performance indicators (KPIs) and evaluating them before and after the change. • Two-way communication (i.e. top down as well as bottom up). • Planning the change within the context of existing processes and organizational systems (ISO, TQM, BSC, etc.); not developing many entirely new and untested methods. • Creation of new positions such as change manager or project manager. • Utilizing experienced leaders from previous processes of change.	• Disagreement among top management. • Change is not communicated clearly with lower managerial positions; their understanding of the importance of change is neglected. • If the internal communication channel is not established, the employees receive the information from external sources which might mislead them and cause misunderstanding, which can end with the employees' frustration and fear about the change content. • Communication with the public is often forgotten; society develops its own perspective and view. • The impact of the change on the organizational culture is postponed or not analyzed; very often the effect of radical change on organizational culture is underestimated. • A conscious or unconscious focus of the top management on particular features rather than seeing the big picture and core issues that will cause the main problems. • Insufficient allocation of all resources. • One-way communication (i.e. top down only). • Limited aim of the transformational change for cost reduction rather than planning for sustainable development and improvement of the competitive position of the company. • Insufficient analysis of the internal and external environment and lack of strategic thinking.

Source: Authors.

Global research in change management was conducted by PROSCI (2014), where 822 organizations worldwide were studied and their best practices were observed. The benchmark report shows what the most common mistakes by managers and supervisors are in times of change. The top five errors in managing the change process were identified by participants as follows:

1. Lack of visible support and involvement; assuming employees would automatically embrace and engage in the change without encouragement and assuming that a project team was responsible for communication and engagement surrounding the change.
2. Failing to understand or listen to employees' concerns; a forum for employee questions, concerns and feedback was not instituted.
3. Insufficient communication to impacted employees: communications were unclear regarding change details, context, drivers, impacts, business cases and benefits.
4. Resisting change by managers: via publicly expressing negative messages about change, indicating to employees that the change was not essential or would not last and deliberately withholding information.
5. Weak and inconsistent leadership, lack of coaching, feedback and supporting of employees throughout the change process.

Due to an absolute absence of conceptual theory that emphasizes the complexity of leadership, we are looking at those areas that represent the essential outcomes of leadership. The expected results of leadership actions are associated with fostering innovation and change, setting the future direction for the organization and encouraging human resources toward their development and higher performance. These required commitments of the leaders are very complex and can be fulfilled through various processes that relate to and overlap each other.

As we have already discussed in Chapter 4, the organization is seen as a system where processes related to leadership focus on developing human potential and thus contribute to the successful performance of the organization. When we use grounded theory to analyze how organizations are dealing with current challenges, an absolute contradiction occurs here. Even though respondents acknowledge the importance of focusing on innovation and establishing new leadership approaches oriented more on people, in some organizations the traditional approach still exists. The system view in most organizations is missing, therefore leaders are struggling to combine two dimensions: innovation/change process and people focus.

Although there is no one approach or model to choose to successfully lead change, our process-relational-based approach is trying to cover the context of leading change and how to communicate with people in order to successfully cope with the process of change. It is based upon the premise that leaders should focus on people's strengths and aspirations rather than on problems and what people are doing wrong. It recognizes that people are most often their own best experts of the circumstances of their own lives, and that their strengths and capacities are the most powerful catalysts for change. It is they who will be affected by the change and who need to be the shared co-owners of that change.

In our research, the second partial process of leading change related to the implementation phase was examined. In Table 6.3 the most significant observations are presented.

While the strengths approach acknowledges that it is crucial to seek expertise, it cautions that sometimes leaders can use power over others, either deliberately or inadvertently, assuming to know not only what is

Table 6.3 Process of implementing change

Pros	Cons and Barriers
• Creating a detailed implementation plan and being consistent with its fulfillment. • Continuous information flow is well established and performed. • Two-way feedback process: providing and receiving feedback is a mechanism to assess and evaluate milestones. • Involvement of all business units and their shared understanding that "we are all in the same boat". • Collecting partial positive achievements and also negative implications related to change (labor reduction, financial cuts on bonuses, etc.). • New and modified procedures have to be explained and the implementation checked. • Continuous development of human resources and training for new jobs or tasks (before, during and after the change is implemented). • Extensive use of various ICT tools to establish internal and external communication with all stakeholders. • Developing and implementing the adaptation plan for all generations. • Modifying or providing new job descriptions; clarifying responsibilities and competencies. • Establishing regular meetings where the fulfillment of partial goals is presented and further actions agreed to. • Being prepared to change the key people and appoint new positions if necessary.	• Nonexistence of a detailed action plan and lack of control. • Partial changes are not connected, interrelated issues and their sequence have not been considered or evaluated. • Misunderstandings over the crucial importance of the organizational culture and the role of human acceptance of the change. • Awareness that standardized and traditional habits and approaches are difficult to change fast; it requires patience and a well-planned communication process. • An absence of a communication plan. • Feedback conducted only one-way (i.e. only from managers to employees).

Source: Authors.

best for others but also about other people's experience, capabilities and skills. This traditional leadership approach, called the power-over attitude, reflects a hierarchical role of leadership that fundamentally disrespects and disempowers people. It can be easily used as an instrument for creating passive dependence, keeping people "in their place", assigning blame and framing people as resistant or uncooperative. This concept has significant obstacles to being successfully implemented in the organizational environment where frequent implementation of various changes and innovation play a crucial role in being successful competitors.

When thinking about leading change as one of the main expectations of what leaders should deliver to the organization, our process-relational-based approach might be a bit confrontational. It explicitly counters the prevailing traditional image of strong leadership with an alternative set of propositions:

- Leadership is a function that is realized within the complexity of an organizational context and reflects all processes conducted in organizational systems.
- The purpose of the leading process is the creation and maintenance of effective, respectful and sustainable change.
- Everyone in every team is, should be and can be an agent of change; that is, involved in leadership.
- The success of any change depends on the ability of individuals to understand the purpose and meaning of change and a willingness to adopt a new behavior.

Change-Driven Organizations and the Role of Leadership

The significance of organizational change is self-evident in times when a large percentage of change projects have failed to deliver the desired outcomes, and the business environment has become more and more adapted to continuous change and unpredictability. This can be confirmed by one of the findings from our initial research, obtained by implementing grounded theory when analyzing the research question, "Which external and internal challenges make an impact on leaders' work?"

This research is supported by facts and evidence, provide a warning that there is significant pressure on organizations. These new realities are examined in the strategic planning process, which is one of the core tasks of leaders. This can be confirmed by our research findings where managers identified "a change in the strategic planning process with more focus on innovation and people is needed".

The research question was raised during our interviews: "What are the sources for change and improvements in surveyed organizations?" Through our coding analysis, we have identified two sources of change and improvements.

An *internal source* of improvements was identified, including experienced senior employees and junior employees with higher education and IT skills who contributed considerably to enhancements. Here we can mention that internationally based companies share their changes and improvements (via electronic systems) with other manufacturing plants worldwide. At the same time, companies calculate the costs of each innovation and how the innovation can decrease current costs. After introducing the innovations, they analyze their impact on the environment or safety.

One CEO gave an example of the improvements proposed by employees from the printing industry:

> *I would highlight mainly the changes in the production process (book printing). Employees proposed a new process of ink drying (which was necessary to shorten). New materials for printing are tested which is not possible without experienced printers. They (technicians) are also proposing how to reach the most effective parameters of machines when we talk about their speed and productivity. We have implemented Kaizen—ongoing improvements in the production.*

The *external source* of improvements for companies is its customers and business partners, as well as information from international conferences, fair trade and mother companies. As an example of improvement, we can mention the suppliers of car producers who proposed new "strategic materials" (colors and adhesives, use of high-tensile-strength steel for cars to improve their characteristics and consequently the car's performance). In some cases, competitors also give new incentives to companies to move forward to survive in the market.

Through our coding process, we identified *two main groups of changes and improvements proposed by employees*: *improvements based on digitalization* of all processes (mainly production, accounting, customer service) and with it, the accompanying training focusing on people (customer service improvement and communication) and employees (teamwork and leadership, workplace). Young employees generally have better IT skills, and they propose changes using cloud services, new apps or software. Because of these changes, companies save time, costs and often reduce repetitive procedures. The second group of changes is focused on *the improvement of working conditions and relations* (reconstruction and redesigning of working space), relations in teams (employees proposed new teambuilding activities) and teamwork (employees suggested the optimization of task tracking in the CEE region), and changes in leadership style (from autocratic to more liberal).

The managers we interviewed agreed that every new idea, every improvement, is encouraged in their organization.

One of our principles is the ongoing improvement "Invent and simplify". According to this approach, we support employees to propose new ideas, improvements. We have a special program— "Innovator"—many improvements are from daily activities.

(PR manager, retail industry)

When an organization needs a change, expectations of leadership action are often a key topic. Leaders are expected to communicate the vision and mobilize the capacity for change. Since the focus of this monograph is on the process of leading rather than describing the capabilities of successful leaders, the leadership approach to change creation and its implementation is defined in the next few sections.

As organizational design becomes less hierarchical because the digital influence is moving toward a more democratic and flat structure, the process of leading change involves groups of employees from all levels of an organization. Employees, under the guidance of suitable leadership, can participate in planning and implementing large-scale organizational change and thus create an organization characterized by flexibility and continuous learning. Given the rapidly changing environment in which organizations operate, there is little doubt that the leadership's ability to guide and manage change successfully needs to be a core competency for organizations.

When we refer to findings from grounded theory analyzing how leaders are addressing challenges, the importance of active and open communication systems was observed. Communication in continuously changing environments is highly essential. Organizations need to facilitate dialogue within and across groups to sustain the free flow of information, diversity of ideas, high levels of cooperation and substantive involvement in decision making.

Some of the authors already presented focus on the role of dialogue and communication within this changing stage (Ford and Ford, 1995; Jabri, 2004; Kellet, 1999; McDaniel, 1997), and their work provides summarizing key guidelines and characteristics:

- Building relationships within and across the organization and creating trans-organizational relationships develops networks and achieves creativity, innovation and shared meaning.
- Dialogue provides a database for collective thinking and creates a thoughtful exchange, generate mutual understanding and facilitates discussion of issues people care about.
- A process of reflective questioning relies on our ability to listen, value others and address deep issues.
- Dialogue is a meaningful approach for developing a vision and mission statement jointly, understanding what needs to change and how the change aligns with other factors in an organization.

As we stress the importance of dialogue within the relational approach, there are two sides to it. According to Kellet (1999), dialogue encourages a diversity of ideas on what critical actions are for continuous change in organizations. Diversity brings both conflict and multiple voices to be heard.

Implementation of the Reflective Leadership Model in the Process of Change

The organization is not only responding to external forces which impose change internally, but it also anticipates it, prepares for its planning process and incorporates it in an organizational strategy. Lewin defined organizational change through more dynamic perspectives that also provide some concepts, tools and techniques for leading the change process. Lewin (1951) is best known for his "force field analysis", a method which described change as a planned process. He saw a change as a multistage process in a social field, moving from the present level to a desired one. He analyzed the dynamics in change processes by identifying the drivers for and resistance to change. He proposed a change processes through successive phases of "unfreezing", "change" and "refreezing", referring to the psychological determinants of change rather those external factors that trigger change within organizations.

Lewin's previous work provided a foundation for other related models developed by other authors. Kanter et al. (1992) and Kotter (1996) see the purpose of the unfreezing stage as establishing a sense of urgency and identifying the crisis. This stage involves discussing the current or potential crisis and defining significant opportunities that may galvanize or inspire change.

According to Hickman (2016), both crisis and opportunity can create revitalized momentum in an organization, especially when members of the organization acknowledge them. Many people fear and resist change, feeling a high level of uncertainty, and can refuse the new state.

The organizational "status quo" is one of the main obstacles to overcome for leaders. When people are satisfied with current practices and procedures, they may have little or no interest in making changes. The question is how to explain to people that the process of continuous improvements should be the main driver for every member of the organization. The main factor in the unfreezing stage is making employees understand the importance of change and how their jobs will be affected by it. Creating awareness of the need for change in employees is the responsibility of the leadership of the organization (Moorhead and Griffin, 2012).

The model which relates the most to our system approach is the System Model of Change, defined by Kinicki and Fugate (2012). It is based on the notion that any change has a cascading effect through the organization.

A system model of change offers a framework to use for diagnosing what to change and how to evaluate the success of the change effort. There are four main components: inputs, strategic plans, target elements of change and outputs.

The organization is an open system where it tries to adapt and reflect its environment. The open system view of change emphasizes the following aspects:

- Change in a system requires an understanding of the entire system and how different parts of the system influence each other.
- Change in a system involves understanding of the environment and the adaptive processes needed to survive.
- Change in a system requires an understanding of organizations as basic feedback systems, where information is processed and used in a managerial process. Change should be viewed as a structured process where data is fed into the change process from the beginning to the final evaluation of the change effort.
- Change in a system requires an understanding of the point of entry (i.e. the origin of the change attempt), which could be a managerial decision or any event that triggers a change effort (Eriksson-Zetterquist et al., 2011).

The limitations of Lewin's model are due to its simplicity, which can make it difficult to convert into specific actions of leaders. Therefore, we refer to Kotter's fundamental model of leading change, which provides some guidelines on how to approach such a process. Kotter's Eight Steps for Leading Change (1996) offers suggestions on how to communicate the change progress effectively and what the expected benefits are of such a process.

We have applied the Reflective Leadership Model to Kotter's fundamental process of leading change to show how close these models are. The important similarities and overlap between these two models are presented in Figure 6.3. The process which frames the Reflective Leadership Model corresponds to the main steps of Kotter's process of leading change. We analyze those processes and compare them with crucial questions which were raised to international leaders to assess and evaluate their leadership actions.

The *Process of Continuity* reflects the importance of the current situation, analyzing past successes and foreseeing the future. This process represents the starting point of every change. When conducting change, it requires that all involved members have a clear picture of where the change is taking them. The question "Do I understand the big picture?" addresses the ability of the leader to reflect on the external environment that affects the organization and what has to be considered. People in an organization need a sense of purpose when they see how and what has

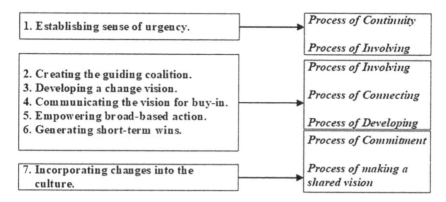

Figure 6.3 Overlapping Kotter's model and the Reflective Leadership Model
Source: Authors on the basis of Kotter (1996).

to be done. It is essential for leaders at the very early stages to realize the defenses between people. However insignificant it might appear, everyone wants to contribute or at least to have a vision about the future. Our researched leaders reached the highest scores of 59 on average in this process, even though they are still 8 points below the standard 77. Here the maximum value (in the range of 95–99) was achieved by three leaders.

The *Process of Involving* starts a dialogue, and various points of view are exchanged. As already mentioned, this debate can cause some conflicts, but still it is essential to have diverse personalities. Different perceptions of change are a valuable resource to generate variety to overcome difficulties and predict some problematic issues at the very beginning of the change process. One of the questions raised related to this process was "Do I give and receive feedback?" Feedback is a dialogue: a two-way learning process. We were rather surprised that in this process, which immediately followed the process with the highest scores, leaders admitted to having the lowest value with only 44 points on average. It was the biggest gap between the leader's score (average among 77 leaders) and the standard value of 79. This was the highest standard value defined because we believe that feedback is a technique that is commonly used by leaders. The explanation for this finding can be based on an observation that leaders know what feedback is, but they are not very familiar with how to use it. Another obstacle for them is the fact that constructive and useful feedback consists of two-way flow: to give feedback and also to receive it. How many leaders are asking for feedback from their subordinates? Among all assessments conducted for this question, there were also the lowest values in the maximum (80) and minimum (15) scores.

The debate continues to the stage when change starts to be implemented. This is crucial for building the relationship between leaders and followers, which enhances the mutual trust between them. This is the main focus of the *Process of Connecting*, which fosters the social relationships where trust, reciprocity and shared values are built. Change is never value-free. It is always necessary to identify the values that are implied in what may seem to be a simple technological or structural adjustment. The question "Do I think about what is going on?" ranked with a trend value of 52 compared to the standard value of 67.

The *Process of Developing* is a third crucial process in the stage where change is still led and leaders need to cope with resistance and people's difficulties in accepting the new situation. Very often they are asked to learn new skills or acquire new expertise. The question addressing this process, "Do you share information and knowledge?", reflects the leader's ability to establish a network for new knowledge sharing, which contributes to individual and team development. We were not surprised by the average result of 54, with the smallest difference of only 11 points compared to the standard level. It confirms that most of the researched subjects still perform more like managers than leaders. Therefore, this question was given a weight of 6 for its impact on the successful leadership process. On the other hand, we can also comment that providing information to followers is made mainly in one direction, and this corresponds to a lack of feedback with two-way dialogue.

The third stage in the change process is connected with change implementation in the *Process of Commitment*, with leaders emphasizing what should be needed to make the change process clear to everyone. It is important that change is specified with measurements of progress or completion. The important question asked in this part should be "Do I evaluate process and progress both in a quantitative and qualitative way?" Our research findings showed that leaders are not dedicated enough to establish such measurements as evidence of change results. In this question, their score was the second lowest 48 (average value) with the second smallest gap (–27) compared to the standard level. However, this part of the leading action was given the highest impact weight of 10. Providing quantitative and also qualitative assessment requires developing such a system and implementing it into all organizational processes of change. The lack of this procedure is evident from the negative results based on the CRA when the implementation of changes grew by 38%, and improvements were not higher in absolute number between the two studied periods of 2014 and 2015 (see Table 6.1).

The final process is called the *Process of making a shared vision*, where the focus is on developing a common concept. This action requires time for reflection, sharing, seeing one's individual role in the new situation and clear understanding. The question "Do I design simple and clear systems?" refers to the leader's ability to develop a system which is an organized collection of actions. Systems organize things that are critical to the team's work. Because of their importance, systems need to be clear, purposeful and consistent. Based on the reflection of respondents, their average score was 49, which is 13 points below the standard (62). Although a few leaders gave themselves 95 points, there was also the lowest minimum score (10). The lowest weight of 5 was given for this question.

Change permeates every aspect of organizational life, making long-term stability an artifact of the past. That's why, for most organizations, the ability to change is among the few remaining long-term competitive advantages. To be change focused, organizations need to have leaders who can develop change-capable people. Based on the results of our longitudinal research and several consulting assignments in practice, we implement the Reflective Leadership Model in the process of leading change. It is a useful tool for leaders to build the confidence and flexibility of their employees toward constant organizational change. The implementation of the Reflective Leadership Model in the change process (see Figure 6.4) enlarges the original model with an additional three functions that lead change and emphasize the leadership task of developing change capability in the organization.

The six fundamental processes of the Reflective Leadership Model (creating continuity, involving, connecting, developing, creating commitment,

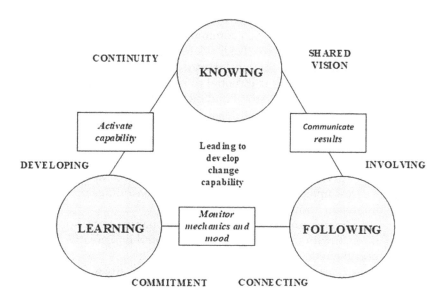

Figure 6.4 Reflective Leadership Model in the process of leading change
Source: Authors.

and shared vision) are implemented in the process of leading to enhance the change capability in an organization.

The specific actions when developing change capability as the prerequisite for any innovation are proposed. The framework of the L-K-F-L model (Figure 5.5) overlaps those particular tasks of leading the change process and are as follows:

LEARNING: *Activate capability* focuses on the central practices that point out external realities and activate change capability inside of an organization:

- Expand the awareness of business realities to help people see the need for change and motivate the focused effort.
- Spotlight strengths and successes to generate confidence and momentum and diffuse pessimism.
- Embrace experimentation to foster an environment that allows for high levels of involvement and learning.
- Encourage meaningful commitment to build a sense of ownership, make better decisions and bring better results.

KNOWING: *Communicate results* emphasizes the creation of dynamic dialogue that promotes action and results:

- Provide information to others about change at the right time and in a form that works for them. Employees want the correct information, and this unit shows how to capture their hearts as well as their minds when communicating.
- Encourage constructive feedback to know what people think and feel about change. Straightforward dialogue is central to change results; therefore, it is essential to know firsthand how provided information is understood and interpreted.

FOLLOWING: *Monitor mechanics and mood* establishes the commitment to making change happen and to make the transition process successful.

- Make progress clear to all by creating a system of regular small progress updates and reality checks that encourage open, candid discussion about development.
- Coordinate resources that support the change effort: how to stay in touch with changing resource needs and find creative ways to meet them.
- Revisit systems, practices and policies to identify any that hinder progress and act to adjust or replace them.
- Respond to resistance by applying various managerial techniques (coaching, critical thinking, feedback, mentoring, etc.) to create conditions that reduce resistance and encourage commitment to change.

The most successful leaders have been characterized as perpetual learners. The explanation for this is that knowing how to lead people is a skill that can be learned; the leader's work is under the influence of continuous changes and new situations which, now more than ever, require new and creative decision-making skills; and the final argument is that good leaders coach their followers toward higher performance results and self-realization.

To be change capable, the organization needs leaders who can develop the change focus, and capable people who can lead the process from the realization for the need for change, activating new ideas and transforming them in new and innovative ways. The success of every change initiative depends on individuals who are willing to adopt new behaviors and a new proposed vision.

Conclusion

This chapter focused on two main investigations. The first focus was given to observing the process of forming and implementing changes in various sectors. Moreover, the use of the Critical Reflection Analysis provided an opportunity to assess and evaluate the type of changes and what improvements have been obtained. Over a three-year period, there was an increase in the implementation of all specific types of radical changes (transformational, strategic, organizational, system and process, cultural and behavioral). On the other hand, steady improvements did not correspond to the trend of change dynamism. The increased number of changes brought smaller impacts to an organization. Moreover, the number of incremental changes in studied period has been decreased.

The second research focus was to identify the source of innovation and change in organizations and consequently the types of changes and improvements proposed by employees.

As a result of our coding, we identified two sources of change and improvements. The first one, an internal source, was represented by experienced senior employees and junior employees with higher education and good IT skills. The second group, the external source of improvements for companies, was their customers, business partners, information from international conferences, fair trade and mother companies. In some cases, there were also competitors who gave new impulses to companies to move forward to survive in the market. This was somewhat visible in the IT or polygraphic industry.

Based on our coding process, we identified two main groups of changes and improvements proposed by employees. First, improvements based on digitalization of all processes (mainly production, accounting, customer service) and with it, the accompanying training focusing on people (customer service improvement, communication, workplace, teamwork and leadership). The second group of enhancements was focused on the improvement of working conditions, relations in team and teamwork and changes in leadership style (from autocratic to more liberal).

We can conclude that most of the changes contributed by different groups of people (employees, customers, suppliers, etc.) are incremental ones. When radical change is formed and planned to be successfully implemented, then collective action of leaders and their followers is needed. Kotter's process of leading change has been studied across diverse organizations. The best practices gathered through research contributed to the implementation of the Reflective Leadership concept into the process of leading change. The six principles of creating continuity, involving, connecting, developing, creating commitment, and shared vision offer guidelines for a leader to enhance change and innovation.

Bibliography

Armstrong, M. (2006). A *Handbook of Management Technique: A Comprehensive Guide to Achieving Managerial Excellence and Improved Decision-Making.* London: Kogan Press.

Astrom, K. J., Murray, R. M. (2008). *Feedback Systems: An Introduction for Scientists and Engineers.* Princeton, NJ: Princeton University Press.

Beerel, A. (2009). *Leadership and Change Management.* London: Sage.

Burns, J. M. (1978). *Leadership.* New York: Harper & Row.

Dess, G. G., Lumpkin, G. T., Eisner, A. B. (2008). *Strategic Management: Creating Competitive Advantage.* New York: McGrow-Hill Irwin.

Eriksson-Zetterquist, U., Mullern, T., Styhre, A. (2011). *Organization Theory. A Practice—Based Approach.* New York: Oxford University Press.

Ford, J. D., Ford, I. W. (1995). The Role of Conversations in Producing Intentional Change in Organizations. *Academy of Management Review*, 20(3), 541–570.

Hamel, G. (2000). Resource Attraction. *Executive Excellence*, 17(8), 3–4.

Handy, C. (1989). *The Age of Unreason.* Boston: Harvard Business School Press.

Handy, C. (2014). The Shamrock Organization. *Business Strategy Review*, 25(4), 81–81.

Hickman, G. R. (2016). *Leading Organizations: Perspectives for a New Era.* London: Sage.

Jabri, M. (2004). Team Feedback Based on Dialogue: Implications for Change Management. *Journal of Management Development*, 23(2), 141–151.

Jarvenpaa, S. L., Stoddard, D. B. (1998). Business Process Redesign: Radical and Evolutionary Change. *Journal of Business Research*, 1998, 41(1), 15–27.

Kanter, R. M. (1983). The Change Masters. *Human Resource Management*, 22(3), 313–317.

Kanter, R. M., Stein, B. A., Jick, T. D. (1992). *The Challenge of Organizational Change: How Companies Experience It and Leaders Guide It.* New York: Free Press.

Kellet, P. M. (1999). Dialogue and Dialectics in Managing Organizational Change: The Case of a Mission-Based Transformation. *Southern Communication Journal*, 64(3), 211–213.

Kinicki, A., Fugate, M. 2012. *Organizational Behavior*. New York: McGraw-Hill.

Kotter, J. (1996). *Leading Change*. Boston: Harvard Business School Press.

Kotter, J. (2014). *Strategy Acceleration Tool*. Boston: Kotter International Inc.

Lewin, K. (1951). *Field Theory in Social Science. Selected Theoretical Papers*. New York: Harper.

McDaniel, R. R. (1997). Strategic Leadership: A View from Quantum and Chaos Theories. *Health Care Management Review*, 22(1), 21–37.

Monge, P., Contractor, N. (2003). *Theories of Communication Networks*. New York: Oxford University Press.

Moorhead, G., Griffin, R. W. (2012). *Managing Organizational Behavior*. South-Western: Cengage Learning.

PROSCI. (2014). Best Practices in Change Management. Benchmarking report. Prosci Inc.

Yukl, G. A. (2009). Leading Organizational Learning: Reflection on Theory and Research. *The Leadership Quarterly*, 20(1), 49–53.

Yukl, G. A., McDonald, R. A. (2003). Effect of Multisource Feedback and a Feedback Facilitator on the Influence Behaviour of Managers Towards Subordinates. In Seifert, C. F. (ed.), *Journal of Applied Psychology*, 88(3), 57–63.

7 Reframing Current Leadership Approaches to Include Diversity

Introduction

Different views on diversity exist around the globe due to different historical backgrounds and experiences among societies and geographical regions. For a number of traditionally multicultural European countries, such as the United Kingdom or Belgium, or outside Europe, such as Australia, the topic of diversity is commonly understood. Nevertheless, diversity has not been widely discussed yet in countries like Slovakia (as well as in other CEE countries which experienced the similar historical experience of transition from a centralized planning to a market economy at the end of the 20th century), which is also recognized as homogenous with respect to race, religion and ethnicity. The perception and understanding of the core aspects of diversity occurred after the 1990s, when foreign direct investments appeared to a larger extent in CEE countries. Globalization and internationalization of business has diversity as a core managerial competency. The increased number of foreign workers at all organizational levels has opened the issues of cultural differences and how to manage this type of team. At that point in Slovakia, diversity was mainly emphasized on cultural dimensions; other aspects related to age, social context, educational background or race were omitted.

In this chapter, we will concentrate on various diversities in organizations. Moreover, the influence of diversity on business will be analyzed—more precisely, the contribution of diversity to innovation and creativity.

The four-layered diversity model will be presented in order to explore diversity features in the organizations we researched. In this chapter, we follow the broader understanding of diversity which is based not only on demographic features but also includes informational differences, reflecting a person's education and experience, values and goals. This was influenced by the specificity of the CEE region which was rather isolated in the second half of the 20th century. As a result, a different perception of diversity was formed in these countries. In addition, we wanted to find out how organizations perceive diversity, and moreover if a positive or negative perception prevails. Currently, various generations are represented in the workplace, each with its own values and priorities. This provides a unique opportunity to increase productivity, creativity, problem solving and learning.

Finally, the role of leadership in supporting innovation and creativity will be examined.

The Complexity and Ambiguity of Diversity

Diversity is rather complex, consisting of a number of factors and characteristics. In order to obtain a more complex overview and understanding of diversity, there are several definitions and levels of diversity. We will mention a few of them (which fit the focus of the research provided) to understand a number of factors and characteristics that diversity covers and its impact on organizations. The existence of various approaches to diversity (described below) create certain ambiguities and consequently raise difficulties in using this term in different contexts. When focusing on diversity from the business point of view, the related challenge is not only to acknowledge the existence of diversity in the workplace but also to establish the conditions in which every employee can perform and develop.

The ambiguity of the diversity concept is also present in the 28 EU member states, where diversity is understood differently depending on the context. We can highlight the most frequently used understandings of diversity:

- Diversity as "a new concept" means inclusion, tolerance, non-discrimination and an equivalent to "plurality".
- Diversity is directly associated with disadvantaged groups who are at higher risk of discrimination (e.g. immigrants, elderly people, ethnic minorities, women or sexual minorities).
- Diversity in traditionally "homogenous countries" (in our case the CEE countries) represents a certain equivalent in the meaning of "cosmopolitanism" and tolerance toward others (e.g. religion, national traditions) and could represent a certain national dilemma.
- Diversity as multiculturalism (or racial/ethnic diversity) is important in strategies for integration of foreigners, mainly in making some minorities visible, and is materialized (e.g. in language education). However, it can also be an obstacle for social cohesion and equal opportunities.

Historically, many organizations relied on the similarity-attraction paradigm. This resulted in the claim that homogeneous teams are likely to be more effective than diverse teams because of the mutual attraction of similar members. Diverse teams were expected to be less productive and cohesive because of misunderstandings and tensions among team members. Increasingly, in recent years, organizations are learning to value diversity. Diversity can provide a powerful competitive advantage. Mainstream research confirms the benefits of diversity (e.g. Craig and Kelly, 1999; Kurtzberg, 2005); however, some researchers remain skeptical (Tsui et al., 1992; Rothman et al., 2003).

According to the cognitive resource diversity theory, diversity should enhance organizational performance by bringing more perspectives and a wider range of knowledge to bear on problems, increasing creativity and decision-making effectiveness. Leaders have been trying to increase diversity in teams to achieve the benefits of innovation and fresh ideas. The common underlying belief in companies is that diversity has more positive than negative connotation for them.

> *In our company, diversity is perceived as something enriching. We experience mainly age, ethnicity (different nations) and gender diversity. Diversity is about mutual respect. We are from a different environment, learning from each other; this is enriching for us.*
>
> (PR manager, retail industry)

Broader Understanding of Diversity

Although historically *diversity* focused on demographic differences (McGrath et al., 1995), now it encompasses "deeper" or unobservable attributes (Milliken and Martins, 1996) including cultural (Wrench, 2002), technical and cognitive differences. Similarly, Loden and Rosener (1991) highlighted not only primary dimensions (e.g. age, ethnicity, sexual orientation and physical abilities) but also secondary dimensions (e.g. educational background, income, marital status and beliefs) of diversity.

To develop the broader understanding of diversity mentioned above, Gardenswartz and Rowe (2003) proposed a model with four layers of diversity. This approach has influenced and broadened the conversation about diversity. It offers a more complex view of diversity reflecting each person's reality in the organization. The central part of this model (at the first level) focuses on the personality. The second level, internal dimensions, includes age, gender, race, sexual orientation, ethnicity and physical ability. The third level includes external dimensions of a person, such as geographic location, income, personal habits, recreational habits, religion, educational background, work experience, appearance, parental status and marital status. The fourth (outer) layer examines the organizational dimensions incorporating work content, such as division/department unit/group, seniority, work location, union affiliation, management status and functional level/classification.

The creators of the model believe that "a work team has always been diverse" (Gardenswartz and Rowe, 2003) with regard to individual differences (of each team member) and uniqueness. However, they tried to examine how task and relationship issues need to be adapted to ensure goal accomplishment when team composition is diverse. Regardless of the numerous diversities such as work experience, position in the organization, cultural dissimilarities involving language and ethnicity, or some of the less changeable diversities such as age and race, one thing is clear. They believed that the way the differences are managed within a diverse group will have enormous consequences for how the team functions and, furthermore, on its performance. Leaders have no influence on the personality of workers; however, their role is more visible in other levels of diversity which are part of external dimensions.

As we already mentioned, for the purpose of this book we will follow the broader understanding of diversity proposed by Gardenswartz and Rowe (2003), taking into consideration the different perception of diversity in the CEE region. Based on the research findings (see detailed description in Appendix I), our main focus was given to those diversity features which were identified by interviewed managers. Referring to the four-layer model of diversity, they mentioned ethnicity, gender (as a part of internal dimensions), educational background, work experience (as a part of external dimensions) and finally seniority and management status, which are part of organizational dimensions.

In the following sections, our findings will be analyzed, focusing on internal, external and organizational dimensions of diversity. In addition, the actions which might be taken by managers in organizations will be proposed.

Organizational and Social Contexts of Diversity

In this section, attention will be given to managers' perceptions of how diversity influences their business.

As stated by Morrison (1996) and Fleury (1999), diversity is a requirement for organizational survival. Similarly, Tajfel and Turner (1979) examine diversity in organizations and workgroups using social identity theory (SIT). SIT is a cognitive theory which holds that individuals tend to classify themselves and others into social categories and that these classifications have a significant effect on human interactions (Syed and Özbilgin, 2015).

In the earlier works, Alderfer and Smith (1982) proposed embedded intergroup relations theory, which posits that two types of groups exist within organizations: identity groups and organization groups. Members of identity groups share some common biological characteristics (e.g. sex) and/or equivalent historical experiences, and thus have relatively consonant worldviews. Members of organization groups share common organizational positions and participate in equivalent work experiences. The significance of this theory is its attention to the effects of diverse identities within a larger organizational context. It recognizes that employees don't leave their racial, gender or ethnic identities at the door when they enter an organization.

Demographic researchers have established that minority and majority status in diverse workgroups is not experienced equivalently across sex, race or age. Early demography work by Tsui et al. (1992) also supports this statement. They found that white male employees reported adverse reactions to increasing minority representations in workgroups, while women and racial minorities did not. This conclusion was confirmed also in our qualitative research (sample of 65 companies in Slovakia; see Appendix I).

> *Women as workers are more empathetic. When we had problems with the integration of Roma employees, they discussed the prejudices with male workforce (who were not willing to accept their Roma counterparts). We all are human beings, women stated—at the end women helped to improve the working climate. Now all employees are respecting each other.*
>
> (HR manager of an international retail chain)

In qualitative research based on grounded theory, the main emphasis was to identify the perception of how different dimensions of diversity influence business among managers in Slovakia and to observe how they apply features of diversity in their managerial practice. In order to analyze diversity in detail, we proposed eight research questions (which were used as additional questions 2.1–2.8 in the main qualitative research described in Appendix I).

The main identified categories to research questions 2.1–2.8 and those resulting from the coding tree analysis have been identified as follows:

1. Due to a skilled labor shortage, it is difficult to maintain growth and competitiveness.
2. It is important to develop the diversity management framework and implement it into managerial practice.
3. Diverse employees (with different educational backgrounds, work experience, age, managerial status, gender and ethnicity) contribute to innovation and effective global development strategies.
4. A variety of initiatives are introduced with priority on recruitment and retention of the diverse workforce.
5. Specialized and highly diverse human resources are employed where their differences are acknowledged.
6. Lack of formalized processes of diversity policy implementation is visible. They can help to enhance the recruitment, inclusion, promotion and retention of diverse employees.
7. A diverse workforce influences the company's effectiveness on all levels of organizational operations.
8. Talent pool expansion is a strategic priority which fosters performance and innovation within the organization.

By analyzing our coding, we captured the answers as they arose through more broad understandings and sorted them into core categories summarizing managers' different opinions and level of experience.

The aim of this chapter is to find out if the positive links among group diversity, creativity and innovation exist (as stated by Craig and Kelly, 1999; Kurtzberg, 2005; Milliken and Martins, 1996) or this is rather rare in practice.

The contribution of diversity to higher performance in organizations was confirmed by interviewed managers across all industries. Here the diverse workforce was understood as employees with different educational backgrounds, work experience, age, managerial status, gender and ethnicity. Interviewees acknowledged the importance of diversity as an asset for their organization. Work experience as a part of the external dimension of diversity was frequently considered as crucial for proposing innovation.

> *Especially in production, we have employees who spent a few weeks abroad (often outside of the EU). After their arrival, they see things differently and are able to propose improvements based on their work experience abroad.*
>
> (Talent manager, automotive industry)

Current Challenges of Diversity in the Workplace

The greatest challenge (identified by managers) which influences internal and external dimensions of diversity was the lack of skilled labor, regardless of the sector or industry. One of the solutions proposed is to attract foreign workers. This has already considerably influenced diversity in the workplace. Nowadays, the Slovak economy is one of the most dynamic economies in the Eurozone. The majority of companies stated that the main problem of the Slovak economy is the lack of a skilled workforce. This problem was attributed to several causes. First, it is linked with the small proportion of students who are willing to enroll in professional-oriented programs. Second, this problem was aggravated by the negative demographic development in the last decades, following by young people's emigration and the likelihood of the younger generation to study abroad.

As a reaction to the qualified workforce shortage, in 2015 a dual vocational education training system was introduced, but interest among potential participants and companies remains low mainly due to complicated procedures proposed by the Slovak government. The limited number of companies (multinationals from the automotive and machinery industry) which participated in our research are involved in dual vocational education.

> *The dual vocational education is for us the opportunity to adapt to the new "Generation Z". Professionals from our company lead*

training for students in order to understand their different values and approaches to work. At the same time, this is the way junior employees can work in parallel with our key people.

(Talent manager, automotive industry)

One big problem with vocational training is the perceived lack of social and intellectual capital. Take for example the profession of the plumber. Everyone knows that today's plumber is well paid in almost any society, yet few people desire to be plumbers. The plumber is perceived to be less educated, and even with higher pay, they are seen to be less sophisticated. From our ten-year research of students in a university, we measured the degree of undesirability of skilled manual labor. When given an option between a blue-collar job with twice the pay of an office job, the students would still choose the office job. As "dirty" blue-collar jobs tend to be male dominated, we asked women about their desire to marry a blue-collar worker over an office worker. At around 80%, most women would choose a white-collar partner even when his earning potential was significantly less. It is a lack of social panache that drives young people to university. This is especially true for fields that have low earning potential (i.e. degrees outside of science, engineering, technology and medicine). A similar problem was found in attracting young people in the polygraphic industry, as was mentioned by the CEO of a printing company:

Now we cooperate more with schools to show them that the work in our company is different from the past, using new technologies and having the clean environment. We want to persuade young people to come.

Another aspect which aggravated the workforce shortage is the rising number of Slovaks working abroad. According to data from the Statistical Office of the Slovak Republic, about 160,000 people (6% of the working population) worked abroad in 2016 (25% in the Czech Republic, due to cultural, linguistic and historical proximity, followed by Austria and Germany). This number had increased from 103,000 in 2004.

Similar problems with a workforce shortage are reported in other CEE countries, mainly Poland, Slovenia, Lithuania and Latvia (which is especially relevant for the IT industry). In addition, many young people from CEE countries consider studying abroad and consequently, they do not have the motivation to come back (lower wages, higher corruption, insufficient reforms in their home countries). This negative trend has also contributed to the acute shortage of skilled labor in the whole region. Moreover, this development has been exacerbated by emigration. According to Hazans (2013), Latvia has lost about 9% of its population since the beginning of the 21st century. Hazans claims that two-thirds of emigrants are under 35 years old at the time of their departure. Lithuania is in the same situation, where OECD (2016) emphasizes the lack of finances, a high skill mismatch and brain drain as the main factors hindering business innovation activities.

Based on the research elaborated by Gajdzik and Szymszal (2015), in the Polish labor market serious problems with the generation gap are present. They believe that changes in labor market demographics were caused by a restructuring of the economy and consequent changes in demand and supply of human resources. Employment reductions led to changes in the age structure of personnel. The Polish market shows a clear disproportion between the number of young and older workers. This is visible especially in the steel industry, where about 50% of workers are in the 50+ age group.

The demographic decline in the last few years in the whole CEE region also contributed to the labor shortage to some extent. The total number of inhabitants in the EU-28 rose at a modest pace during the period 2011–2016, with annual population growth within the range of 0.2%–0.4% per annum (Eurostat statistics).

After Slovakia joined the European Union and its economy transformed into a market economy, human capital became a key factor of success in the competitive fight between organizations in the business and public administration sectors, specifically in schools (Lusková and Hudáková, 2015).

The availability of the labor force in the future seems to be rather skeptical. Eurostat data (*People in the EU*) shows that within the next 30–40 years the total number of inhabitants in the EU-28 is projected to stagnate and then decline after 2045. Similarly, according to UN data, the population of the Visegrad Four (Slovakia, Czech Republic, Hungary and Poland) will fall about 13% in 2050 compared with the year 2017. In the years 2015–2020, we are witnessing population stagnation in these countries and even a slight decrease in Poland and Hungary.

Nevertheless, fostering diversity in the workplace is associated with the costs of intercultural communication, difficulties with coordination and potential conflicts. Even though companies in Slovakia are becoming more global, they still prefer to hire and train local people. Managers (from the machinery, automotive, transport, chemical and retail industries) have the experience that local people from the region are more loyal than people from remote regions (companies struggle to offer them appropriate accommodations due to lack of rental flats).

> *We employ people from various regions but we struggle to offer them accommodation to support their mobility.*
>
> (CEO from a metallurgical company)

The experience (positive as well as negative) with foreign workers is shared among companies from the telecommunication, machinery, construction and IT industries.

*We are afraid to employ some foreigners. Our business partners
employed foreigners, they had the bad experiences with them.*
(CEO from a metallurgical company)

As for negative experience with foreign labor, managers often mentioned employees from other EU countries (Romania or Bulgaria) who are not motivated to work in other CEE countries where the wages are only slightly higher than in their home country. After a short time, they move on to Western European countries. On the contrary, they have good experience with employees from Ukraine, who are more loyal. Their wages in the CEE countries are considerably higher than in their home country. At the same time, they appreciate better working conditions, additional benefits and a lower level of corruption in the private sector than they experienced at home.

The managers also pointed out that legislation is not flexible enough to employ people from third countries (non-member states of the European Union). According to the data from the Central Office of Labor, Social Affairs and Family, companies in Slovakia employed about 60,000 employees from abroad (about 10,000 from Serbia, more than 9,000 from Romania, more than 5,000 from Hungary and Ukraine; www.upsvr. gov.sk). Half of the foreign workers are from other EU countries and the rest are from third countries. Slovakian employers are allowed to employ people from third countries (outside of the EU) only if the position is on the list of lacking positions for a chosen region (dentists, warehousemen, truck drivers, etc.). The shortage of workforce in the CEE region provokes an increase in wages (especially in the lacking positions mentioned above). At the same time, companies try to propose new benefits to stabilize existing employees and attract new ones as well. Currently, referring programs are popular in Slovakia and the Czech Republic, where employees are rewarded with up to 1,000 euros when they recommend a potential new employee for a company. Moreover, companies employ a variety of tactics to engage new employees. As an example, a special campaign was introduced by an international retail chain in Slovakia in August 2018—a special double-decker bus visited various places to promote the company and find new employees.

As a result of de-industrialization and globalization, leaders started integrating diversity into their corporate strategy.

In the model of communicative interactions in culturally diverse workgroups, Larkey (1996) utilized Cox's (1991) continuum of organizational types, from monolithic organizations (which are homogenous with few minority employees, and where formal policy alone is utilized to incorporate diversity) to multicultural organizations (where the integration of minority employees and perspectives is ideal). According to Syed and Özbilgin (2015), organizations began to leverage diversity as a way to drive their business, tap into new markets and clients and ultimately to impact their bottom line. In the access-legitimacy paradigm, employees are typically trained to accept diversity.

All respondents except one company had no formalized processes of diversity policies implemented in order to enhance recruitment, inclusion, promotion and retention of diverse employees. The general legal requirements on equal rights are implemented in their human resource policies and documents, such as a fully-fledged Labor Code, Antidiscrimination Act and standards of business ethics. In spite of the fact that innovation needs strategy, the absence of formalized diversity policies was observed especially in medium, small and micro companies (mainly from education and the food and retail industries). Respondents justified this fact by the diversity's novelty, insufficient knowledge and lack of experience with a multicultural environment in Slovakia, which is a homogenous country. On the other hand, managers recognize the future necessity and benefits which are related to diversity issues. Therefore, they actively support and organize training focusing on cultural differences and communication, and their employees take part in workshops and conferences discussing diversity.

The opinion emerged that the competitive advantage of diversity lies in a customer-centered approach, contributing to improving the leading market position. Respondents acknowledge that by applying diversity issues into a company's culture, competitiveness can increase in three possible ways: (1) entering the global marketplace by better client insight, (2) setting up strategic priorities for talent pool expansion and (3) boosting the company's performance.

Nevertheless, the greatest challenge addressed by respondents is insufficient knowledge and lack of experience of how to put a diversity management framework into practice. The main arguments are related to the company's inability to define its objectives and strategies for diversity, and consequently the costs of implementation and time.

Diversity and Its Contribution to Innovation and Creativity

The perception that different ideas, perspectives and competencies increase the potential for innovation is not completely new. This was presented by Triandis et al. (1965) and confirmed in later works, for example by Bachmann (2006), who added that different ideas bring solutions to organizational problems, and by Chin and Trimble (2015), who believe that diversity brings innovation to a team.

In our qualitative research (based on grounded theory), we analyzed how diversity contributes to creativity and innovation in organizations. The formulation of the final category confirms that the benefits of diversity prevail in the organizations we researched. Gender diversity especially creates competition, which contributes to creativity and innovation.

On the other hand, age diversity accelerates the development of junior employees. Cultural diversity contributes to new solutions combining different points of view. Moreover, diverse thinkers help a team think out of the box and bring in different perspectives for more creative solutions. Referring to the previous qualitative research, we found that culture, age and gender diversity open new perspectives and disrupt existing schemes. Although diversity triggers rare misunderstandings or conflicts (as confirmed by other scholars, e.g. Chin and Trimble, 2015), it contributes to team synergy and mutual respect and enables the fulfillment of the organization's goals. In this context, Gratton et al. (2007) studied whether gender proportion impacts a team's ability to be innovative. Their findings confirmed that greater gender diversity impacts innovation by increasing a team's psychological safety, willingness to experiment and take risks, and efficiency. Here, it is necessary to mention that in the organizations surveyed, the labor force consisted mainly of men (62% of companies where men prevailed) due to the type of industry (16% machinery, 8% chemical, 8% IT). Traditionally in these types of industry (not only in the CEE region but also globally), more positions are occupied by men than women. An interesting point of view was presented by one production manager from a machinery company:

> We deliberately nominate women to higher managerial positions because they are more determined due to their complicated path to the career. [They are] more responsible, qualified, experienced and provide more diverse solutions.

Generally, companies that were part of our research have good experience employing more women (who have often better language skills) in male teams. In their opinion, it brings better results. Male employees propose mainly technically based innovation. As for the link between gender diversity and innovation, all respondents confirm that *both women and men contribute equally to innovation and creativity.*

In connection with creativity, managers often referred to the educational programs which are offered for their employees.

> Our employees are the biggest source of changes and innovations. It is a cycle: a satisfied and appraised employee feels his/her importance and contribution, puts an effort to perform his/her best and contributes his/her creativity to the company's results. We like each other here. When we invest in people, we see their changing attitudes, effort and ideas and consequently creativity increases.
>
> (Manager from the machinery industry)

To analyze the link between diverse workforce and innovation, we included educational background and work experience as a part of the external dimensions of diversity. In this context, we can confirm that the employees with a university degree prevailed especially in the automotive, machinery and IT industries. Of course, it does not automatically mean that only this type of labor is the source of innovation in organizations.

The following was stated by the manager from the engineering section in the paint department of one international automotive company:

> *In production, employees have mainly a secondary education, they are quite practical and hand-skilled oriented. Due to this fact, they do not see the connections between improvements, costs, feasibility, and the return of investment. On the contrary, employees in the engineering sub-department mainly have a university degree, they have the "big picture", but sometimes they lack real-life experience from the production process.*

Similarly, in other organizations, diversity of educational background was seen as a precondition to the generation of innovation. Here the experience from production together with the skills and knowledge of university-educated employees are complementary and therefore contribute to innovation in organizations.

Horwitz and Horwitz (2007) also studied the impact of team diversity on group-level outcomes. They found that there is a positive relationship between task-related diversity and team performance. However, they found no relationship between bio-demographic diversity and team performance.

As we explored in our qualitative research, attention was given to the relationship between bio-demographic diversity and team performance, where the majority of respondents confirmed the positive relationship between them. In this context, diversity provides an opportunity for the company's development, learning and growth. When exposing employees to new cultures and a variety of approaches and skills, they can gain a broader insight into the global environment. Thus, companies can manage to strengthen their market positions, having an ability to quickly adapt to changing conditions in different markets.

According to our research findings, we can make a conclusion that culture, age and gender diversity open new perspectives, disrupt existing schemes and contribute to innovation.

In spite of many studies confirming positive impacts of diversity, there are a number of scholars who present a rather opposite point of view (Tsui et al., 1992; Rothman et al., 2003). Analyzing our research findings, we did not encounter this perception among interviewed managers; however, they admit rare problems do occur in diverse teams (e.g. misunderstandings in communication or small conflicts among different generations).

As a potential barrier to fully benefit from diversity, we can see the lack of specialized training for employees on embracing differences in the workplace. This barrier was underlined by the majority of researched managers.

The Pareto 80/20 theory alludes to the notion that 20% of the workers in a corporation would be responsible for 80% of the profits. This concept is a bit misleading as it ignores some basic laws of physics. If we take for example five bricklayers, each having five years of experience, one bricklayer may be more talented than the other four, but he is unlikely to have four times the efficiency. There is, however, the inverse of the Pareto theory, which could be stated that almost all individuals have a talent that would put them in the top 20% of a certain subgroup (e.g. some individuals would be in the top 20% for artistic skills, athletic ability, math proficiency, emotional intelligence and so on). The challenge for leaders is to cultivate the natural talents that most all individuals excel in. By doing so, the collective would be able to optimize the natural complementary skill sets needed for innovation.

Benefits and Biases of Generational Differences

It is necessary to mention in the context of the CEE countries (and Europe as a whole) the changing demographics of the workforce which are influenced by various factors. Managers in our research highlighted their concerns over the aging of the workforce, changing generations and worker migration. Similar anxiety was identified by the International Monetary Fund (IMF) in a study from May 2017, suggesting that the changing workforce will hinder economic growth in the region.

Nowadays, the situation in companies is rather challenging for leaders. For the first time in history, they need to work with four different generations at the same time. This is due to increased life expectancy, which consequently means that people work longer compared to their counterparts in the past. World Health Organization (WHO) data shows that the average life expectancy of the global population in 2016 was 72.0 years (in the CEE region: Poland 77.8, Slovakia 77.4, Romania 75.2 and Hungary 76.0 years). The global average life expectancy increased by 5.5 years between 2000 and 2016, the fastest increase since the 1960s (*Global Health Observatory Data*). As a result, people retire later.

We summarize key observations from our research (presented in Case Study 2) and significant characteristics and differences in habits and values in Table 7.1. It is harder for leaders to motivate employees or to propose benefits without considering the different preferences of each generation.

However, Wong et al. (2008) argue that the differences between generations have marginal statistical significance, explaining that it is more about the differences in age and individual character rather than the differences between generations.

Table 7.1 The general characteristics, habits and values of different generations

Main Impact-Influence	Traditionalists	Boomers	Generation X	Generation Y	Generation Z
History	WWII	Hippies	End of communism	Terrorism, guns at schools	Globalization and environmental threats
Technology	None	Ignore	Acceptance	Excellency	Born with
Communication	Face-to-face	Telephone	Mobile	Emails, SMS	Social networks
Feedback	No feedback is good feedback	Once a year	"I don't want to bother you but how am I doing?"	Quick and constructive	Discussion 24/7
Motivation	Respect	Recognition	Flexibility and positive environment	Meaningful work	Challenge and aspiration
Personal view	Pragmatic	Optimistic	Skeptical	Optimistic with high self-confidence	Egocentric and childish
Work ethic	Dedicated	Driven	Balanced	Inpatient and excited	Transparent
Authority	Respect	Natural	Polite	Questioning authority	Equality
Leadership	Hierarchical	Consensus	Competence	Collaboration	Digital relationship
Relations	Sacrifice	Self-fulfillment	Flexibility	Diverse, social	Networks
Change	Hesitation	Resistance	Acceptance	Searching	Creating

Source: Authors.

Nevertheless, mainstream research (e.g. Fogg, 2009; Glass, 2007) focuses on the challenges of Generations X, Y and Z working at the same place. This was confirmed in our research in numerous companies. As an example, we can use the statement of a team leader from the retail industry. "There are different approaches between seniors who often state 'I have learned something from others and I am doing it in this way' and juniors who state 'I have learned it myself and I know it' ".

The changing workforce provoked a new debate about how diversity should be managed in organizations. With regard to our findings, the topic of generational differences frequently came up in talking about current challenges.

The Resource-Based View (RBV) recognizes that all workers have an intrinsic value and that economic, social and intellectual investment leads to increased organizational capital, which in time leads to higher strategic returns. At the same time, RBV acknowledges the value added by older workers' skills, abilities and experience (Quiggin, 2001), their individual productivity (Munnell et al., 2006) or their further contribution to productivity by being part of an age-diverse team (Feyrer, 2007). The positive contribution of senior employees in the organization was highlighted in our qualitative research (Appendix I), where the financial manager of a construction company stated: "The presence of senior employees in a team helps to establish continuity. They help junior employees to understand the corporate culture and improve their skills which need to be improved, especially soft skills".

When junior employees are working together with seniors, they proceed faster and young ones gain trust and appreciation from older ones. The surveyed managers stated that junior employees are more flexible and ICT skilled, with better language skills and are open to innovation with new ideas. Managers in surveyed companies perceive that the capability to innovate is strongly connected with a mixture of education skills and willingness to work. In a few cases, the managers mentioned that "young employees are losing their invention because they try to find everything on the internet".

In the majority of companies, the correlation between age and the increasing ability to innovate was not found.

> *We do not see differences in innovativeness between junior-senior employees. For example, there are some inventors who invented really interesting things when they were seniors. So, the age is not the limitation for us. Everyone is welcomed who is willing to propose something, the only limitation is your enthusiasm and desire to change things.*

(PR manager, retail industry)

The results from the survey conducted with respondents from generation Z showed what techniques and approaches are suggested to be used by leaders in order to enhance the learning and development of this generation.

Critical thinking and reflection are the elements that provide a deeper understanding of behavioral models (emotions, perception and motivation) and enable coping with diversity in real life. The continuous learning process across generations is necessary within the entire organizational ecosystem. That is an inevitable source of creativity, change and innovation. The constructive and continuous process of feedback is crucial. The process of feedback is a two-way dialogue between managers and their employees, where raising questions is an essential technique. It is developed as mutual and dual flow actions: providing and receiving feedback between managers and all stakeholders is the way for some change and improvement.

In rare cases, companies mentioned conflicts between generations; new employees were not welcomed by "seniors". To solve this, they introduced a "welcoming culture"—welcoming of new employees. Some scholars (Thomas, 1990) do not see conflicts as something negative; on the contrary they see them as an opportunity to learn. They believe that learning from conflicts generated from diversity and difference is more effective than using training initiatives.

Because of the different backgrounds, perspectives and characteristics of their members, diverse teams seem to be more sensitive to conflicts. Some managers do not see this as problematic. According to their experience, differences among team members are often a source of learning and they find it enriching. Although external and internal dimensions of diversity trigger rare misunderstandings or conflicts, it contributes to team synergy and mutual respect and enables the fulfillment of the organization's goals.

Based on our key findings, we can summarize that age diversity contributes to creativity and innovation, and junior employees proceed faster when learning from senior employees.

The Role of Leadership in Supporting Innovation and Creativity

Referring to studies which confirmed the links between leadership and successful diversity initiatives (Gilbert and Ivancevich, 2001; Bell, 2007), we included this type of question as a part of our qualitative research based on grounded theory.

Success in innovation—whether an individual or an organization—is not just about having a good idea and assembling the resources (people, equipment, knowledge, money, etc.) to make it happen. It is also about having the capabilities to manage them toward results. Innovation is about organizing different pieces of knowledge and particularly about balancing creativity with the discipline of making something happen (Blackler, 1995).

As mentioned in Case Study 3, the CEE countries (including Slovakia) are still considered "moderate innovators". With respect to the Blackler study, in some organizations different pieces of knowledge are not properly organized, which can be a barrier to innovation. The research results indicate that companies do not have a separate "innovation strategy". However, their strategic goals regarding innovation are part of the overall corporate strategy. Surprisingly, any multinational company that was part of the research did not consider having an "innovation strategy" as a special document.

> *We do not have a special "Innovation Strategy"—but we have a principle—"Deep dive"—each idea is analyzed in detail. We are asking how we can improve things. The innovation strategy should be in our employees' DNA. In the recruiting process, we try to choose people who can adapt to our "principles" and who are open fully to new solutions.*
>
> (PR manager, retail industry)

The interviewed managers considered many factors important for supporting innovation and creativity. One of the most important is their *ability to motivate* their subordinates (financial and non-financial benefits, such as public praise). A frequently used practice remains motivation by example. A majority of managers mentioned the fact that leaders should be able to critically scan the processes and identify problems which are necessary to solve. This of course requires the knowledge of all processes across the organization (in the machinery, automotive and chemical industries, production processes were especially highlighted).

Leaders play an important role in facilitating feedback and indirectly giving feedback to employees. As mentioned in Chapter 5, feedback is one of three pillars of the leading process framework. The importance of feedback (in many cases 360-degree feedback) was widely confirmed by respondents regardless of the company's size or the sector in which it operates. However, the qualitative method of feedback was preferred.

> *They (employees) always get the feedback. In many cases, the feedback is within 24 hours. When there is a more complex improvement/idea, it takes longer because more people need to express their professional opinion about that. We do not have a special committee or something like that. The employees always get the feedback also in case the improvement is not implemented.*
>
> (PR manager, retail industry)

To foster innovativeness, managers use different leadership practices. A few examples were given by the HR manager from a retail company:

> *We have various communication tools, e.g. boards, TV screens, scanner or stand up meetings where managers deliver news and*

information to employees present in the shift. Moreover, we have daily feedback or a special talk with managers—all-hands meetings— of the whole team where people can propose improvements.

Respondents confirmed that they try to avoid criticism while encouraging employees to propose new ideas. All these aspects contribute to the *better atmosphere in the workplace* which promotes employees' creativity. Another aspect which contributes to the friendly atmosphere in a company (which was repeated many times) is the policy of "open doors", where everyone is allowed to discuss their ideas with a manager.

At the same time, a precondition for generating new, original ideas is teamwork. As mentioned in previous chapters, clear links between the diverse teams and their contributions to innovation and creativity were confirmed.

Companies with a friendly climate in which employees feel good are able to generate ideas and implement them efficiently and effectively. The degree of organizational innovativeness depends on whether everyone can propose a change, correct it and disagree with it without the consequences of punishment, and that means specific management behaviors (Dess and Picken, 2000).

In the light of digitalization, employees appreciate even more frequent and friendly contact with managers. Quite often employees are afraid to use new technologies, and the role of the leader in such a situation is to transform this fear into a positive attitude. It is necessary to explain to employees (in some cases even demonstrate) how much easier and simpler their work could be using new technology.

Similar research findings were delivered by Taha et al. (2016) analyzing a sample of 200 companies in Slovakia. In this study, the relationship between organizational culture, creativity and innovation was examined. First, the relationship between the alignment of employees' personal values with organizational values and their willingness to propose new ideas was confirmed. Second, identical to our research, open team communication about new ideas positively affects the team's creativity. The creative performance of employees is strengthened by good interpersonal relationships in the workplace. With regard to both types of research, we can confirm that organizational culture supports creativity and innovation.

In another part of our research, we focused on the source of innovation in companies. Here we wanted to find out if the internal (employees) or external sources (customers, suppliers, business partners) prevail. Based on our research findings, the majority of innovations were proposed by employees. In rare cases, suppliers proposed some improvements (especially in the automotive, polygraphic and machinery industries). These improvements were feasible only thanks to ICT. According to interviewees, junior employees generally generally better IT skills, and they propose changes and improvements regarding using cloud services, new applications and software. As a result, companies save time and money and often reduce repetitive procedures. On the contrary, senior employees are often afraid to use new technologies. This might be a potential barrier to innovation, especially in the age of digitalization. The role of the leader is to explain to employees (both senior and junior) how much easier and simpler their work could be using new software or technology.

The implementation of diversity and inclusion (D&I) programs require a responsible leader who has the competencies and capacity to deal with this topic. According to the PwC survey in Slovakia (sampling 31 companies), fewer than one-third of companies have a D&I leader at the top level of the organization. On the contrary, globally, more than one-third of companies have an independent D&I leader at the middle management level. Moreover, 14% of companies globally do not have a D&I leader. In Slovakia, the situation is even worse: 37% of companies do not have a D&I leader (Diversity and Inclusion Survey, Slovakia, Pwc, 2018).

Half of the companies from our research are multinationals where managers have experience leading diverse teams from abroad, which helps them to deal with diversity challenges. Tasking leaders with specific D&I goals is key to driving results. Despite this, the majority of European organizations have not adopted this practice (76%) (Diversity and Inclusion Benchmarking survey, Pwc, 2017). The focus on diversity in organizations (which was part of the research) is visible during the last few years when the shortage of labor was alarming, and therefore companies recruited more employees from abroad (proportionally from other EU countries and outside of the EU).

To deal with the challenges generated by increased diversity in the workplace, leaders can benefit from the Reflective Leadership concept (as it was described in Chapter 5). The aim of this approach is to help better understand the organizational contexts and relationships based on stronger social interactions between actors. The three fundamental pillars of the Reflective Leadership concept are critical thinking and reflection as well as the implementation of the process of feedback among leaders and employees. This can contribute not only to effective information exchange but also foster working relationships.

Some managers that we interviewed highlighted the feedback tool using discussions, appraisals and support.

> *Leadership is important in every element of our organizational activities. We try to conduct all activities to be beneficial not only for the company but also for its employees.*
>
> (Manager from a construction company)

Referring to quick changes and continuous improvement, managers have the impression that feedback needs to be faster too.

Conclusion

Slovakia is a homogenous country where issues related to multicultural-ism and diversity are addressed in social life and business only occasion-ally. In companies in Slovakia, diversity has mainly emphasized areas such as ethnicity, gender, age, educational background, work experience, seniority and management status. Other aspects related to sexual ori-entation, physical ability, geographic location, income, personal habits, recreational habits, religion, appearance, parental status, marital status and race have been omitted.

Diversity and the knowledge surrounding it are continually evolv-ing as demographic challenges and migration are discussed extensively within society. With current demographic trends, companies are facing the challenge to create an environment where different generations will work together despite having different values and attitudes about a bal-ance between work and life. In the business environment, there is the lack of an internal workforce that can sustain economic growth and productivity.

Managers are facing some contradictions: diverse teams are a great source of innovation and can provide competitive advantages to the com-pany, but in rare cases they can produce conflicts that might lower overall company performance. Analyzing the links between diversity, innovation and creativity, the importance of culture, age and gender diversity was highlighted. As a result, these diversities open new perspectives and dis-rupt existing schemes in organizations which contribute to innovation and creativity.

Potential barriers to fully benefit from diversity are the lack of special-ized training for employees, insufficient knowledge and lack of experi-ence of how to implement the diversity framework in company processes. Therefore, formalized diversity policies are needed as a core part of the HR strategy in order to enhance recruitment, inclusion, promotion and retention of a diverse workforce. The multicultural competence and sen-sitivity to diversity among managers and leaders becomes an important element of managerial education.

This requires a shift from production-oriented business toward a people-oriented focus of management. Personal and organizational goals should be linked. The open and effective communication system can become an important tool for reliable information exchange, supporting the devel-opment of critical thinking at all levels. However, managers recognize the future necessity and benefits which are related to diversity. The leaders' role is to foresee future trends and requirements for new specializations, which have to be implemented into personal development and training plans at all staff levels. Diversity becomes the key for obtaining certain specialized skills; however, legislative restrictions at the national level impoverish future diversity.

Bibliography

Alderfer, C.P., Smith, K.K. (1982). Studying Intergroup Relations Embedded in Organizations. *Administrative Science Quarterly*, 27, 35–65.

Bachmann, A.S. (2006). Melting Pot or Tossed Salad? Implications for Designing Effective Multicultural Workgroups. *Management International Review*, 46(6), 721–747.

Bell, M.P. (2007). *Diversity in Organizations*. Mason OH: Cengage.

Blackler, F. (1995). Knowledge, Knowledge Work and Organizations: An Overview and Interpretation. In *Organization Studies*, 16(6), 1021–1046.

Chin, J.L, Trimble, J.E. (2015). *Diversity and Leadership*. New York: Sage.

Cox, T. (1991). The Multicultural Organization. *Academy of Management Executive*, 5(2), 34–47.

Craig, T.Y., Kelly, J.R. (1999). Group Cohesiveness and Creative Performance. *Group Dynamics: Theory, Research, and Practice*, 3, 243–256.

Dess, G.G., Picken, J.C. (2000). Changing Roles: Leadership in the 21st Century. *Organizational Dynamics*, 28(3), 18–34.

Diversity and Inclusion Benchmarking survey, European datasheet, Pwc. (2017). Retrieved from: www.pwc.com/gx/en/services/people-organisation/global-diversity-and-inclusion-survey/european-report.pdf [Accessed 24 January 2018.]

Diversity and Inclusion Survey, Slovakia, Pwc. (2018). Retrieved from: www.pwc.com/sk/sk/publikacie/assets/2018/diversity-inclusion-survey-sk.pdf [Accessed 8 August 2018.]

Feyrer, J. (2007). Demographics and Productivity. *The Review of Economics and Statistics*, 89(1), 100–109.

Fleury, M.T.L. (1999). The Management of Culture Diversity: Lessons from Brazilian Companies. *Industrial Management & Data Systems*, 99(3), 109–114.

Fogg, P. (2009). When Generations Collide. *Education Digest: Essential Readings Condensed for Quick Review*, 74(6), 25–30.

Gajdzik, B., Szymszal, J. (2015). Generation Gap Management in Restructured Metallurgical Enterprises in Poland. *International Journal of Management and Economics*, 47, 107–120.

Gardenswartz, L., Rowe, A. (2003). *Diverse Teams at Work: Capitalizing on the Power of Diversity*. Alexandria: Society for Human Resource Management.

Gilbert, J.A., Ivancevich, J.M. (2001). Effects of Diversity Management on Attachment. *Journal of Applied Social Psychology*, 31, 1331–1349.

Glass, A. (2007). Understanding Generational Differences for Competitive Success. *Industrial and Commercial Training*, 39(2), 98–103.

Global Health Observatory data. World Health Organization. Retrieved from: www.who.int/gho/mortality_burden_disease/life_tables/situation_trends/en/ [Accessed 1 September 2018.]

Gratton, L., Kelan, E., Voigt, A., Walker, L., Wolfram, H. (2007). *Innovative Potential: Men and Women in Teams*. The Lehman Brothers Centre for Women in Business. London: London Business School.

Hazans, M. (2013). Emigration from Latvia: Recent Trends and Economic Impact. In *Coping with Emigration in Baltic and East European Countries*, Paris: OECD Publishing.

Horwitz, S.K., Horwitz, I.R. (2007). The Effects of Team Diversity on Team Outcomes: A Meta-Analytic Review of Team Demography. *Journal of Management*, 33(6), 987–1015.

International Monetary Fund (IMF). (2017, May 11). *IMF Country Focus.* Retrieved from: www.imf.org/en/News/Articles/2017/05/10/na051117-central-and-eastern-europe-a-broaderrecovery-but-slower-catch-up-with-advanced-europe [Accessed 8 August 2018.]

Kurtzberg, T. R. (2005). Feeling Creative, Being Creative: An Empirical Study of Diversity and Creativity in Teams. *Creativity Research Journal*, 17(1), 51–65.

Larkey, L. K. (1996). Toward a Theory of Communicative Interactions in Culturally Diverse Workgroups. *Academy of Management Review*, 21, 463–491.

Loden, M., Rosener, J. (1991). *Workforce America. Managing Diversity as a Vital Resource.* Homewood, IL: Business One-Irwin.

Lusková, M., Hudáková, M. (2015). Making the Process of University Teachers' Motivation More Effective. *Turkish Online Journal of Educational Technology*, Special Issue for INTE, 2015, 308–313.

McGrath, J. E., Berdahl, J. L., Arrow, H. (1995). Traits, Expectations, Culture and Clout: The Dynamics of Diversity in Work Groups. In Jackson, S. E., Ruderman, M. N. (eds.), *Diversity in Work Teams*. Washington, DC: American Psychological Association.

Milliken, F., Martins, L. (1996). Searching for Common Threads: Understanding the Multiple Effects of Diversity in Organizational Groups. *Academy of Management Review*, 21, 402–433.

Morrison, A. M. (1996). *The New Leaders: Guidelines on Leadership Diversity in America.* San Francisco: Jossey-Bass.

Munnell, A., Sass, S., Soto, M. (2006). *Employer Attitudes Towards Older Workers: Survey Results. Issue in Brief.* Chestnut Hill, MA: Center of Retirement Research at Boston College.

Organization for Economic Co-Operation and Development (OECD). (2016). *OECD Reviews of Innovation Policy: Lithuania.* Paris: OECD. Retrieved from: https://doi.org/10.1787/9789264259089-en [Accessed 17 August 2018.]

People in the EU—statistics on demographic changes, Eurostat statistics. Retrieved from: https://ec.europa.eu/eurostat/statistics-explained/index.php?title=People_in_the_EU_-_statistics_on_demographic_changes#Population_change_in_the_EU [Accessed 3 September 2018.]

Quiggin, J. (2001). Demography and the new economy. *Journal of Population Research*, 18(2), 177–193.

Rothman, S., Lipset, S. M., Nevitte, N. (2003). Does Enrollment Diversity Improve University Education? *International Journal of Public Opinion Research*, 15(1), 8–26.

Statistical Data. (2018). *Central Office of Labor, Social Affairs and Family.* Retrieved from: www.upsvr.gov.sk/statistiky/socialne-veci-statistiky/2018/2018-socialne-davky.html?page_id=771091&lang=en [Accessed 31 July 2018.]

Syed, J., Özbilgin, M. (2015). *Managing Diversity and Inclusion.* London: Sage.

Taha, F. A., Sirkova, M., Ferencova, M. (2016). The Impact of Organizational Culture on Creativity and Innovation. *Polish Journal of Management Studies*, 14(1), 7–17.

Tajfel, H., Turner, J. C. (1979). An Integrative Theory of Intergroup Conflict. In Austin, W. G., Worchel, S. (eds), *The Social Psychology of Intergroup Relations*. Monterey, CA: Brooks/Cole, pp. 33–47.

Thomas, R. (1990). From Affirmative Action to Affirming Diversity. *Harvard Business Review*, 68, 107–117.

Triandis, H.C., Hall, E.R., Ewen, R.B. (1965). Member Heterogeneity and Dyadic Creativity. *Human Relations*, 18, 33–55.

Tsui, A.S., Egan, T.D., O'Reilly, C.A. (1992). Being Different: Relational Demography and Organizational Attachment. *Administrative Science Quarterly*, 37, 547–579.

Wong, M., Gardiner, E., Lang, W., Coulon, L. (2008). Generational Differences in Personality and Motivation: Do They Exist and What are the Implications for the Workplace? *Journal of Managerial Psychology*, 23(8), 878–890.

World Population Prospects. (2017). United Nations. Retrieved from: https://esa.un.org/unpd/wpp/Download/Standard/Population/ [Accessed 3 September 2018.]

Wrench, J. (2002). Diversity Management, Discrimination and Ethnic Minorities in Europe: Clarifications, Critiques and Research Agenda. *Occasional Papers and Reprints on Ethnic Studies*, 19, 1–179.

8 How Emerging Technologies Transform Leadership

Introduction

The emergence of information and communication technology (ICT) has led to the acceleration of innovation and its diffusion, generating not only new opportunities but also risks. Innovation is driven by the ability to see connections, to spot opportunities and to take advantage of them. Innovation matters, not only at the level of the company but also increasingly for national economic growth.

The constantly changing environment and emerging technologies have triggered so-called new teams: virtual, global and self-managing. This evolution has been strongly influenced by growing computer literacy and the explosion of ICT. The process-relational leadership model (as described in Chapter 4) explains which skills are required to tackle new challenges. New technologies such as social networking and virtual collaboration play a crucial role in the leadership process. Increasingly, more interactions are occurring in cyberspace than in the real environment. This revolution has brought potential benefits (e.g. reduction of costs for organizations) and has fostered capabilities of a diverse workforce. High-performing organizations operating in the digital environment are trying to move beyond diversity and focus more on inclusion. This chapter deals with leadership challenges triggered by digitalization and examines how organizations tackle these challenges; —more precisely, how organizations embrace new ideas, accommodate different styles of thinking, create a more flexible work environment, enable people to connect and collaborate and encourage different leadership approaches. There is also a high level of complexity which leads to the necessity of interactivity among all innovative actors.

The Rise of Digitalization

Digitalization and the growth of the platform economy have been unbalanced. Despite an early and more than respectable start in developing its digital infrastructure, Europe has lagged behind significantly in riding the wave of digital innovations offered by the platform economy. As a result,

Europe is missing out on the technology champions of the new millennium while the United States, and increasingly China, are largely dominating these innovations which are transforming the global economy, redefining industries and creating job opportunities (Science, Research and Innovation Performance of the EU 2018, European Commission Report).

The European Commission is proposing to create the first "Digital Europe program" and invest 9.2 billion euros to align the next long-term EU budget (2021–2027) with increasing digital challenges. Focus will be on supercomputers, artificial intelligence (AI), cybersecurity and digital skills. About 700 million euros will ensure that the current and future workforce will have the opportunity to easily acquire advanced digital skills through long- and short-term training courses and on-the-job traineeships, regardless of their member state of residence. This is a regulatory framework for the "Digital Single Market Strategy" (launched in 2015), which has the ambition to shape Europe's digital transformation to the benefit of citizens and businesses (European Commission—Press release, June 2018).

The countries with the highest growth rate of BERD (business research and development expenditures) in the ICT sector were Poland and Slovakia (from the CEE region), while Finland, Greece and Luxembourg showed a negative change. R&D researchers and R&D personnel in the ICT sector were especially high in three CEE countries: Lithuania, Poland and Slovakia (JRC Technical Reports, 2018).

However, Slovakia as an EU member state has not obtained effective outcomes from investments in ICT compared to countries such as Denmark, Finland and Spain. The reasons for this are seen in the inability of various organizations (government, universities and business) to use ICT to support innovativeness that can achieve outcomes having a multiplier effect.

In 2015, the EU ICT service sector represented 3.6% of its GDP, but ICT manufacturing only accounted for 0.3%. Thus, the total ICT sector amounted to 3.9%. In this time, the EU ICT sector value added (VA) was 581 billion euros, employing 5.8 million people and spending 30 billion euros on BERD. The ICT sector represented 3.9% of the EU value added in 2015, and 2.5% of employment. The largest ICT sectors in the EU in relative size (ICT sector value added/GDP) were Ireland, Malta, Luxembourg, Sweden and Romania, all of which were above 5.0%. In terms of employment, the largest EU ICT sectors were Estonia, Malta, Ireland and Finland, with a share over total employment higher than 3.7% (JRC Technical Reports, 2018).

Emerging Technologies as a Source of Transformation and Disruption

Referring to our research findings, social networks and virtual collaboration tools were considered crucial for the transformation of processes in organizations. Collaborative software can include not only simple applications to ensure sharing of information and data between team members, but also a more complex group support system that creates an environment for interactions, encourages creativity and brainstorming or facilitates group decision making. The development of these systems triggered new, so-called virtual teams which have slowly replaced "traditional" (face-to-face) teams (this transition will be explained in the next section).

Analyzing the challenges in the digital era (with research based on grounded theory), we found that digitalization of all processes is present across all industries. Moreover, new technologies influence the production processes (e.g. new automated cooling systems, use of robots—mainly in the automotive industry) even more than in the past.

The majority of managers agreed that the digital era disrupts the traditional processes in organizations. An example of vast digitalization was presented by the innovation manager from an automotive company:

> *We have a special innovation department where we focus on the analysis of big data. The digitalization and automatization have already been here for years; today big data and the internet of things are the issues for each company. In the light of Industry 4.0, our ambition is to build a digital enterprise which will be fully automated with only e-documentation.*

Similarly, the manager from a telecommunication industry stated: "Due to digitalization, we completely changed the ordering system in our company".

Respondents acknowledge that digitalization requires more employee involvement and participation in redesigning of some processes in the company to enhance organization performance and results. This interesting point of view was presented by the majority of managers regarding the impacts of digitalization and automatization. Surprisingly, digitalization has not automatically triggered the dismissal of employees. In this stage of digitalization, companies are able to shift workers to other positions within the organizational structure. However, it will reduce the future demand for the labor force.

As for virtual collaboration tools, the companies we studied mainly make use of communication tools (Skype, online internal chats, social networks), which are slowly replacing traditional ones (email, phone calls) that are considered outdated. Moreover, Microsoft SharePoint is used by some companies (e.g. companies in the automotive industry) in order to store, organize, share and access information from any device. Companies had good experience with this software, which is safe and facilitates the circulation of information in real time. In this way, the traditional way of sharing information (intranet or email) is perceived as less efficient, mainly among junior employees. The majority of companies already have experience with cloud services (data backup solutions or file sharing).

Growing digitalization triggered new challenges for companies, such as data security, intellectual property rights (IPR) and personal data protection. As an example, we refer to a quote from the CEO of a chemical company:

> *Data and know-how protection are more and more difficult in the open digital world.*

The use of new technologies, on the one hand, saves companies money (via simplification and automatization of processes, e-documentation) and generates higher profits; on the other hand, it creates new costs (additional trainings and workshops for employees, investment in new systems), threats and challenges for managers. In spite of advanced technologies, people are still important to organizations. The introduction of new technologies and automatization is still rather limited in some industries, as presented by the CEO from a metallurgical company:

> *Our production is specifically based on physical labor; people are crucial for us. In metallurgy, digitalization and automatization of some processes are rather limited.*

Although technological development is a positive phenomenon, it frequently leads to the erosion of employees' skills. This was confirmed by the majority of managers from our research.

> *They (employees) rely on technologies even for easy tasks and lose or weaken their existing skills.*
>
> (CEO from a machinery company)

Similarly, the negative influence of digitalization was seen by a manager from the construction company:

> *I agree that digitalization is our future and it works. This is evident with the decrease in human labor in our industry. We rely more and more on technologies. At the same time, I have the impression that digitalization makes us less intelligent.*

About half of the researched managers perceive that the use of ICT also brought some negative aspects to their daily work. One manager from a construction company explained this perception:

> *For me as a manager, I need to be always online. In spite of new technologies which surely facilitate my work, I need to work still more and more. The working hours seem to be endless.*

In some cases, interviewees said that employees are losing the capability to talk face-to-face. This is rather visible in companies where they are part of a virtual (project) team. Another factor which is perceived negatively by employees is that digitalization has brought the notion that an *employee is only a number for a company.*

> *The huge challenge is the loss of the human aspect at work. Instead of real experience, we have the digital one. We focus only on data, we do not see the reality. The key performance indicator (KPI) is crucial, not people.*
>
> (Manager from the machinery industry)

Moreover, according to managers, employees feel that they have less privacy, as they are constantly surveyed using electronic tools. As an example, we can use this statement of a manager working for an IT company:

> *The digital era makes us more opened but within the borders—we let you see our kitchen but not our stomach.*

Another aspect that was underlined is the *acceleration of technological development* and changes, which is rather challenging to keeping up with for the companies we surveyed. In spite of advanced technologies, people are still important to organizations. Managers find that personal contact, discussions and interactions with all employees across the organization are even more crucial in the digital era. In the companies we researched, managers who develop and care about people are preferred.

Leading Virtual Teams vs. Traditional Teams

Advances in communication technologies (which were mentioned partially in the previous section) have dramatically changed the nature of teamwork. Traditional (collocated) teams are currently giving way to virtual (distributed) teams linked through technology, reaching across space, time and organizational boundaries (Lipnack and Stamps, 2000). The most critical factor that has enabled the expansion of virtual teamwork is advances in ICT which occurred during the 1990s. Another important impulse according to Townsend et al. (1998) is the development of default technology for the creation of virtual work. There is the development of desktop video conferencing systems that offer virtual teams the possibility of using direct, face-to-face communication, and the development of systems to support collaboration.

In addition to the concept of the virtual team in our research, the terms "distributed team", "remote team" or "geographically dispersed team" were also used in a similar context. For the purpose of this book, the term "virtual team" will be used.

According to Townsend et al. (1998), the virtual team is a group of geographically and/or organizationally dispersed coworkers who are united by the use of a combination of telecommunication and information technologies to perform organizational tasks. Lipnack and Stamps (1999) add to this definition: "extra spatial distance and temporal distance define virtual teams as, teams use technology to bridge time zones, distances and border organization".

Dubé and Paré (2004) do not consider spatial remoteness of team members a definitional characteristic of virtual teams. Although virtual team members are often separated by many miles or even continents, they can also be placed in adjacent offices in the same department if they decide to communicate mainly through ICT. The virtual image is defined by a team using communication, collaboration, sharing information and coordinating their activities mainly using computer-mediated communication infrastructures.

The transition from traditional to virtual teams is visible mainly in multinational companies (especially in the automotive, IT, telecommunication and financial services industries), where employees often cooperate on the same projects with their counterparts in branches abroad.

Generally, "virtual" currently indicates the use of electronic information and electronic communication tools. All companies, regardless of the industry in which they operate, indicated the shift from paper to electronic documentation. In some companies (e.g. operating in the automotive or retail industry), paper documentation has already disappeared.

The increase of the virtual teams globally (and also in the CEE region) was also due to the presence of multinational companies where virtual communication is vastly used in daily work. Naturally, the rise of virtuality in teamwork is inevitably connected with more diverse teams which are highly challenging to lead. The main challenges of leading virtual (diverse) teams will be analyzed in the second half of this section.

However, the boundaries between traditional and virtual teams are not entirely clear. As mentioned earlier, not every virtual team must possess dispersed location, and traditional project teams rarely exist without computer-aided communication. For this reason, authors offer an alternative viewpoint, suggesting that is more appropriate to focus on the extent to which team members use virtual tools to coordinate and execute team processes (Kirkman and Mathieu, 2005; Hertel et al., 2005).

To summarize aspects which can distinguish virtual teams from traditional teams, there are several unique characteristics defining virtual teams:

1.　Members are chosen based on skills, not proximity.
2.　Commitment is proliferated across time and place.
3.　Collaboration is carried out electronically.
4.　Supervision is driven by electronic methods (Guillot, 2002).

In the context of traditional and virtual teams, companies were mainly referring to their teams working together on projects.

Denis Lock (2007) defines several advantages of the traditional project team. Short-term leadership and motivation are considered to be one of the main advantages of the traditional project team when compared to the virtual project team. Team members are responsible to one manager, they know exactly who they report to, and there is a little chance of their being given conflicting instructions from more than one superior. The roles and responsibilities of individuals are clear and recognizable. Good cross-functional communication is another advantage of the traditional project team. Specific projects require people with specific skills or from professional disciplines to work together. The project manager should ensure that strong and fast communication links exist up, down and across the project organization. Security and confidentiality are also advantages of traditional project teams. If work is being conducted for any project that requires a secret or confidential environment, the establishment of the traditional project team helps organizers to contain all the work and its information within closed, secure boundaries. The advantages of the virtual project team, on the other hand, are also numerous, including efficiency of project execution, the integration and optimization of competencies, removal of physical boundaries and the ability to form new partnerships (Chinowski, 2003). Virtual teams overcome the limitations of time, space and organizational integration that traditional teams face. This allows team members to work constantly, which increases work performance and makes it possible for work time to be 24/7. The majority of managers consider virtual teams more beneficial, however, they require a different approach than traditional teams.

> *In our company, the whole project team meets rarely face-to-face. It brings positives and negatives as well.*
>
> (HR manager from a telecommunications company)

Increased utilization of employee time, round-the-clock workforce availability and the opportunity to leverage knowledge and expertise around the world are also advantages of virtual project teams, contributing to the general efficiency of project execution. At the individual level, potential advantages of the virtual working environment are higher flexibility and time control together with higher responsibilities and empowerment of team members. This kind of project team also increases response time to tasks, provides flexible hours for employees, and a greater sense of responsibility is developed (Precup et al., 2006; Hertel et al., 2005; Clear and MacDonell, 2011; Piccoli et al., 2004).

There are several occasions when traditional (collocated) project teams might be inefficient or even inconvenient for a project. Lock (2007) gives examples, such as inflexibility and inefficiency in the use of resources.

When a project is not big enough, it can be difficult to find enough tasks to keep all members of the team occupied all the time. Another example of a disadvantage in the traditional project team is the isolation of specialists. Specialists in small project teams are less able to discuss problems with their peers or have access to professional data. Administrative difficulties are also one of the disadvantages of the traditional project team, according to Lock. Even though the project is of sufficient size, it might be impossible to place all participants under one roof. There is no further purpose of the specific project team after the project is complete. When various aspects of the project are finished, the team will be reduced in size until finally disbanded. Therefore, life after the project might also be considered to be a disadvantage of the traditional project team.

Challenges of Leading Virtual Teams

Requirements for successfully implementing virtual teams into the organization include supportive company policies, a rewarding system and team empowerment for virtual team members and leaders.

Every team created for any particular reason struggles with plenty of challenges. All of these challenges can be exacerbated by not being in the same room or not working with colleagues at the same time. Leaders should be comfortable with giving up traditional control over their employees while remaining committed to mentoring and evaluating them. Additionally, leaders must pay particular attention to the challenges posed by the physical separation between members. The physical distance between team members is the most obvious contrast between traditional and virtual teams. However, other contrasts like missions, tasks or goals are not necessarily different in the two types of teamwork. The methods and processes of how tasks are accomplished and the specialties faced in the work bring challenges to leading and participating in the virtual team (Hunsaker and Hunsaker, 2008). Managers also may find it difficult to coach and advise, assess training needs and give feedback to team members who are not on site. Technology and cooperation can resolve many of these problems, but team members have to work hard to overcome the gaps left by their inability to communicate face-to-face.

Virtual project teams usually consist of members from different parts of the world, thus from different nations with different traditions and habits. Each culture has a different impact on the performance of an individual. Therefore, this challenge is particularly crucial for the project manager to handle. The ability to successfully meet this challenge requires a thorough analysis of the intercultural aspects of international projects (Kormancová, 2012).

Leadership skills such as critical thinking, crucial communication and organizational change management will be important parts of project management competencies in the future (Kormancová and Kovaľová, 2013).

If the leader operates in a company where people are working from different parts of the world, it is necessary for them to adapt to changes and demands required by the situation. The first step in effective leadership of a team composed of people from other cultural conditions is realizing what the culture actually means and how it determines the behaviors and mindsets of people. A leader from one culture may perceive a situation positively, and at the same time managers from another culture may interpret the same situation with different meanings and emphasize different factors. Communication and cooperation between all of the project team members are extremely important to pay attention to, since they are greatly influenced by their own cultures.

Malhotra et al. (2007) categorized these challenging tasks in leadership of virtual teams:

1. Creating and obtaining trust with help of communication technologies.
2. Ensuring diversity in the team is understood, appreciated and supported.
3. Managing project lifecycle and virtual meetings.
4. Measuring the performance of the team with IT technologies.
5. Appreciating team members within a team but also outside of it.
6. Allowing team members to benefit from being part of the team.

In traditional teams, project leaders can see where members are strong and where they need support. On the contrary, in a virtual team, monitoring and measuring productivity can be problematic.

The Changing Role of Leadership in the Digital Era

As mentioned in previous chapters, leaders need to reflect the shift to digital organizations and the rise of diversity in the workplace which requires new approaches to employees.

As mentioned in Chapter 1 (in the section New Leadership Challenges: Transforming Business Models), the key role of leadership in the digital era is to make people involved in organizational processes and to build relations. This conclusion takes into consideration the following challenges identified above:

- Disruption of traditional processes in organizations.
- Employees' perception of being less important for a company.
- Employees' perception of having less privacy in the workplace.
- Erosion of employees' skills.
- Acceleration of technological development.
- Increasing data security, intellectual property rights (IPR) and personal data protection.

Managers from some industries (mainly telecommunications and the automotive industry) experienced the digital era disruption of the traditional (existing) processes in their organization. They acknowledge that it requires more employee involvement and their participation in redesigning some processes in the company to enhance organizational performance and results. In some cases, mainly in the automotive industry, suppliers participate in redesigning internal processes as well.

With regard to the challenges which were generated by accelerating technological development, the role of a leader is to assure people that they are still humans, not numbers or machines for their employer. The employees' perception of being less important for a company occurred often, across all industries. Increasing use of technology brings less privacy for employees as they often feel like they are being surveyed. In spite of vast digitalization and automatization, the human workforce remains irreplaceable for many tasks and is therefore still valuable for organizations. This statement was also confirmed by the CEO from a printing company:

> *In spite of the high level of automatization, we cannot live without people. I often experience that other companies are not able to deliver products/services on time because they lack people. We want to avoid the same problem, introducing automatization as much as possible, but still, you cannot print a book without human labor.*

Managers acknowledge this perception and try to contribute to an employee-friendly environment. They try to meet personally with their subordinates and build an atmosphere of trust in the workplace. In addition, benefit packages are proposed to ensure employees that they are still the main asset for their employers.

The role of leadership is to help employees to understand and cope with all changes and inspire them to actively participate in the organization. This requires bringing together both digitalization of all organizational processes and accommodating the human resources in those processes.

> *For me as a senior leader, I do not see people only as a source of profit. For me, people are not machines. We need to set back from managing and to move to real leadership.*
>
> (Manager from an electronics company)

Here the crucial role of a leader is to recognize an interrelation between the ongoing investments into the latest technologies and human resources and understand how well-developed employees can contribute to the continuous process of innovation which is crucial for maintaining the company's competitiveness.

The Implementation of Reflective Leadership in the Digital Era

In light of the transition to "digital enterprise/factory", a new generation of managers has emerged. They are influenced by the digital era and are often considered "digital leaders". To cope with the new challenges which appeared as a result of vast digitalization, they prefer a different leading style accompanied by a rather different mindset. Regarding the background of current leaders, expertise in a technology field is required and seems to be inevitable.

In this section, six key processes which contribute to Reflective Leadership in the digital era will be presented.

1. *Process of Involving*: In general, diversity is recognized as a valuable source for innovation; therefore a strategy for how to implement it in an organizational system is crucial. This requires that leadership focus on individual strengths to capture the best talents that a diverse workforce can offer. Even though communication is mainly via ICT, personal interactions (either meetings or face-to-face debates, appointments or visits) are important occasions for continuous feedback and exchange of different ideas. Leaders at all hierarchical levels and their employees are giving and receiving feedback which has to be structured with both quantitative and qualitative parameters. This enables the evaluation and assessment of performance across the entire organization. All processes are simplified as a result of ICT implementation. The leader's role is to assist people to adjust to changes and plan a staff's continuous learning and development.

2. The *Process of Continuity* reflects the value and understanding that the past affects the present and the future. The organization respects what worked, positive aspects are acknowledged and assessed objectively, and if they fit the new environment, they are kept. Leaders explain the interrelations between the actions/performance in the past and present, thus they might direct their decisions in the future. Since organizations are living systems, some rules, job positions or roles have to be changed or modified. It is important to indicate any new roles and any perceived gaps in skills as soon as possible. Here the ways in which they are identified and addressed need to be precise. There is a significant necessity to be flexible enough to justify those new procedures and policies toward new trends and requirements of customers, clients or society. Knowledge and information creation and sharing are essential in this process. The digital era is accompanied by an overload of information. People struggle to filter what is important and what impacts are associated with the use or absence of a certain piece of information. Leaders need to be digitally

skilled to be able to advise and consult on vital information and how to share it within the organizational system so that everyone has the right information at the right time. The main challenge current leaders are dealing with is how to implement innovation in an agile way.

3. The *Process of Commitment* stands for an understanding of the purpose of change and innovation. If it is not communicated clearly, then this uncertainty often causes employee frustration, rejection and demotivation. In recent years, new ICT has been considered a universal remedy for organizational problems. Now, leaders acknowledge new challenges which appear in the light of increased digitalization. In order to turn it into a positive, individual involvement and participation in the process of innovations are vital. When leading teams, it is important to set up team tasks and goals, monitor and manage the working process, set up measurements of progress and provide ongoing support. In a team, the work of each individual contributes to the whole. When team members see how the results of their actions contribute to the final result, they are more likely to be committed. When leading virtual teams, it is inevitable to establish the framework consisting of ICT tools for effective communication and collaboration and for evaluation of all processes and partial progress.

4. The *Process of Connecting* stresses that a good process can build relationships. This is rather challenging especially in the digital age where the shift from traditional to virtual teams is highly presented. People gain a sense of identity from their relationships with others. In the case of virtual teams, it is recommended to have, at least at the beginning of the cooperation, an introductory face-to-face meeting in order to create an atmosphere of confidence based on shared values in the virtual workplace. This is even more difficult considering increasing team diversity, which is often combined with some degree of virtuality. The various levels of team virtuality can decrease task interdependence, which makes coordination of these processes even more important for a leader. In addition, it is more difficult to coach and advise, assess training needs or give feedback to team members who are not on site. On the contrary, thanks to digitalization, constant feedback and connection are possible.

5. The *Process of Developing* explains that a good process will value, support and develop the potential for learning that each individual brings. The increasing diversity of teams is a huge source of learning for each team member. The different points of view often lead to new ideas or problem solutions compared to their homogeneous counterparts. Although this difference may trigger some conflicts among team members, they can contribute in the end to improvements. Such a real-time experience is enriching for each team member but at the same time requires a high level of tolerance and understanding.

6. The *Process of Making a Shared Vision* concentrates on sharing the "big picture" with everyone. To introduce this picture, which is called a shared vision or a common purpose, is more difficult in virtual teams where direct contact is limited. However, developing a shared vision requires time for reflection, sharing things from all perspectives and creating networks. Various dimensions of diversity facilitate looking at things from different perspectives, which is highly valued in organizations. On the contrary, it is rather challenging to involve employees who are part of the virtual team and persuade them to identify themselves with the company's vision. Due to their perception of isolation while being part of a virtual team, this is rather limited.

As mentioned in the previous chapter, the majority of innovations in the researched companies were proposed thanks to emerging technologies. This interconnection was extremely strong. Therefore, the positive attitude of employees toward ICT is appreciated. However, the importance of the experience of employees cannot be omitted. Employers create attractive benefits packages, try to ensure that employees have a reasonable work-life balance, offer health insurance and create an employee-friendly work environment. The results indicate that despite vast digitalization, the human factor is the main challenge for companies across all industries. In this context, the erosion of employees' skills was underlined. To deal with this challenge, companies propose organizing regular workshops and training for their employees and leaders as well. Much attention is given to face-to-face communication and building personal relations among employees. At the same time, the leader needs to reestablish the employees' self-confidence with their own capabilities and common sense.

As mentioned above, vast digitalization generates not only benefits but also potential risks for companies. Introducing ICT into a workplace requires new investments in data security, intellectual property rights (IPR) and personal data protection. In the majority of companies, security measures were far stricter than required according to European and national legislation (e.g. GDPR: general data protection regulation, which was implemented in May 2018). Companies offer regular workshops to employees at all levels to educate them on how to prevent data loss or data misuse. In large and medium-sized companies, a special position for this purpose exists. The role of a leader is to ensure the implementation of the latest legislation in corporate strategy and other internal processes. At the same time, he/she needs to persuade employees that following the security measures in this regard is in their own interest. Often the security measures regarding data security are considered as formal by employees.

As mentioned in Chapter 5, new technologies influence the approaches of leaders, and they need to be incorporated into new corporate strategies. However, this remains challenging due to fast ICT development.

Conclusion

Organizations in Slovakia are no longer only assembly partners to multinational enterprises. Many of them operate in technologically driven and dynamic sectors including the automotive, aluminum and ICT industries and have brought their research and innovation activities to local production facilities. The current industrial focus vastly depends on digitalization and is closely linked to new challenges which require a properly skilled and qualified workforce. Introduction of ICT to companies profoundly shaped the way they function and brought potential benefits (e.g. reduction of costs, simplification of processes, and fostering of capabilities of a diverse workforce). However, emerging technologies often trigger the redesigning of internal processes, less privacy for employees in the workplace to some extent or erosion of employees' existing skills. Due to the acceleration of technological development, leaders need to adapt quickly to new conditions and help their employees to accept them too. In spite of the presence of digitalization in all corporate processes, employees remain a valuable asset and key driving force for further development based on different types of innovation. The digital leader should be able to deal with the challenges of digital transformation and propose how to implement innovations in an agile way.

The majority of companies acknowledge that their employees are their main source of innovation. Even during the recruitment process, they try to analyze the innovative potential of their potential employees and their capability to adapt to changes.

Investment in R&D is crucial, especially now when companies deal with increasing digitalization of all processes across all industries. In our research (sample of 65 companies in Slovakia), we identified new challenges triggered by digitalization. Managers underlined the ongoing transformation to a "digital enterprise". This shift is accompanied by rising virtuality, which is represented by the use of virtual collaborative tools and the shift from "traditional" to "virtual" teams. On the one hand, this development facilitates routine operations and saves them time; on the other hand, it triggers new challenges for leaders. As a result of vast digitalization, employees often perceive themselves as numbers or being less important for the company than in the past. Moreover, the acceleration of technological development brings some negative consequences, including the erosion of employees' existing skills. The accelerating technological development has consequently changed the nature of teamwork which resulted in the creation of "virtual" teams. The rise of virtuality in teamwork is inevitably connected with more diverse teams which are highly challenging to lead.

The key role of leaders in the digital era is to make people involved in organizational processes and to build relations. In order to balance ongoing digitalization, it is necessary that leaders meet personally with their subordinates and build an atmosphere of trust in the workplace. Employees, even more, appreciate feeling important to the company and being part of the team.

Case Study 3 The CEE as the Catching Up Innovation Region

Europe is failing to transform its high scientific excellence into leadership in innovation and entrepreneurship. European states are strong in incremental innovation and medium-tech (e.g. transport, health or energy sector) innovation. However, their position is being eroded in several emerging technologies that are leading to breakthrough innovations and enabling transformational entrepreneurship (Science, Research and Innovation Performance of the EU 2018, European Commission Report). According to the Global Startup Ecosystem Report (2017), Europe has five start-up entrepreneurial ecosystems in the top 20. However, their value was nearly one-quarter of the seven American ones that rank in this list, and lower than those of China. Some of the factors that hinder the support of stronger innovation creation and diffusion are low business investment in research and development (R&D) and other intangible assets, a fragmented European market that hinders firms' abilities to quickly scale up innovations, rigidities in the functioning of markets that deter stronger innovation diffusion across sectors, fragmented or uncertain regulatory frameworks, fewer entrepreneurial universities and an uneven geographical spread of innovation.

Moreover, in the European Union context, we need to take into consideration the fact that companies deal with 28 different tax systems. While the differences concerning the nominal tax rates are obvious, another aspect of tax base rule differences is less visible, although they can play a relevant role in stimulating innovation activity. In some countries, the tax base composition is affected by the existence of R&D tax incentives concerning the company's income tax, but the situation differs according to each EU member state (Lacová and Huňady, 2018).

Research and Development Expenditures

Eurostat data show that gross domestic expenditure on R&D (GERD) stood at 303 billion euros in the EU in 2016, which was a 0.4%

increase over the year before and 40.0% higher than ten years earlier (in 2006). When we make a global comparison in 2015, the level of expenditure on R&D in the EU-28 was equivalent to two thirds of that recorded by the United States, while the EU-28's R&D expenditure was 48.5% higher than in China, more than double the expenditure in Japan, and more than five times as high as in South Korea.

The ratio of GERD to GDP, one of five key Europe 2020 strategy indicators, is also known as R&D intensity. There were nine member states that reported R&D expenditure that was below 1% of their GDP in 2016; each of these were member states that joined the EU in 2004 or later, with the lowest R&D intensities recorded in Romania, Poland, Croatia, Lithuania, Slovakia, Bulgaria and Latvia, which are part of the CEE region. Other CEE countries, including the Czech Republic, Hungary and Estonia, are slightly above 1%. The best-performing country from the CEE region is Slovenia, with 2% of its gross domestic product (GDP) (in 2016).

However, the highest EU R&D intensity growth rates over 2007–2015 occurred in Bulgaria, Poland and Slovakia, all of which had growth rates at least four times higher than the EU average (mainly due to the increased use of European Structural and Investment Funds). More precisely, Slovakia significantly increased its R&D investment intensity over the past decade, but business R&D investment remains low. In addition, there was an increase from 148.5 million euros (52.7% from the private sector) in 1994 to 640.8 million euros (50.4% from the private sector) in 2016 (Slovak Republic in Numbers, 2017). The development of R&D investment in the past explains the current rather poor placement of these countries in global and European comparison reports.

Innovativeness of CEE Countries

The post-transitional economics of the CEE region (12 countries including Albania, Bulgaria, Croatia, the Czech Republic, Hungary, Poland, Romania, the Slovak Republic, Slovenia and the three Baltic states of Estonia, Latvia and Lithuania) are still overcoming a history that was heavily bureaucratized and resistant to change and yet the EU seems to have the same problem. The "new" EU members (joining the EU in 2004 and later) carry traditional and rather bureaucratic organizational models from their former centrally planned economies (the process of transition was described in detail in Case Study 1).

Their management systems need to be more change oriented and more proactive.

According to the *Global Innovation Index 2018 Report*, Europe holds the leading position in innovation on the global level. The Global Innovation Index (GII) provides detailed metrics about the innovation performance of 126 countries which represent 90.8% of the world's population and 96.3% of global GDP. Its 80 indicators explore a broad vision of innovation, including the political environment, education, infrastructure and business sophistication. In the top 20 countries, there are 11 European countries (Switzerland 1st place, Netherlands 2nd place, Sweden 3rd place). As for the CEE countries, Slovakia is considered a moderate innovator (36th place), together with Estonia (24th place), the Czech Republic (27th place), Hungary (33rd place), Latvia (34th place) and Bulgaria (37th place).

Slovakia still lags behind the leading EU countries in innovation. Slovakia's relative strengths for innovation systems are in areas such as employment impacts, sales impacts and human resources. Relative weaknesses were highlighted in the enhancement for innovators, intellectual assets and existence of attractive research systems. The lack of intellectual assets can be explained by increasing migration of the labor force (especially fresh graduates) abroad which triggered a generation gap in the local labor market. This is a common problem of the whole CEE region. In spite of this, the strength of Slovakia is the higher proportion of doctoral students compared to the EU average. On the other hand, the quality of scientific publications is below the EU average (Investment in R&D in Slovakia, 2017). According to some researchers (e.g. Horehajová and Marasová, 2018), apart from enterprises, there is a crucial role for regional authorities, which through innovation policies can considerably influence the development of innovation potential in regions.

Additionally, in Romania, the relative strengths of the innovation system are in intellectual assets, employment impacts and human resources. As for weaknesses, we can mention the low number of innovators, finance, support and attractive research systems.

As for innovation, the highest position among all CEE countries is Slovenia. The relative strengths of its innovation system are human resources, firm investments and an innovation-friendly environment. Relative weaknesses are in finance, support, sales impacts and innovators.

Some of the main challenges in Hungary are the worsening innovation performance and a growing shadow economy (ICEG European

Center, 2016). According to the *ICEG European Center Report*, the main strengths of Hungary's economic performance are the export of goods, its cost-of-living index and tourism receipts, while the main weaknesses are the diversification and resilience of the economy, (low) employment, GDP per capita and youth unemployment. In addition, the main strengths of business efficiency in Hungary are compensation levels, working hours and a female-dominated labor force, while the main weaknesses are the attitude toward globalization, flexibility and adaptability, competent senior managers and brain drain as well as skilled labor and worker motivation.

Based on the *Global Competitiveness Report 2016–17* (World Economic Forum), Latvia is reported to lag in institutions, infrastructure and innovation, and business sophistication. It is recognized as being at a transition stage between an efficiency-driven and an innovation-driven economy.

The process of innovation in Polish companies is slow and entrepreneurs are cautious and distrustful of innovations bearing risk, which they usually cannot afford to take (Francik et al., 2018).

As mentioned above, the weak position of the CEE countries as innovators is caused partially by migration of some innovators/innovative companies to other EU countries where better conditions for start-up businesses are offered. Based on the survey "Startup Heatmap Europe 2017" which analyzed the startup migration flows within Europe in 2016 and 2017 (more than 1,000 entrepreneurs were involved), the CEE region loses 5% of Entrepreneurs to the United Kingdom, Ireland and the Baltic states, where start-up founders usually emigrate.

According to the special Eurobarometer on Public Perceptions of Science, Research and Innovation, at least half of the respondents expected that in 15 years, science and technological development would have a positive impact on their lives, notably in relation to health (65%), education and skills (60%) and transportation (59%). Health and medical care were the first priority in 10 countries (including the Czech Republic, Estonia and Slovakia).

Conclusions and Recommendations

Based on statistical data and our research we can summarize that the main reasons that CEE countries are still "moderate innovators" are as follows:

- Lower R&D investment compared to their counterparts from other EU countries.
- Migration of innovators/innovative companies to other countries.
- The transition from centrally planned economies to market economies (most of the CEE companies started to integrate themselves into the world economy at the end of the 20th century).

Here we can mention that despite the presence of multinational companies in this region, they do not considerably contribute to better innovation performance. Foreign investors benefit mainly from cheap labor, but they do not consider (with a few exceptions) relocating their R&D centers to the CEE region. However, the situation is slowly changing (e.g. in the automotive industry).

Finally, the companies we researched take a variety of actions to benefit from employees' innovative potential:

- Innovation days: special events where the best employee improvements are presented for business partners or the general public.
- Corporate idea management: a system where employees from production directly propose improvements of daily work in paper form. In later stages, each idea is analyzed by an evaluator who decides if the improvement will be elaborated on further.
- Innovative corporate culture: where all formal and informal barriers to innovation for employees are minimized in order to encourage them as much as possible. The policy of open communication and open doors is widely introduced (addressing the fact that some employees were afraid to present their ideas directly to top management).
- Database "lessons to learn": best practices from other branches that might be a source of inspiration for local employees are stored here.
- Corporate business systems/"invent and simplify": online systems of continuous improvements for employees.
- Stand-up meetings: short daily meetings of employees and their superiors where ad hoc small improvements are proposed.
- Employee boards: special boards for employees in production to propose improvements, with feedback given within 24 hours.

Bibliography

Blackler, F. (1995). Knowledge, Knowledge Work and Organizations: An Overview and Interpretation. *Organization Studies*, 16(6), 1021–1046.

Clear, T., Macdonell, S. G. (2011). Understanding Technology Use in Global Virtual Teams: Research Methodologies and Methods. *Information and Software Technology*, 53(9), 994–1011.

Chinowski, P. (2003). *Virtual Teams: Guide to Successful Implementation.* Retrieved from: http://morfconsulting.com/articles/star/Virtual_Teams_A_Guide_To_Successful_Implementation.pdf [Accessed 20 June 2018.]

Digital Program Press release. (2018). *European Commission.* Retrieved from: http://europa.eu/rapid/press-release_IP-18-4043_en.htm [Accessed 28 June 2018.]

Dubé, L., Paré, G. (2004). The Multi-Faceted Nature of Virtual Teams. In David Pauleen (Ed.), *Virtual Teams: Projects, Protocols and Processes.* Hershey, PA: Idea Group Publishing, pp. 1–39.

European Center Report. ICEG European Center, 2016. Retrieved from: www.imd.org/globalassets/wcc/docs/hungary.pdf [Accessed 8 August 2018.]

Eurostat Statistics Explained. (2018). *European Commission.* Retrieved from: https://ec.europa.eu/eurostat/statistics-explained/index.php?title=File:Gross_domestic_expenditure_on_R_%26_D,_2006_and_2016_(%25,_relative_to_GDP)_FP18.png [Accessed 31 August 2018.]

Francik, A., Szczepańska-Woszczyna, K., Dacko-Pikiewicz, Z. (2018). Innovation as an Impetus to Change in Organization Management. In Szczepańska-Woszczyna, K., Dacko-Pikiewicz, Z. (eds.), *Innovation Processes in the Social Space of the Organization.* New York: Nova Science Publishers.

The Global Competitiveness Report 2016–2017. Geneva: World Economic Forum. Retrieved from: http://www3.weforum.org/docs/GCR2016-2017/05FullReport/TheGlobalCompetitivenessReport2016–2017FINAL.pdf [Accessed 16 August 2018.]

Global Innovation Index 2018 Report. (2018). Cornell University, INSEAD, and the World Intellectual Property Organization (WIPO). Retrieved from: www.globalinnovationindex.org/analysis-indicator [Accessed 13 August 2018.]

Global Startup Ecosystem Report 2017. European Commission Report. Retrieved from: http://europa.eu/!Qu38pf [Accessed 28 June 2018.]

Guillot, T. L. (2002). Team Building in a Virtual Environment. *American Society for Training & Development.* Retrieved from: http://studylib.net/doc/8443456/virtual-consulting-teams [Accessed 3 September 2018.]

Hertel, G. T., Geister, S., Konradt, U. (2005). *Managing Virtual Teams: A Review of Current Empirical Research.* Retrieved from: http://cogprints.org/7814/1/2653-2669.pdf [Accessed 3 September 2018.]

Horehajová, M., Marasová, J. (2018). The Regional Innovation Policy: The Situation of Slovakia. In Dias, A., Salmelin, B., Pereira, D., Dias, M. (eds.), *Modeling Innovation Sustainability and Technologies.* Springer Proceedings in Business and Economics. Cham: Springer.

Hunsaker, P., Hunsaker, J. (2008). Virtual Teams: A Leader's Guide. *Team Performance Management*, 14(1/2), 86–101.

Investment in R&D in Slovakia. (2017). *European Commission.* Retrieved from: http://ec.europa.eu/research/horizon2020/pdf/countryperformance/sk_research_and_innovation_performance.pdf#zoom=125&pagemode=none [Accessed 3 September 2018.]

Kirkman, B. L., Mathieu, J. E. (2005). The Dimensions and Antecedents of Team Virtuality. *Journal of Management*, 31(5), 700–718.

Kormancová, G. (2012). *Špecifiká medzinárodných projektov a ich vplyv na úspech projektu.* [Specifics of international projects and its influence on project success] In *Management of Organizations in Real and Virtual Environment: Opportunities and Challenges IV: Proceedings of scientific papers.* Banská Bystrica: EF UMB.

Kormancová, G., Kovaľová, M. (2013). *Fundamentals of Project Management.* Banská Bystrica: Matej Bel University Banská Bystrica.

Lacová, Ž., Huňady, J. (2018). The Consequences of Tax Base Rules on Enterprise Innovation in the European Union. In Dias, A., Salmelin, B., Pereira, D., Dias, M. (eds.), *Modeling Innovation Sustainability and Technologies.* Springer Proceedings in Business and Economics. Cham: Springer.

Lipnack, J., Stamps, J. (1999). Virtual Teams: The New Way to Work. *Strategy & Leadership*, 27(1), 14–19.

Lipnack, J., Stamps, J. (2000). *Virtual teams: People Working Across Boundaries with Technology.* New York: Wiley.

Lock, D. (2007). *Project Management.* Bodmin: MPG Books Ltd.

Malhotra, A., Majchrzak, A., Rosen, B. (2007). Leading Virtual Teams. *Academy of Management Perspectives*, 21(1), 60–70.

Mas, M. et al. (2018). *JRC Technical Reports: An Analysis of ICT, R&D in the EU and Beyond.* Retrieved from: https://ec.europa.eu/jrc/sites/jrcsh/files/jrc111895.pdf [Accessed 8 June 2018.]

Piccoli, G., Powell, A., Ives, B. (2004). Virtual Teams: Team Control Structure, Work Processes, and Team Effectiveness. *Information Technology & People*, 17(4), 359–379.

Precup, L., O'Sullivan, D., Cormican, K., Dooley, L. (2006). Virtual Team Environment for Collaborative Research Projects. *International Journal of Innovation and Learning*, 3(1), 77–94.

Public Perceptions of Science. Research and Innovation, Eurobarometer Report 2014. Retrieved from: http://ec.europa.eu/commfrontoffice/publicopinion/archives/ebs/ebs_419_en.pdf [Accessed 28 June 2018.]

Science, Research and Innovation Performance of the EU 2018. European Commission Report. Retrieved from: https://ec.europa.eu/info/sites/info/files/srip/rec-17-015_srip-brochureb5_en_v10_outec_20180412.pdf [Accessed 28 June 2018.]

Slovak Republic in Numbers. (2017). *Statistical Office of the Slovak Republic.* Retrieved from: https://enviroportal.sk/uploads/files/zelene_hospodarstvo/publikacie/Slovenskarepublikavcislach2017.pdf [Accessed 2 September 2018.]

Startup Heatmap Europe 2017. (2017). *European Startup Initiative.* Retrieved from: https://www.startupheatmap.eu/assets/pdf/startups-heatmap-europe_2017_executive-summary.pdf [Accessed 28 June 2018.]

Townsend, M. A., DeMarie, M. S., Hendrickson, R. A. (1998). *Virtual Teams: Technology and Workplace of the Future.* Retrieved from: http://economia.uniroma2.it/cdl/biennio/clem/corso/asset/YTo0OntzOjI6ImlkIjtzOjI6IjE2IjtzE2IjtzOjM6ImlkYSI7czozOiI5MDgiO3M6MjoiZW0iO047czoxOiJjIjtzOjU6ImNmMY2QyIjt9 [Accessed 2 September 2018.]

9 Leading in the Era of Innovations and the Appearance of New Values

Critical Views, Implications and Final Thoughts for Future Actions

Introduction

This final chapter has the ambition to pinpoint the main findings from previous chapters and propose future research questions. The relevant aspects that shape future leadership development, including creativity, innovativeness and diversity, will be highlighted. Current evolution requires a different leadership approach underlying the importance of social identities of all members of a company and their relations within the organization.

The primary objective of this book was to develop a new leadership concept which explains the connections between both process-oriented and relational approaches that foster organizational innovation.

One theme that surfaced throughout this book is that the past and the present can direct us to the possible future. Identifying the Modified Reflective Leadership concept and reframing existing approaches toward diversity, change and innovation, we can provide not only new knowledge and research about leadership framework (which fits the new era) but also consider its application for leaders and organizations.

Main Goals of This Book

The primary aim of all of the work we conducted (i.e. literature review as well as the different forms of research) was to examine the process of leadership that corresponds with the challenges brought to leaders in any organization by the digital era. Leaders are expected to deal with a high degree of uncertainty coming from the external environment, with the increasing diversity of the workforce and with strong requirements to implement changes and innovations quickly. The digital era is also associated with the need to balance the focus on innovation on one hand and realize the importance of human beings on the other.

A significant element of the digital era is the compression of the product lifecycle and the need to quickly react to the changing market. As the CEO of Accenture, Pierre Nanterme, stated, "Digital is the main reason just over half of the companies on the Fortune 500 have disappeared since the year 2000" (Digital disruption has only just begun, World Economic Forum, 2016). For a company to succeed, leaders need a system of transformation as only dedicated employees will be able to respond to the changes.

As the need for transformative skills in an organization is paramount for survival, the big question is how to be adaptive in the digital era. Harvard's VUCA principle (see Chapter 1) describes a landscape where change happens rapidly (volatile), future predictions have no precision (uncertainty), causes and solutions are multifaceted (complex) and there is little clarity of events (ambiguous).

In Part I of the book, we provided an overview of theories and concepts focusing on emerging views on leadership. As elaborated further in Chapters 2 and 3, the organizations in the digital era function as a complex ecosystem where the need for new leadership values and approaches arise. They shared both social responsibility and ethics for leading the organization that is framed by the leaders and modeled through the behavior of followers.

An overall concept that was used throughout this book was the idea that individuals are aware of their fleeting moment on Earth and are keen to leave an appropriate legacy when they are gone. This legacy includes family, community and also work. Good leaders are those whose legacy becomes part of the company's culture after they leave the company. There were several responses from the interviews we conducted that highlighted that leaders are always expected to provide a good example. For instance, how they behave, what their performance results are, what values and habits they are passing on to their people, what ethical principles they implement and many other signs of leadership actions are watched and followed by people in an organization.

From an ethical point of view, few would like to be remembered as being corrupt, evil or unethical, yet the concepts of ethics are fluid. For many organizations the rules for ethical practices are found not in stated goals but in revealed practice. It does no good to have a list of rules that is ignored, especially when breaking the rules is rewarded in practice. As such, measuring ethical adherence is difficult, as few would voluntarily admit to doing something wrong. Humans have a high capacity to take advantage of whatever suits them or to lie, especially to themselves. People are considered to be an essential resource for any organization, which can create a distinctive capability as a prerequisite to achieve a competitive advantage once they are led and appropriately developed. The crucial role of leadership in the digital era is to make people aware of what is happening outside and inside of the company, to involve them in organizational processes and to build relations by using all sorts of influential forms. The concept of the "big picture" (elaborated in Chapter 4) helps leaders to show people the interconnections between the internal and external environments where various stakeholders exist.

Each decade has brought new challenges to corporate social responsibility (CSR). Worker rights and safety have been joined by other concerns such as the environment, community involvement and cultural diversity. The responsibility of the corporation has historically been viewed from as a pendulum swinging between the two poles of stakeholder vs. stockholder. These two viewpoints are harmoniously complementary rather than opposing. Without a profit, a corporation could not exist. Without the input of the various stakeholders, a corporation could not survive.

Societal digitalization has added new concerns to CSR. The individual is facing a new form of harm, often through products being provided by the corporation. Responsibility for this harm is shifted to the individual as a form of moral failing. Individuals, of course, must be responsible for their health, but it would be foolhardy to suggest that the corporation has no responsibility in this new paradigm. At some point in the future, the corporation will be asked to share responsibility.

Every sector of the economy has its decisions to deal with and to adapt to, and it is the leader's job to articulate a vision for the company and to steer the organization through the needed changes (see Chapter 6). A large amount of energy, however, is spent addressing resistance to change. Max Weber (2012), in his book *The Protestant Ethic and the Spirit of Capitalism*, argues that organizations adopt a system of bureaucratization that is so irresistible and powerful that it becomes an iron cage of constraint. In today's world, there are a few industries where a change of the status quo is undesired. For the most part, industries will continuously need to reinvent themselves to survive. How to do this effectively, and what the leader's approaches to change and innovation are, are the eternal questions.

The quest for how to lead in the digital age must move beyond the platitudes offered up by the university setting. Merely stating that a leader needs to be visionary, change oriented and inventive offers little in the way of guidance. Hickman's Leading Organizations Framework (2016) did move closer with his guidelines for leadership. A reinterpretation of his findings (mentioned in Chapter 1) can be summarized in the following points:

- Ensure the organization is in a good economical position, as capital investors will quickly punish those that have lost profitability.
- Finding and developing critical human capital is paramount. The 80/20 Pareto distribution theory states that 80% of your outcomes will come from 20% of your efforts. Concerning human capital, it can be said that a company's survival will depend on the top 20% of the human talent and constant optimization of the entire talent pool.
- A company's success depends on the relationship with external stakeholders. Few companies today could genuinely be vertically/horizontally integrated, doing all aspects of production in-house. Today's

economy is indeed a "LEGO world", with many external stakeholders contributing their components to a greater product. No company today could genuinely go it alone.

• Communicate the strategic direction with established values. The strategic direction must also be aligned with the core values of society and never lose the faith of its current and potential customers.

The results of all of our conducted research activities show that *the key leadership challenge in the digital era is to propose how to enhance continuous innovation, to create a dynamic change flow in all organizational processes and inspire people to take a proactive role within those processes.*

As elaborated in Chapters 5 and 6, change should not be limited only to technological innovation. Social dimensions and relational interactions become essential elements in the process of leading change.

The intangible nature of the internet and all its iterations make it incomparable to past inventions, as it is the most far reaching and personal invention ever created and is today's biggest challenge for the corporation. From a societal standpoint, a significant change in lifestyle occurred around 2012–2013. It was at this time that the smartphone surpassed the standard mobile phone in sales. This meant that information moved from the desk to the hand and therefore absolute mobility. At the same time, a cultural shift is afoot as people are opting for a more traditional, less raucous lifestyle—that is, people in general are becoming quite staid when compared to the latter part of the 20th century. In Chapter 6 these changes are examined in companies we observed from the period 2013–2015. Trends showed that companies shifted from small, incremental improvements toward transformational changes, system and process changes.

From the researched companies, we can see the shift from the traditional desktop/laptop platform to mobile platforms and the internet of things. This, however, was followed up by leaders' focus on people. Changes in tech will not deliver the desired results without including employees (Chapter 8).

Today, change is as profound as that in the early steam age where processes were automated for exponential efficiency gains. Unlike in the past, white-collar workers are also facing a threat from automation. This can bring resistance and a modern Luddite aversion to change. For change to be effective, the technological approach must also be accompanied by an adaptive approach where people within the organization will support this change.

Diversity does enhance creativity, but diversity does not always improve quality. Manufacturing centers like Japan and China are profoundly monocultural and yet have delivered the lion's share of influence on the world.

It needs to be said that diversity in the CEE cannot be measured by the Western European or North American model, as little diversity will be found. This is to be expected, as Central Europe historically was a feeder region to the world's immigration magnets like the United States, the United Kingdom and Germany. Few could successfully argue that the CEE region could ever become a worldwide cultural melting pot. As such, there is always an innovation limitation because of monocultural-ism. Europe is unique in that it is both a union with a common identity (the EU and Europeanism) and a diverse collection of nations with vari-ety. This variance enhances creativity on a broader level just as it does in multicultural countries. Societies such as those found in the CEE region need a different measurement for diversity.

Because of the economic success of the CEE region, there is a need for labor immigration. Because of locality and closeness of the Slavic culture, much of this immigrant labor force is coming from neighbors to the east. Wojciech Kononczuk, head of the Department for Ukraine, Belarus and Moldova at the Center for Eastern Studies in Warsaw (*Poland fears eco-nomic hit as EU opens door to Ukrainians*, 2018), estimates 1–1.5 million Ukrainians are working in Poland. Areas of Ukraine at one time were part of both Poland and Czechoslovakia, and since the languages are similar, this could hardly be considered "brain diversity"; rather it is the fulfill-ment of economic needs from both sides. Slovakia and Poland need work-ers, and Ukrainians, Serbians and Romanians need better opportunities than what can be found at home. This sort of international diversification of workforces cannot be compared to more extreme cases such as those in France or Germany, with immigrants from Africa, Asia and beyond.

Our focus on diversity in Chapter 7 raises questions which are con-cerned with the purpose of diversity in the corporation. We feel that the most critical element is the reduction in historical institutionalism. Each person in society has his or her own historical background and comfort zone. Each societal group is conditioned to protect their interests based on their historical experience. Historical institutionalism emphasizes the constraints institutions placed on decision making and individual discre-tion (North, 1990). One way to describe historical institutionalism is in the saying, "this is the way we have always done it, why do we need to change?" This thought may be considered a form of Luddism, with an older generation refusing to change, but it is also found in the younger generation which is likely to say something like "we have a new way to do things that is different (meaning better and likely to be digital)". The diversity of labor, the multitasking element of almost every job and externalities that are hard to predict make changing the process of lead-ing companies even more urgent.

Buckminster Fuller (1973) used the term "ephemeralization", which means that technological advancement allows a firm to do "more and more" with "less and less". The younger generation is smitten with the concept of an ephemeralized world, where most processes can be handled with a few swipes on a mobile phone. For many, there is a lack of understanding that inputs into a computer must direct some output, which is most likely a tangible product. The older generation understands the basics of a world interconnected by infrastructure, with each contributing their share. Age diversity is essential, and according to our research, the younger generation is eager for hands-on guidance.

The concept of technological advances destroying jobs, especially blue-collar jobs, has become so ingrained that the newer generation perceives security in the form of a face-to-screen workplace, usually associated with a desk. This tends to skew the education process more toward a digital landscape to such an extent that no other options are considered. From our corporate survey, we can see tech on the shop floor reaching a pinnacle with still more digitalization to be seen in administration. Companies are reporting a shortage of workers who possess manual dexterity, an area in which computers and robots are ill-suited. Tesla Motor Company, for example, ended up replacing robots with humans in order to increase production capacity. Digitalization has been conspicuously absent from the construction field, where the labor shortage will not be alleviated by robots.

At the same time, paperless documentation has become a euphemism for the digitalization of all non-production processes such as sales, payments, design and so forth. This means a reduction of office staff. When project teams are needed, they are often formed only to be dispersed when the project is completed. This becomes a challenge to corporate loyalty and the benefits of continuous feedback. In Chapter 8 the concept of virtual teams is presented as they function in that way, but with some other limitations. With this comes a challenge of having a system that becomes so specialized that there are few who truly understand the overall process, causing a shortage in advanced ICT skills.

The digital era is profoundly changing the way leaders interact with subordinates by weakening the power of labor, employees and even whole regions of countries.

As digitalization has brought many advances and a new speed of fast change, the average consumer has enjoyed the spoils of abundance regarding quality, quantity and price. It has also brought a certain level of alienation and anxiety as digitalization and globalization can make any individual redundant in a heartbeat. If this emasculating process of marginalization through digitalization occurs across a broader landscape, a revolt will ensue. Much of the current political turmoil can trace its roots to people who feel marginalized. As a matter of principle, human beings, sovereign individuals, must be at the top of the hierarchy in corporate decision making.

A common fallacy today is the idea that most current problems an organization faces have a digital solution. If the only tool in the toolbox is a computer, then leaders will see all issues as having a coding solution. This, by its very nature, leaves out the more necessary human-centered approach.

Digitalization and innovation of an organization runs a risk of regression if the knowledge required (the input of learning) exceeds the output of what has been learned. Any innovator needs to know the history of their field. The past, however, grows longer with each innovation. This requires more and more time in the education process in order to innovate. This is the very nature of professionalization and results in a winnowing down of the number of knowledgeable individuals through a lengthening education process. At some point, innovation will stop as there are too few people capable of carrying on the process. One answer to this dilemma is intergenerational sharing of knowledge, where an older generation, steeped in the historical traditions of a field, can exchange knowledge with the younger generation that brings with them a new perspective on an old problem. From our perspective, all organizations should have a strong intergenerational exchange of knowledge and age diversity. It is the role of leadership to facilitate this exchange of knowledge through a constant exchange of feedback.

The framework of the Reflective Leadership Model presented in Chapter 5 consists of six main processes which establish a balance between the processual and relational dimension of leadership. These are as follows:

1. Process of Continuity.
2. Process of Involving.
3. Process of Connecting.
4. Process of Developing.
5. Process of Commitment.
6. Process of Making a Shared Vision.

This concept has been elaborated in the broader organizational ecosystem that recognizes the fact that organizations should provide fair, or substantive, equality of opportunity for all individuals in the organization. Going back to the primary objective of this book, we propose the modified version of the Reflective Leadership concept which addresses the current challenges of the digital era where innovation plays a key role. It is developed in order to highlight the essential tasks for leaders as well as to suggest how these tasks can be implemented in the diverse organizational environment.

Reflections on the Qualitative Analysis

This book focuses on leadership issues studied in the CEE region covering 12 countries with particular emphasis on the Visegrad Four countries (Poland, the Slovak Republic, the Czech Republic and Hungary). It may seem an odd choice for study, especially when one considers the current state of politics. The results of the broad research presented in this book, together with a focus on the CEE region, provide a unique, once-in-a-lifetime opportunity to deeply examine the leadership process starting in 2013, when many companies were recovering from the financial crisis, and finishing in 2017, when the strong emphasis on innovation and digitalization has come to many businesses.

The CEE countries' transition and significant development is described in three case studies at the end of each part. The case studies aim to show how historical, political and economic changes might impact the culture and how that influences the corporate world. The corporation establishes rules for its functioning reflecting cultural differences and the region's uniqueness as well as all externalities. It is essential for the corporation to understand both cultures and values of any society they serve. The underlying assumption of this book was to follow the increasing complexity of leadership which needs to adapt to constant changes not only in the workplace but also in society as a whole.

For many in the CEE region, EU governance is reminiscent of past times, and the current elected officials are a warning against visionary excess. Despite the noisy politicians, economic development, led by corporate leaders, is raising the standards in CEE countries and carving a path toward economic parity with Western Europe.

When considering historical, political and economic influences, leadership in the CEE region cannot be successful through flamboyance and theatrics as there is too much cynicism toward anyone displaying a cult of personality. The inspirational leader of the past with a gift of charisma will not likely succeed today anywhere in the world. Leaders are not expected to be autocratic, powerful individuals who get respect because of their hierarchical position. The results and judgment of the leader's work and its moral and ethical implications will be assessed by the broader society, the community and different stakeholders.

The CEE region has enjoyed the success that corporations and their leadership have brought, yet the citizenry has also been signaling they want and demand a place in decision making. Tomorrow's leaders will need to create a world to which the common man wants to belong. Ignoring this basic principle comes with great peril, as no one wants to be made irrelevant. An outdated machine can be discarded and replaced with a new, more advanced model—a discarded or disregarded employee breeds resentment. As such, leadership must be transformative with regard to new expectations and compelling learning opportunities.

Moreover, the leading process seems more like a social interaction rather than a quantifiable action. Social relations and interactions of followers within the environment created by leaders are difficult to measure using quantitative methods. Qualitative research methods are offering more in-depth analysis to investigate leaders' actions and their impact on people's behavior and organizational performance. Since 2013 Critical Reflection Analysis (CRA) was implemented in many case studies and in interviews with managers, with the primary aim to examine their leadership competencies. CRA is a very useful tool to assess and evaluate specific processes which contribute to effective leadership performance. It also establishes the basis for managers to reflect on their understanding of the leadership role and how they can implement it well in everyday work.

The research results indicate some controversial tasks for leaders. On the one hand, the implementation of ICT across all organizational operations is inevitable; thus, it reduces costs and simplifies work. The pacing of the latest digitalization trends and their fast implementation represents one of the key leadership challenges in the digital era. On the other hand, the understanding of real leadership by respondents is to help people to understand and adjust to new conditions, accept changes and actively participate in new processes. The external and internal environments are changing dramatically, and they are making an impact on organizational systems and leadership actions.

Emerging technologies often trigger the redesign of internal processes and to some extent this results in less privacy for employees in the workplace or erosion of employees' existing skills. Due to the acceleration of technological development, leaders need to adapt quickly to new conditions and help their employees accept them.

Macroeconomic uncertainty was identified as the critical category reflecting external challenges. Additionally, change as a multiple and complex factor was highlighted as the biggest internal challenge for leaders, with no relation to industry or sector.

Currently, the situation in companies is somewhat challenging for leaders. For the first time in history, they need to work with four different generations at the same time. It is harder for leaders to motivate employees or to propose benefits without considering the various preferences and values of each generation. To conclude, there is a changing structure and quality of human resources in the global world, and that requires new leadership approaches. From all the responses, one major theme has appeared: to succeed and maintain a competitive advantage, companies inevitably need to invest in innovation and people. Innovation and people can jointly contribute to the success of the organization.

The necessity for change will most likely be a decision that comes from the top, as leaders have a bigger picture of the environment. The implementation of change will come from the followers, who most likely are comfortable with the status quo—a bias in favor of the known over the unknown. Change planning can meet with resistance. This is especially true when there is the view that "the top level gains while the lower levels get pain".

As a reaction, the Modified Reflective Leadership Model (Figure 9.1) was designed (explained below) to overcome this resistance by being all-inclusive.

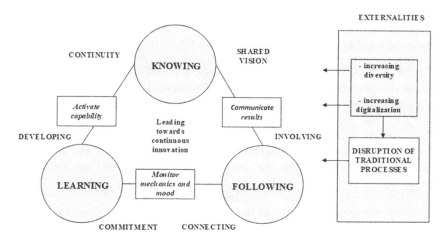

Figure 9.1 Modified Reflective Leadership Model
Source: Authors.

The Reflective Leadership Model can be seen as a complex set of inter-related actions which strengthen people's participation in all processes and functions in the organization. If leaders succeed with involving their followers and helping them understand what their role within the organizational system is, then the core base for any innovation and change will be established.

Our research aimed to find out how people interact (in diverse teams, often virtual, with different perceptions of ethical behavior) and how leaders can effectively support the human capacity to enhance innovation.

The Modified Reflective Leadership Model is based on a process of a shared vision that can be implemented by followers. Moreover, the proposed concept reflects the challenges brought by the digital era. Our process-relational leadership model explains which skills are required to tackle these challenges.

The "process of knowing" gives leaders as well as their followers all essential resources to understand the broader organizational ecosystem. An indispensable element for innovation is a shared knowledge base and the need to innovate as well. This must be communicated and shared across all levels of the organization.

One analogy that could be used to describe leadership is that it is a two-way filter between internal and external processes, conditions and new information. Internally, the organization is generally compartmentalized with different subgroups, each contributing a component to an end product. Externally, customers, suppliers, competitors and society in general factor into the decision-making process. As such, it is the leader's job to see the "big picture" or "helicopter view". These two terms may not be the best description for leadership, as they imply separation and aloofness and hark back to charismatic leaders. A better metaphorical term would have the leader making observations by walking along the gangways, catwalks and rooftop trusses of the corporation to view the overall landscape as well as the internal processes. This implies that the leader understands that the subordinates are there to be guided by someone who understands both the working environment and life outside the company's gate.

Our research responses to the "big picture view" suggest that surveyed leaders, for the most part, have a full understanding of their particular industry. On the other hand, OECD research (Andrews et al., 2015) of frontier companies (those companies in the top 5% of their economic sector) create innovations and insights that are not being shared with laggard firms. As such, this suggests a certain amount of leadership hubris, especially among larger players.

The feedback process of discovery is an exercise that is easy in theory and hard in practice. The digital landscape and its ability to quickly alter standard operations (to disrupt) has added a layer of apprehension to discovery. This could be quantified in the known knowns and unknowns of the other—there are things I know, and you don't, and there are things you know that I don't. If a leader rules by fear, the discovery process to remove unknowns will collapse.

This give-and-take between leaders and followers is a two-way feedback process where both qualitative assessment and evaluation are conducted to improve people's performance, which results in overall organizational success. Too much of current leadership has trended toward quantitative maximization with the notion of reducing labor to the bare minimum, often with the result of customer alienation (i.e. communicating to a machine rather than a person).

The "process of following" allows the continuous observation of whether people are coping with new changes and what support they need. To be effective, most leaders require change-capable people in the organization who are a source of innovation and improvements. Based on our research, increasing diversity and digitalization were identified as emerging challenges for leaders in the age of innovation. Increasing digitalization disrupts the traditional (existing) processes in the organization. It requires more employee involvement and their participation in redesigning some processes in the company to enhance organizational performance and results.

The digital era is profoundly changing the way leaders interact with followers. Our research makes clear that the key role of leadership in the digital era is to make people involved in organizational processes and to build relations among them (as proposed in Figure 9.1). To do this, there must be constant interaction between leaders and subordinates. The focus on people repeatedly occurred throughout the entire research. Our proposed model acknowledges the importance of the individual in the digital age. Excellent leadership puts followers above both machines and processes. Thus, the crucial role of a leader is to recognize an interrelation between ongoing investments into the latest technologies and human resources and understand how well-developed employees can contribute to the continuous process of innovation.

The "process of learning" promotes actions and results by having continuous feedback. Feedback is two-way communication and consists of separate but also interrelated processes of giving and receiving feedback. The managers we interviewed admitted that they lack the ability to establish this two-way process of feedback. The reason can be both their limited experience and lack of systematic guidelines on how to give and receive feedback or time limits. The two-way process of constructive feedback is a time-consuming effort when there is no systemic support for it in an organization.

At the same time, leaders need to be digitally skilled to be able to advise and consult on what information is vital and how to share it within the organizational system so that everyone will have the right information at the right time.

One of the challenges addressed by respondents was insufficient knowledge and lack of experience of how to put a diversity management framework into practice. To tackle this challenge, leaders need to actively support and organize training focusing on cultural differences and communication, and employees need to take part in workshops and conferences discussing diversity. Implementing diversity issues into a company's culture can considerably increase the company's competitiveness.

The leader's role is to foresee future trends and requirements for new specializations, which must be implemented into personal development and training plans at all staff levels.

From our survey, we discovered that corporate leaders did not rate themselves highly with regard to "giving and receiving feedback" and "evaluating process and progress quantitatively and qualitatively". Considering the self-serving bias tends to skew numbers toward a positive light, we can assume an outcome that is even worse than what our numbers suggest. This also means that ratings on "having a shared vision" were also quite low. It does seem that the communication process between organizational levels is weak and that leaders are assuming the role of giving orders and followers are felt to be weaker. As such, change implementation remains weak. If we take this dynamic to its conclusion, resistance to change will grow, and the working environment will become hostile. The image of a firm, decisive leader with a dictatorial flair may seem appealing on one level, but it is unsustainable in the long run.

There is a continuous feedback loop of learning, knowing and following. The most successful leaders are perpetual learners. To be effective, most leaders need change-capable people in the organization.

Reflective Leadership recognizes the fact that organizations should provide fair, or substantive, equality of opportunity for all individuals in the organization. John Rawls (1971) argued that advantaged positions should be open to all, not only formally but also in such a way that each person has a fair chance of attaining them. Regarding decision making, this suggests that followers do have an opportunity to give input. It in no way indicates that there should be an equality of outcome (i.e. decisions made by leaders should reflect the opinions of the followers, but followers' opinions can be overruled as the overall view can only be seen from the top).

This research makes it clear that a defining principle of Reflective Leadership is the need to prioritize the individual over institutional considerations with regard to decision making. To do this, there must be constant interaction and well-established relationships between leaders and subordinates. Good leadership put followers above both machines and processes.

Thoughts and Recommendations for Future Research Directions

The thrust of this book has been to develop the Reflective Leadership Model which brings together the two dimensions of process and relations. We would like to express our personal feelings and share our observations of the organizational world and leaders' behavior. The literature related to leadership issues is vast, therefore in our book we offer a different view. We intended to describe the organizations as living systems and study leadership through different processes which fulfilled the core task of any leader: to lead people toward the main organizational goals and purposes.

We believe that the synthesis of selected theories, the methodology of qualitative research where two conceptual and reflective approaches were implemented, bring some interesting thoughts and insights into the new leadership approach. Notably, the research design and the integrated research methods offer valuable results and create an excellent network among academia and practice not only in the CEE region but also internationally. We also believe that the suggested Reflective Leadership Model and a few conceptual tools apply to leaders as well as for future empirical research, suggesting that implementation of complementary research methodologies are beneficial.

When starting to study the leadership issues, understanding of the organizational environment is crucial. Even though leaders are aware of interconnecting features of the internal and external environment, organizations are still managed the traditional way, where business models are mainly based on balancing costs, and price and growth is supported by entering new markets and increasing production. Opposite to these traditional concepts, business models based on innovations are trying to balance digitalization while maintaining and developing talent.

Our research design began with the global challenges that examine the organizational environment and finally reflect leaders' actions. We hope to combine the local and international dimension and develop the Reflective Leadership Model in general while also including different research methods. We believe that subsequent efforts should continue in multiple directions to enable us to study more in-depth influences of the external environment. Moreover, we want to focus on the implementation of changes and their links to the leadership approach in different sectors or organizations. This research will also yield more meaningful findings if conducted by teams in different countries that will allow cross-country comparisons. Another dimension of this research is to examine the leadership of multicultural teams. There are an increasing number of organizations that tackle increasing cultural diversity. Future organizations will have diverse employees, managers and leaders who want to succeed in an increasingly volatile and unpredictable global environment.

Bibliography

Andrews, D., Cruscuolo, C., Gal, P. (2015). *Frontier Firms, Technology Diffusion and Public Policy: Micro Evidence from OECD Countries.* OECD 2015. Retrieved from: www.oecd.org/eco/growth/Frontier-Firms-Technology-Diffusion-and-Public-Policy Micro-Evidence-from-OECD-Countries.pdf [Accessed 10 October 2018.]

Buckminster Fuller, R. (1973). *Nine Chains to the Moon.* London: Cape.

Digital Disruption Has Only Just Begun. (2016). *World Economic Forum.* Retrieved from: www.weforum.org/agenda/2016/01/digital-disruption-has-only-just-begun/ [Accessed 29 October 2018.]

Hickman, G.R. (2016). *Leading Organizations: Perspectives for a New Era.* Thousand Oaks, CA: Sage.

Lemert, C.C. (1993). *After Modern Social Theory: The Multicultural and Classic Readings.* Boulder, CO: Westview Press.

North, D.C. (1990). *Understanding the Process of Economic Change.* Princeton, NJ: Princeton University Press.

Poland Fears Economic Hit as EU Opens Door to Ukrainians. (2018). Retrieved from: www.dw.com/en/poland-fears-economic-hit-as-eu-opens-door-to-ukrainians/a-42367764 [Accessed 10 October 2018.]

Rawls, J. (1971). *A Theory of Justice.* Cambridge: The Belknap Press of Harvard University Press.

Theodoulides, L., Jahn, P. (2013). *Reflective Method: Tool for Organizational Learning.* Bratislava: Iura Edition.

Weber, M. (2012). *The Protestant Ethic and the Spirit of Capitalism.* Cambridge, MA: Start Publishing.

Appendices

Appendix I
Research Description Based on Grounded Theory

Sample Description

Overall, 65 managers from 65 companies in Slovakia were surveyed.

Table A1.1 Sample description—type of position

Type of Position	Number of Interviewees
CEO	20
Finance Manager	7
HR Manager	8
Production Manager	10
Marketing/Sales	11
Team Leader/Low Management	6
IT Manager	3
Σ	65

Source: Authors.

Table A1.2 Sample description—years in this position

Years in This Position	Number of Interviewees
More than 20	7
15–20	4
10–14	14
5–9	15
Less than 5	25
Σ	65

Source: Authors.

Table A1.3 Sample description—industry

Industry	Number of Companies	%
Education	2	2
Machinery industry	11	16
Automotive industry	2	6
Electronics industry	2	6
Chemical industry	2	8
Energy industry	1	2
Metallurgical industry	2	6
Construction industry	2	5
Food industry	2	6
Textile and clothing industry	3	3
Retail industry	2	2
Agricultural industry	2	2
Telecommunications industry	2	6
Transport industry	3	3
Mining	2	2
Financial services industry	2	2
Cosmetics industry	2	2
Polygraphic industry	2	5
Postal service industry	2	2
Furniture industry	3	3
IT	6	8
Consulting and trade	2	3
Σ	65	100

Source: Authors.

Table A1.4 Sample description—company size

Company Size	Number of Companies	%
Large—more than 250 employees	40	62
Medium—max. 250	15	23
Small—max. 50	8	12
Micro—max. 10	2	3
Σ	65	100
Slovak	30	46
Multinational	35	54

Source: Authors.

Methodology

The data were gathered through in-depth interviews (consisting of nine research questions) with leaders from 65 companies (both international and local) based in Slovakia. Each interview lasted 60–90 minutes on average and was digitally recorded for further analysis using grounded theory. Grounded theory as a qualitative research method and theory-building platform was used for data analysis. This method seeks to build theoretical explanations of observed phenomena by constructing these explanations from the data itself (as opposed to theory testing). All data were analyzed using the open coding technique to allow definitions of new categories and elaborate on new theoretical frameworks from the research questions. The data collection phase of this research was done from October through December 2017.

The main aim of the research was to identify new approaches and values for leadership in the digital era. The nine questions were:

1. What are the diversity features in your organization?
2. How does diversity influence your business?

    2.1. What are the main challenges related to diversity?
    2.2. How does your organization address these challenges?
    2.3. What impact of diversity on the company performance can be envisioned?
    2.4. What is the composition of the diverse workforce?
    2.5. Which categories of diversity are the most important to develop a talent pool in the organization?
    2.6. Does your organization have diversity policies implemented to enhance recruitment, inclusion, promotion and retention of employees who are diverse?
    2.7. How does the diverse internal workforce affect organizational performance?
    2.8. How can diversity be a competitive advantage for an organization?

3. How does diversity contribute to creativity and innovation in your organization?
4. Which changes and improvements were proposed by your employees?
5. What are the sources for change and improvements in your company?
6. What are the leadership challenges in the digital era?
7. How does your organization deal with challenges in the digital era?
8. What is the role of leadership in supporting innovation and creativity?
9. Did you experience any unethical, unfair or illegal practices inside or outside of your business?

Appendix II
Framework of the Critical Reflection Analysis

The CRA framework used in our research consists of five steps which can be elaborated further as:

1. Describing the content.
2. Designing systems and/or subsystems.
3. Confronting key processes.
4. Identifying and assessing key parameters/criteria.
5. Reconstructing.

The first step in CRA involves the gathering of data to accumulate enough information to understand the internal and external environment of the studied case. The main methods of information collection are those which are usually used in qualitative research through case studies such as an interviewing, observation and experimenting. Additionally, many reports, internal documents and financial data are also provided and examined in order to comprehensively become familiar with the specific industry, sector and segments of the studied organization.

The design of the organizational system and subsystems represents the second stage of the CRA framework. Questions starting with "what?" arise in order to understand the organizational environment (external and internal) where the leaders play a crucial role. Some various forms of reflective actions and decisions are generated in the immediate and longer term.

Stage three of the CRA, confronting key processes, is the place to deal with the information that emerges from the reflections. The questions that arise in this stage start with "how?" to identify the key processes and interactions within them. Critical thinking and more reflections are used in this stage, thus providing a more profound understanding of which processes are essential to consider for analysis.

Stage four becomes a reflection on the identified processes in the previous stage concerning those parameters or criteria which are the most important for successful results within the examined processes. The assessment and evaluation of the selected parameters are conducted here by using the value metrics which are presented in Appendix III.

The assessment and evaluation consists of a matrix structure with these main attributes: evaluated parameters/criteria, weighting (or priority influence) scale, assessment/value of individual reflective parameters and final assessment values/results.

The most important tool in CRA is the feedback which enhances the qualitative improvements of all processes within the organizational system. Feedback is conducting during the final stage of CRA, which is called reconstructing. The core actions, changes and new ways to improve processes are envisioned. Both assessment and evaluation analysis provide knowledgeable analysis and feedback that help the decision-making process and determine which parameters to change or improve.

The Evaluated Parameters or Criteria

The system and evaluated processes are influenced by a number of parameters, variables and criteria. The impact of some of them is negligible, therefore the aim is to identify those which affect the processes and system significantly. In our research, these parameters were formulated in two different studies. The first one was change typology, to examine what changes have been implemented and what improvements were seen made in organizations in two observed years (2014 and 2015). A variety of parameters were identified differently based on the type of change performed in the researched organizations.

The second study was conducted within the CEE region in 2015, where the evaluated criteria were formulated in order to examine the core leaders' actions, and those results contributed to a new leading approach (i.e. the Reflective Leadership Model).

Weighting or Priority Impact

Selected parameters which are significant for the evaluated processes have a different priority or level of influence. To distinguish from the most influential impact on organizational performance to the least important criterion, a weighing scale from 1 to 10 was suggested. The range was set up within three primary levels, as follows:

1. Significant impact (weighting from 8 to 10): parameters strongly influence the process; they represent the critical performing criteria, greatest expected results or have the highest priority in the organization.
2. Standard impact (weighting from 4 to 7): parameters have a standard, regular influence on the examined process; they continuously exist in the organization, and their relevance depends on the

particular conditions, circumstances or current situation in a specific period.

3. Additional impact (weighting from 1 to 3): parameters have only substitutional influence on the evaluated process; they usually appear as unrelated parameters rather than the fundamental ones or found in certain crisis situations.

Appendix III

Reflective Assessment and Evaluation Table

Table A3.1 Evaluation matrix for Critical Reflective Analysis

1st Level of Assessment		2nd Level of Assessment		Outcomes and Qualitative Evaluation of the Observed Processes
Verbal Assessment	*Point Range*	*Point Range*	*Difference*	
Very bad *(poor results, serious mistakes and weaknesses, incomplete or formally unfulfilled expectations)*	1–29	1–9	9	*Expression does not correspond with goals, expectations and requirements that create the base of evaluation.*
		10–19	10	*Small signs of setting goals which lead to completing required expectations.*
		20–29	10	*Little connection between personal potential and completion of the required goals and expectations.*
Bad *(mistakes and weaknesses, positive signs occurring)*	30–44	30–34	5	*Formal expressions of completing the proposed goals/criteria.*
		35–39	5	*Meaningful activities which lead toward completion of the required goals/criteria.*
		40–44	5	*Signs of fulfilling expectations in the line of formal and real compliance. Final evaluation is negative.*
Zone of indecision *(acceptable expressions, partially completing standards)*	45–54	45–48	4	*Expressions of set expectations oscillate around a level of formal and real compliance. Upon completion, evaluation of positive expressions is seen.*

(Continued)

Table A3.1 (Continued)

1st Level of Assessment		2nd Level of Assessment		Outcomes and Qualitative Evaluation of the Observed Processes
Verbal Assessment	Point Range	Point Range	Difference	
		49–51	3	*Expressions of set expectations oscillate around the line of formal and real compliance In its overall evaluation is dominated by positive expressions.*
		52–54	3	*Fulfillment of expectations is in line with real compliance. In response to activity, there is positive evaluation.*
Good (sticking to the standards, fulfilling of set expectations)	55–79	55–62	8	*Fulfillment of set goals oscillates around the line of set standards (expectations).*
		63–71	9	*Fulfillment of set goals oscillates above the line of set standards.*
		72–79	8	*Fulfillment of set goals oscillates above the line of set standards and show a permanent qualitative increase.*
Very good (exceeding standards, innovating and shifting boundaries)	80–99	80–86	7	*Fulfillment of expectations reaches a permanent superior state and shows efforts toward a change of set results.*
		87–92	6	*Fulfillment of expectations reaches a permanent superior state and shows efforts toward a change of set goals.*
		93–99	7	*High fulfillment of expectations permanently exceeds set lines; the result of which is the setting of new goals, requirements and expectations.*

Source: Theodoulides and Jahn (2013).

Contributors

David Cole was born and educated in the United States, but has been living in Slovakia for 15 years and is currently a Slovak citizen. He earned his PhD at Matej Bel University studying migration, mobility and European citizenship. He has long been active in Slovakia as a lecturer and researcher at the Faculty of Economics of Matej Bel University. David's research is focused on behavioral economics based on the theories of Nobel laureate Daniel Kahneman and Amos Tversky in applications toward regional and rural development, primarily focused on sociological aspects of economic problems, namely non-fiscal transaction costs. This study also focuses on ethical standards in corporations.

Gabriela Kormancová is assistant professor at Matej Bel University, Faculty of Economics (Slovakia). She studied Corporate Security Management at the University of Zilina (Slovakia), International Relations at Matej Bel University (Slovakia), Analysis of Conflicts and Violence at Versailles Saint-Quentin-en-Yvelines University (France) and wrote her PhD thesis about the security services forecast. Her research interests focus on virtual teams' performance and innovative performance.

Lenka Theodoulides is assistant professor at Matej Bel University, Faculty of Economics (Slovakia). She studied Economics and Management at Economic University in Bratislava (Slovakia), Business Administration at Swinburne University of Technology, Melbourne (Australia) and earned her master's in Business Administration at Cyprus Institute of Management (Cyprus). She wrote her doctoral thesis about entrepreneurial networks. Her research interests focus on socioeconomic perspectives of organizational theory, such as leadership, change dynamics and reflection.

Index

Abel, A. L. 33
accountability 11, 44, 58–61, 63–64, 71
Ackoff, R. L. 35
Alderfer, C. P. 177
Amir, O. 46
Ancona, D. 128
Andrews, D. 73, 228
Anseel, F. 116
Ariely, D. 46
Armstrong, M. 122, 151
Arrow, H. 176
Astrom, K. J. 121
Avery, G. C. 30
Avolio, B. J. 23–24, 31, 105

Bachmann, A. S. 183
Baldoni, J. 51
Bartell, T. 113–114
Bass, B. M. 23–24, 31, 105
Bazerman, M. 53
Beck, C. D. 7, 135
Beer, M. 31
Beerel, A. 26, 156
behavior 18, 28–29, 36, 38, 43–44, 54, 67, 99, 101, 104, 116–117, 121–122, 127, 134, 152, 156, 158; unethical 45, 54–53, 57–58
Bell, M. P. 189
Bennis, W. G. 19
Benson, S. 113
Berdahl, J. L. 176
big picture 1, 12, 47, 53, 98–100, 107–108, 127, 131, 133–135, 159, 166, 185, 209, 219, 228
Blackler, F. 189–190
Blair, J. 71
Blanchard, K. 20
Bless, H. 50

Boardman, N. E. 45
Bodily, S. E. 79
Bolus, N. E. 113
Bracek-Lalic, A. 4
Bradbury, H. 103
Bradley, R. 70
Brocas, I. 60
Brown, M. E. 104
Buchholtz, A. K. 69
Buckminster Fuller, R. 222
Burns, J. M. 18, 22–23, 30–31, 151

Camagni, R. 72
Cannella, A. A. 31
Carlsmith, J. M. 50
Carrillo, J. D. 60
Carroll, A. B. 69, 71
CEE region 2, 4–6, 8–10, 41, 56, 71–74, 90–91, 108, 135, 141, 163, 174, 177, 181–182, 184, 186, 198, 202, 212–215, 222, 224–225, 230, 239
Central Europe 79, 81–84, 136, 139, 222
change 2, 5–6, 8–10, 12–14, 21–22, 32–33, 35, 38, 55, 76, 90–92, 94–95, 100, 105, 126, 133–134, 137, 147, 149–153, 155–162, 164–166, 168–172, 186, 189, 191, 218–222, 226–227, 229; organizational 91. 149, 158, 162, 164–165, 169, 204
Chin, J. L. 32, 183–84
Chinowski, P. 203
Cilliers, F. 101
Clarke, S. 127
Clear, T. 203
Cleveland, J. N. 22
Coakes, E. 127

Cochran, P. 82
Cole, D. 95
Collier, J. 96
Collins, J. 19
Conger, J. A. 24, 104
Contractor, N. 112
Coons, A. E. 103
Corbin, J. 6
Cormican, K. 203
corporate social responsibility 11,
    66, 220
corruption 81, 180, 182
cost-benefit analysis 45
Cottrell, S. 115
Coulon, L. 186
Covey, S. M. R. 112
Cox, T. 182
Craig, T. Y. 176, 179
creativity 2, 8, 13–14, 29, 37–38, 92,
    119, 132, 143, 149, 164, 174–176,
    179, 183–184, 189–191, 193, 199,
    218, 221–222
critical reflection analysis 6, 8–9,
    96, 99, 108, 130–131, 156, 171,
    226, 238
critical thinking 7, 12, 29, 36, 89,
    107, 111, 113–115, 120–121, 124,
    129, 170, 189, 192–193, 204, 238
Cruscuolo, C. 73, 228
Curphy, G. 89

Dachler, P. 103–104
Dacko-Pikiewicz, Z. 214
Daft, R. L. 94
Dalio, R. 52–53
Davidi, I. 121, 128
DeMarie, M. S. 201–202
Dess, G. G. 150, 191
Diekmann, K. 53
digitalization 13, 37, 107, 113, 141,
    143, 163, 171, 191, 197, 199–201,
    206, 208, 210, 223–225, 228, 231
diversity 1–2, 8, 10, 13–14, 17, 27,
    38, 128–129, 132, 165, 174–179,
    181–185, 188–189, 192–193, 197,
    205, 207, 218, 221–222, 228–229,
    237; age 184, 189, 223–224;
    cultural 13, 149, 184, 220, 231;
    gender 176, 183–185, 193; social
    13, 149
Doliński, D. 49
Dooley, L. 203
Dowd, S. B. 113

Drucker, P. F. 101, 105
Dubé, L. 202
Dundis, S. 113

Egan, T. D. 176, 178, 185
Eisenstat, R. A. 31
Eisner, A. B. 150
Ekiert, G. 4
Elder, L. 113–114
Ellis, S. 121, 128
Ellsberg paradox 61
environment 2, 4–5, 13, 19, 21, 26,
    28, 31–32, 35, 54, 57–58, 63,
    94–96, 103, 118–119, 126–127,
    149, 163, 166, 170, 193, 199, 220,
    225–226; business 5, 13, 25, 31,
    33, 49, 57, 142, 149, 162, 193;
    external 5, 12–13, 25–26, 31, 33,
    36, 38–39, 90, 92, 95, 99, 103,
    112, 115, 133, 150, 153, 158–159,
    166, 218, 231, 238; internal 20,
    25–26, 98, 103, 107, 129–130,
    159, 231, 238; organizational 5, 7,
    10, 12, 20, 25, 28, 30, 35–36, 38,
    89, 95, 123, 126, 162, 231, 238
Eriksson-Zetterquist, U. 28, 150, 166
Esteban, R. 96
Ethical triad 62–63, 131
ethics 25–26, 43, 47–48, 54, 57–58,
    60–61, 98, 219
Evans, J. 20
Ewen, R. B. 183

Facione, P. A. 114
Fairhurts, G. T. 105
feedback 12, 14, 23, 29, 94, 113,
    116–119, 121–126, 128–129, 132,
    142, 160–161, 167–168, 170, 187,
    189–192, 204, 207–208, 215, 224,
    229, 239; 360-degree 123, 190
Ferencova, M. 191
Festinger, L. 50
Feyrer, J. 188
Fiedler, F. E. 31
Fiedler, K. 50
Fleury, M. T. L. 177
Fogg, P. 188
Folwarczny, M. 49
Ford, I. W. 164
Ford, J. D. 164
four layered diversity model 13
Francik, A. 214
Freeman, R. E. 70–71

Friedman, M. 70
Fugate, M. 150, 165
Furnham, A. 30, 32

Gajdzik, B. 181
Gal, P. 73, 228
Gardenswartz, L. 176–177
Gardiner, E. 186
Gawdiak, I. 84–85
Geister, S. 202–203
Gergen, K. 103–104
Geweke, J. 61
Gibson, C. 128
Giddens, A. 44, 74, 95
Gilbert, J. A. 189
Gilmore, T. N. 103
Gino F. 46
Gioia, D. A. 104
Glass, A. 188
Gneezy, U. 47
Goleman, D. 26, 111, 126
Gordon, A. 7, 135
Gordon Hullfish, H. 116
Graen, G. B. 103
Grant, T. 71
Gratton, L. 184
Gray, D. E. 116
Grayson, L. E. 79
Green, B. 19
Green, R. 61
Greene, D. 53
Greenfield, P. 48
Greyvenstein, H. 101
Griffin, R. W. 150, 155, 165
Grint, K. 18
Grzybała, P. 49
Grzyb1, T. 49

Hall, D. T. 116
Hall, E. R. 183
Hamel, G. 19
Handy, CH. 151
Harrison, J. 31
Hazans, M. 180
Hendrickson, R. A. 201–202
Hertel, G. T. 202–203
Hickman, G. R. 2, 22, 25–26, 36, 151, 165, 220
Hill, CH. V. L. 3
Hitt, M. A. 31
Hofstede, G. H. 83–84, 143
Hogan, R. 89
Horehajova, M. 213

Horwitz, I. R. 185
Horwitz, S. K. 185
Hosking, D. 103–105
Hoskinsson, R. E. 31
House, P. 24, 53
Hudáková, M. 181
human resources 21, 27, 33, 91, 93, 107, 112–113, 155, 160, 181, 206, 213, 229
Huňady, J. 211
Hunsaker, J. 204
Hunsaker, P. 204
Hunt, J. 105
Huy, Q. 31

Inch, E. 115
Ingham, H. 116
innovation 4–8, 10, 13–14, 19, 21–22, 25, 29–30, 34–35, 37–38, 68, 90–94, 98, 100, 105, 127–128, 133, 135, 147, 149–150, 160, 162–164, 170, 172, 174–175, 178–179, 183–186, 188–193, 197, 208, 213–214, 218, 220, 224–225, 226–227; organizational 1, 218
Ireland, R. D. 31
Ivancevich, J. M. 189
Ives, B. 203

Jabri, M. 164
Jackall, R. 49
Jahn, P. 116, 120, 242
Jarvenpaa, S. L. 155
Jennings, M. 51
Jerz, V. 95
Jick, T. D. 165
Johari Window 118, 121, 129
Josephson, M. 57–58

Kahn, W. A. 107
Kahneman, D. 50
Kanter, R. M. 151, 165
Kanugo, R. N. 24
Kelan, E. 184
Kellet, P. M. 164–165
Kelley, R. E. 29, 107
Kelly, J. R. 176, 179
Kendrick, M. 94
Kim, W. CH. 31
Kinicki, A. 150, 165
Kirkman, B. L. 202
Klimovski, R. 32
Knight, F. 60

Kokavcova, D. 119
Kolb, D. A. 119–120
Kolb's learning cycle 119
Konradt, U. 202–203
Kormancová, G. 204
Kotter, J. 13, 26, 111, 150, 156, 165–167, 172
Kovaľová, M. 204
Krantz, J. 103
Krzyszycha, K. 49
Kurtzberg, T. R. 176, 179
Kurubacak, G. 113

Lacová, Ž. 211
Lang, W. 186
Larkey, L. K. 182
Latham, J. R. 128
Latour, S. M. 107
Leading-Following model 28–29, 129
Leading-Knowing-Following-Learning model 130–131
leadership 1–2, 5, 9–10, 12, 17–21, 25–26, 28, 30, 35–36, 45–46, 51, 58, 89–90, 99–105, 111, 116, 126–129, 134, 138, 144, 149, 155, 162–163, 171, 189, 192, 197, 211, 219–220, 225, 227–228, 230, 237; corporate 11, 43–44; transformational 22–25, 28, 30, 48
learning organization 26
Leary, T. 77–78
Levy, P. E. 123
Lewin, K. 165–166
Lichtenstein, B. 100, 103
Lievens, F. 116
Lipnack, J. 201–202
Lipset, S. M. 176, 185
Lock, D. 203–204
Locke, E. A. 128
Loden, M. 176
London, M. 123
Luft, J. 116
Lumpkin, G. T. 150
Lusková, M. 181
Lustig, R. 77

Macdonell, S. G. 203
Majchrzak, A. 205
Malhotra, A. 205
Marasova, J. 213
Marion, R. 95, 104–105
Martins, L. 176, 179
Martynowska K. 49

Mas, M. 198
Mathieu, J. E. 202
Mauborgne, R. 31
Mazar, N. 46
McDaniel, R. R. 164
McDonald, R. A. 123
McGrath, J. E. 176
McKelvey, B. 95
Milgram, S. 48–49, 57, 63
Milliken, F. 176, 179
Mitchell, C. 34
Mitchell, R. 70
Monge, P. 112
Monroe, M. J. 31
Moorhead, G. 150, 155, 165
Morley, I. E. 105
Morrison, A. M. 177
Mullern, T. 28, 150, 166
Mumford, M. D. 116
Munnell, A. 188
Murphy, K. R. 22
Murray, R. M. 121

Nanus, B. 19
Natale, S. 115
Neal, S. 33
Nevid, J. 50
Nevitte, N. 176, 185
Nix, T. 71
Nonaka, I. 127
North, D. C. 222

O'Reilly, C. A. 176, 178, 185
Osborn, R. N. 101, 105
Ospina, S. 105
O'Sullivan, D. 203
Özbilgin, M. 177, 182

Paese, M. 33–34
Paré, G. 202
Paul, R. 113–114
Pearce, C. L. 104
Pendleton, D. 30, 32
Petress, K. 115
Petrie, N. 32
Piccoli, G. 203
Picken, J. C. 191
Plowman, D. 100-
Pope, J. A. 4
Powell, A. 203
Precup, L. 203
process 5, 12, 18, 20, 25, 28, 30–31, 35, 70, 89–90, 94, 104–105, 108,

115, 117, 133, 156–157, 166–168, 171, 207, 223–224, 230, 239–240; of commitment 132, 168, 208, 224; of connecting 133, 168, 208, 224; of continuity 132, 207, 224; of developing 133, 168, 208, 224; of involving 131, 167, 207, 224; leadership 1, 7–10, 14, 17, 21, 34–35, 90–91, 94, 98, 100, 107, 115, 129–130, 168, 197, 225; learning 101, 107, 128, 189; of making a shared vision 133, 168, 209, 224

Purg, D. 4

Quiggin, J. 188

Raguz, I. V. 35, 98
Rast, V. J. 107
Rawls, J. 230
Ray, R. L. 33–34
reflection approach 6, 9
Reflective Leadership model 124, 126, 130–132, 165–167, 169, 224, 227, 230–231, 239
resource-based view 188
Ricci, F. 115
Roeckelein, J. E. 48
Romano, C. 107
Rosen, B. 205
Rosener, J. 176
Ross, L. 53
Rothbard, N. P. 107
Rothman, S. 176, 185
Rowe, A. 176–177
Rustichini, A. 47

Sakal, P. 95
Salt, J. 139
Sass, S. 188
Scandura, T. 103
Schnackenberg, A. 59
Schnitzer, M. 80
Schollaert, E. 116
Schultz, W. 77
Scott, J. C. 3
Senge, P. M. 19, 26, 35, 95, 128
Shamir, B. 24
Silver, N. 80
Silverman, D. 6
Sinar, E. 33–34
Sirkova, M. 191
Smith, A. 33–34

Smith, K. K. 177
Smith, P. G. 116
Smither, J. W. 123
Soto, M. 188
Stamps, J. 201–202
Stein, B. A. 165
Stockdale, M. 22
Stoddard, D. B. 155
Stogdill, R. M. 103
Strack, F. 50
Strange, J. M. 116
Strauss, A. L. 6
Styhre, A. 28, 150, 166
Syed, J. 177, 182
Szcepańska-Woszczyna, K. 214
Szymszal, J. 181

Taha, F. A. 191
Tajfel, H. 177
teams 14, 25, 90, 94, 102, 120, 126, 128, 135, 141, 150, 163, 176, 184, 197, 202–204, 208, 223, 231; diverse 7, 175, 185, 189, 191–193, 202, 210, 227; functional 102; homogeneous 175; intergenerational 144; traditional 199, 201–203, 205; virtual 199, 201–205, 208–210, 223
Tenbrunsel, A. 47, 53
Theodoulides, L. 35, 98, 116, 120, 242
Thomas, R. 189
Todeva, E. 104
Tomlinson, E. 59
Towsend, M. 201–202
transparency 11–12, 58–59, 62–64, 71, 89
Triandis, H. C. 183
Trimble, J. E. 32, 183–184
Trojanowski, J. 49
Tsui, A. S. 176, 178, 185
Turner, J. C. 177
Tversky, A. 50

Uhl-Bien, M. 95, 104–105
universality 11, 58, 61, 63–64, 71–73, 78

Van Ark, B. 34
Vermeulen, F. 128
Vershinina, N. 94
Voelpel, K. 127
Voigt, A. 184
Von Krogh, G. 127

Wade-Benzoni, K. 53
Walker, L. 184
Warnick, B. 115
Wartick, S. 82
Watson, S. 128
Watt, B. 33–34
Weber, M. 220
Wellins, R. 33–34
Whitehead, J. 71
Whitmore, J. 125
Williams, J. R. 123
Willis, D. 127
Wilson, F. M. 20
Wilson, S. 77
Wolfram, H. 184
Wong, M. 186
Wood, D. 70

workforce 2, 9, 14, 20, 31, 35, 37–38, 91, 93, 131, 134–135, 138, 140, 144, 150, 178–180, 182, 184, 186, 188, 193, 197–198, 203, 206–207, 210, 218, 237
workplace 1, 12–13, 37, 89, 129, 143, 163, 171, 175, 179, 181, 186, 191–192, 205–206, 208–211, 223, 225–226
Wrench, J. 176

Yeo, R. K. 113
Yukl, G. A. 7, 26, 31, 105, 123, 128, 135, 156

Zaccaro, S. J. 32
Zavadsky, J. 95

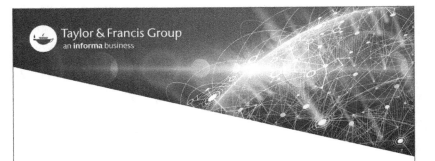